LIBRARY OF NEW TESTAMENT STUDIES

457

Formerly the Journal for the Study of the New Testament Supplement series

Editor
Mark Goodacre

ISRAEL'S
ONLY SHEPHERD

MATTHEW'S SHEPHERD MOTIF AND HIS SOCIAL SETTING

WAYNE BAXTER

t & t clark

Published by T&T Clark International
A Continuum Imprint
The Tower Building, 11 York Road, London SE1 7NX
80 Maiden Lane, Suite 704, New York, NY 10038

www.continuumbooks.com

© Wayne Baxter, 2012

Wayne Baxter has asserted his right under the Copyright, Designs and Patents Act, 1988, to be identified as the Author of this work.

British Library Cataloguing-in-Publication Data
A catalogue record for this book is available from the British Library

ISBN: HB: 978-0-567-06661-9

Typeset by Free Range Book Design & Production
Printed and bound in Great Britain

CONTENTS

vi   *Contents*

ILLUSTRATIONS

Figures and Tables

ABBREVIATIONS

For abbreviations of ancient texts, see Alexander, P. H., et al. (eds), *The SBL Handbook of Style for Near Eastern, Biblical, and Early Christian Studies* (Peabody: Hendrickson, 1999).

AB	Anchor Bible
ABRL	Anchor Bible Reference Library
AFNTC	The Apostolic Fathers: A New Translation and Commentary
AJEC	Ancient Judaism and Early Christianity
ANE	Ancient Near East/ern
ANRW	W. Haase and E. Temporini (eds), *Aufstieg und Niedergang der römischen Welt* (Berlin: de Gruyter, 1979–)
BAGD	W. Bauer, W. Arndt, F. Gingrich, and F. Danker, *A Greek–English Lexicon of the New Testament* (Chicago: University of Chicago Press, 1979)
BASOR	*Bulletin of the American Schools of Oriental Research*
BDB	F. Brown, S. Driver, and C. Briggs (eds), *Hebrew and English Lexicon of the Old Testament* (Oxford: Clarendon, 1907)
BDF	F. Blass, A. Debrunner, and R. Funk, *A Greek Grammar of the New Testament* (Chicago: University of Chicago Press, 1961)
BJS	*British Journal of Sociology*
BLS	N. Gottwald and R. Horsley (eds), The Bible & Liberation Series
BTB	*Biblical Theological Bulletin*
BWANT	Beiträge zur Wissenschaft vom Alten und Neuen Testament
BZAW	Beihefte zur Zeitschrift für die alttestamentliche Wissenschaft
BZNW	Beihefte zur Zeitschrift für die neutestamentliche Wissenschaft
CB	Christ-believing
CB/NTS	Coniectanea Biblica/New Testament Series
CBQ	*Catholic Biblical Quarterly*
CGLCIL	Cambridge Greek and Latin Classics Imperial Library
CNT	Commentaire de Nouveau Testament

CSCT	Columbia Studies in the Classical Tradition
CT	Cahiers Théologiques
DJD	Discoveries in the Judean Desert
DJG	J. Green, S. McKnight, and I. Marshall (eds), *Dictionary of Jesus and the Gospels* (Downers Grove: IVP, 1992)
DSSSE	F. García Martínez and E. Tigchelaar, *Dead Sea Scrolls Study Edition*
EBC	Expositor's Bible Commentary
FRLANT	Forschungen zur Religion und Literatur des Alten und Neuen Testaments
GAP	M. Knibb (ed.), Guides to Apocrypha and Pseudepigrapha
GNTG	J. Moulten, *A Grammar of New Testament Greek* (Edinburgh: T&T Clark, 1993)
HAR	*Hebrew Annual Review*
HSS	Harvard Semitic Series
HTR	*Harvard Theological Review*
ICC	International Critical Commentary
Interp	*Interpretation*
JBL	*Journal of Biblical Literature*
JGRCJ	Journal of Greco-Roman Christianity and Judaism
JNSL	*Journal of Northwest Semitic Languages*
JSJSS	Journal for the Study of Judaism Supplement Series
JSNT	*Journal for the Study of the New Testament*
JSNTSS	Journal for the Study of the New Testament Supplement Series
JSOT	*Journal for the Study of the Old Testament*
JSOTSS	Journal for the Study of the Old Testament Supplement Series
JSP	*Journal for the Study of the Pseudepigrapha*
JSPSS	Journal for the Study of the Pseudepigrapha Supplement Series
LCL	Loeb Classical Library
LNTS	Library of New Testament Studies
MBC	Mellen Biblical Commentary
NCB	Non-Christ-believing
NICNT	New International Commentary of the New Testament
NovT	*Novum Testamentum*
NRSV	New Revised Standard Version
NTS	*New Testament Studies*
NTSS	Novum Testamentum Supplement Series
OTP	*Old Testament Pseudepigrapha*
RevQ	*Revue de Qumran*

SBLDS	Society of Biblical Literature Dissertation Series
SBLEJL	Society of Biblical Literature Early Judaism and Its Literature
SBLMS	Society of Biblical Literature Monograph Series
SBLSP	Society of Biblical Literature Seminar Papers
SCSS	Septuagint and Cognate Studies Series
SEAJT	*South East Asia Journal of Theology*
SJT	*Scottish Journal of Theology*
SNTSMS	Society for New Testament Studies Monograph Series
SNTW	Studies in the New Testament and Its World
SSEJC	Studies in Scripture in Early Judaism and Christianity
ST	*Studia Theologica*
STDJ	Studies on the Texts of the Desert of Judah
SVTP	Studia in Veteris Testamenti Pseudepigrapha
TDNT	G. Kittel and G. Friedrich (eds), *Theological Dictionary of the New Testament* (Grand Rapids: Eerdmans, 1964–74)
TDOT	G. Botterweck and H. Ringgren (eds), *Theological Dictionary of the Old Testament* (Grand Rapids: Eerdmans, 1974–)
TS	*Theological Studies*
TSAJ	Texts and Studies in Ancient Judaism
VT	*Vetus Testamentum*
VTS	*Vetus Testamentum* Supplements
WBC	Word Biblical Commentary
WMANT	Wissenschaftliche Monographien zum Alten und Neuen Testament
WUNT	Wissenschaftliche Untersuchungen zum Neuen Testament
ZNW	*Zeitschrift für die neutestamentliche Wissenschaft*
ZTK	*Zeitschrift für Theologie und Kirche*

Chapter 1

GENERAL INTRODUCTION

1.1 *Purpose*

'"When did Christianity and Judaism part company and go their separate ways?" is one of those deceptively simple questions which should be approached with great care.'[1] The so-called 'Parting(s) of the Ways' represent(s) one of the most intensely researched problems in biblical studies today: how, when, where, and why did the Jewish Jesus movement develop into a religion separate from Judaism? Although this is an extremely complicated issue, an increasing number of scholars have come to recognize that its complexity is comprised largely of smaller questions revolving around individual communities and their texts. One such group is the Matthean Christ-believers,[2] and their text, the Gospel of Matthew.[3]

Matthew's Gospel has been at or near the centre of the debate for quite some time. On the one hand, some commentators argue that because the Gospel is the most Jewish text in the New Testament, it offers evidence of a Christ-believing (= CB) community still closely related to Judaism. Others, on the other hand, assert that it was composed by a non-Jew who sought to distance himself from Jews and Judaism. No consensus, however, has been reached.[4] Furthermore, a lack of precision in the oversimplified terminology that scholars regularly employ in the discussion adds to the confusion and limits the relevance of the conclusions drawn.

---

1   P. Alexander, "The Parting of the Ways' from the Perspective of Rabbinic Judaism', in *Jews and Christians: The Parting of the Ways AD 70 to 135*, ed. J. Dunn (Tübingen: J. C. B. Mohr Paul Siebeck, 1992), 1.

2   The term 'Christ-believer' and its derivations (Christ-believing, non-Christ-believer, etc.), employed throughout this study, refer to first-century people who believed that Jesus of Nazareth was the messiah and who consequently followed his teaching. Generally speaking, many people 'followed' Jesus (e.g. the crowds in Matthew), but not all who followed would have believed or been convinced that he was the Christ, i.e. they followed but would not have been 'Christ-believers'.

3   For the sake of convenience, 'Matthew' shall refer to the author of the Gospel; apostolic authorship is neither assumed nor implied. Furthermore, 'Matthew', 'Evangelist', and 'author' will be used interchangeably for stylistic variation.

4   For further discussion of these views and their respective scholarly representation, see section 1.2.1 below.

Commentators have used diverse approaches for determining the relationship between Matthew and the variegated Judaism of the first century,[5] that is to say, Matthew's 'socio-religious location' or 'socio-religious orientation' – one of the more prominent categories comprising 'social setting' or 'social location'.[6] Few scholars, however, have recognized the important piece that the Evangelist's Christology brings to the puzzle. Of Matthew's various Christological strands, his Shepherd Christology offers significant potential for exploring his socio-religious orientation.[7] The present investigation contends that there are distinctive tendencies in usage in the shepherd metaphor's appropriation by non-Christ-believing (= NCB) Jewish, NCB Roman, and CB authors which reflect certain patterns of thought.[8] By comparing Matthew's deployment of this metaphor (which reflects certain tendencies of its own) with its appropriation by these groups of authors, clues to the Evangelist's socio-religious orientation may be discerned, and its social-historical implications traced.

Thus, the present study, on the one hand, examines Matthew's often overlooked shepherd motif to determine how it contributes to the overall theological framework of the Gospel, specifically its Christology and soteriology.[9] On the other hand, the study uses the motif to ascertain Matthew's socio-religious location; but rather than adopt the problematic language of other inquiries to describe the author's socio-religious orientation,[10] this book will describe it in terms of occupying a certain place on a spectrum. Therefore, the study will contribute to the understanding of Matthew's theology, and of his relationship with first-century Judaism. Although this book does not deal with the larger discussion of the separation between Jews and Christ-believers, Matthew's socio-religious location does have direct bearing on the 'Partings' debate, as well as other social-historical implications, which shall be outlined in the second part of the study. The following review of previous scholarship

---

5   'Judaism' in this study refers to the Adonayistic religion (i.e. worship of YHWH) originating with the Jewish people, primarily characterized by the Temple cult, religious festivals, circumcision, Sabbath observance, and adherence to the Torah and its diverse regulations, including purity, dietary, and tithing laws. For a detailed discussion of the practices and beliefs of (Second Temple) Judaism, see E. P. Sanders, *Judaism: Practice & Belief*, 63 BCE–66 CE (Philadelphia: Trinity Press International, 1992).

6   Other categories include date of composition, place of composition, and the destination or community addressed.

7   For a detailed explanation of how, see section 1.4.5 below.

8   For an explanation of 'patterns of thought', see section 1.4.4 below.

9   'Shepherd metaphor' and 'shepherd motif' have slightly different meanings in the present study. Shepherd 'metaphor' refers to the occurrence of the metaphor in a text. Shepherd 'motif', however, implies a developed use of, and hence, a particular interest on the part of the author in the metaphor, i.e. it acts as a theme or sub-theme within the document.

10   See discussion in section 1.2.1 below.

will indicate the various fields of research needed to address the questions of the theological contributions of Matthew's shepherd motif, and its implications for the Evangelist's socio-religious orientation.

1.2 Survey of Scholarship

1.2.1 The social location of Matthew

When discussing the 'Parting(s) of the Ways,' earlier scholars tended to map a rather simplistic, once-for-all parting between Jews and Christ-believers.[11] Recent proponents paint a more complicated picture of the process.[12] This type of simplistic configuration of social realities, not surprisingly, also characterizes most discussions of Matthew's socio-religious location.

In the history of Matthean scholarship there have been and still are two basic positions among commentators concerning the relationship between Matthew and first-century Judaism.[13] Perhaps the more frequently advocated position throughout the history of research would be the '*extra muros*' view. Scholars of this persuasion contend that although Matthew and his community shared a common heritage with Judaism, a definite breach had occurred between the Mattheans and NCB Jews with the result that the Mattheans no longer participated in the Jewish 'synagogue' environment.[14] Thus, for example, K. Stendahl writes, 'Matthew's community now existed in sharp contrast to the Jewish community in town. For in this church things Jewish meant Jewish and not Jewish Christian versus gentile Christian.'[15] If, as Stendahl asserts, to be 'Jewish', i.e. to adhere to aspects of Judaism, is not to be 'Christian',

---

11   P. Fredriksen notes that scholars typically claim that the 'Parting' took place in either c. 28–30 CE, c. 50 CE, c. 70 CE, c. 135 CE, or 200 CE ('What "Parting of the Ways"?: Jews, Gentiles, and the Ancient Mediterranean City', in *The Ways that Never Parted: Jews and Christians in Late Antiquity and the Early Middle Ages*, ed. A. Becker and A. Y. Reed, TSAJ, ed. M. Hengel and P. Schäfer, vol. 95 [Tübingen: Mohr Siebeck, 2003], 35).

12   E.g. J. Dunn asserts, '"The parting of the ways", properly speaking, was very "bitty", long drawn out and influenced by a range of social, geographical, and political as well as theological factors. ... we must beware of thinking of a clear or single "trajectory" for either Christianity or Judaism' ('Concluding Summary', in *Jews and Christians: The Parting of the Ways AD 70 to 135*, ed. J. Dunn [Tübingen: J. C. B. Mohr Siebeck, 1992], 367).

13   A summary of the different views can be found in G. Stanton, 'The Origin and Purpose of Matthew's Gospel: Matthean Scholarship from 1945 to 1980', in *ANRW* II.25.3 (Berlin: de Gruyter, 1985), 1910–21, and D. Hagner, 'The *Sitz im Leben* of the Gospel of Matthew', in *Treasures New and Old: Recent Contributions to Matthean Studies*, ed. D. Bauer and M. A. Powell, Society of Biblical Literature Symposium Series, ed. G. O'Day (Atlanta: Scholars Press, 1996), 32–40.

14   For further discussion of this environment, see section 5.3.4 below.

15   K. Stendahl, *The School of St. Matthew and its Use of the Old Testament*, 2nd edn (Philadelphia: Fortress Press, 1968), xiii–xiv.

then other scholars, like K. Clark, push this position even further by arguing that the author of the Gospel was not even Jewish but Gentile.[16]

More recently, commentators like G. Stanton, D. Hagner, and P. Foster have argued for what could perhaps be called a 'soft *extra muros*' position.[17] Stanton insists:

> Matthew's communities are *extra muros*, but they are still responding in various ways to local synagogues and they still hope that even if Israel has been rejected by God, individual Jews will be converted. On this view the gospel can be seen, at least in part, as an apology – a defence of Christianity over against non-Christian Judaism.[18]

In this view, then, although the Mattheans abide as a distinct group outside the public synagogue environment (similar to [most] Gentile Christ-believers), they are still engaged to some degree with Jews within it.

While the *extra muros* view has represented the scholarly consensus throughout the history of Matthean scholarship, the '*intra muros*' position has come on quite strongly in the last fifteen years.[19] The *intra muros* viewpoint contends that Matthew and his community, despite the obvious conflicts they were experiencing with their Jewish rivals, still firmly existed within the public synagogue environment. G. Bornkamm thus characterizes the Matthean community: '[According to Matt 24.9] the picture of the Jewish-Christian congregation arises, which holds fast to the law and has not yet broken away from union with Judaism.'[20] For Bornkamm, Matthew aligns more closely with Torah-observant, first-century Judaism than with Torah-free 'Christianity'.[21] The *intra muros* position became influential through the works of Bornkamm (who coined the term '*intra*

---

16   K. Clark, 'The Gentile Bias in Matthew', *JBL* 66 (1947): 165–72. Besides Clark, other scholars advocating this minority view of Gentile authorship include G. Strecker, *Der Weg der Gerechtigkeit: Untersuchung zur Theologie des Matthäus*, FRLANT, vol. 82 (Göttingen: Vandenhoeck & Ruprecht, 1971); S. van Tilborg, *The Jewish Leaders in Matthew* (Leiden: Brill, 1972); J. Meier, *Law and History in Matthew's Gospel* (Rome: Biblical Institute Press, 1976), 14–21.

17   G. Stanton, *A Gospel for a New People: Studies in Matthew* (Edinburgh: T&T Clark, 1992), and P. Foster, *Community, Law and Mission in Matthew's Gospel*, WUNT, vol. 177 (Tübingen: Mohr Siebeck, 2004). Stanton refers to this position as a 'mediating position' between the *extra muros* and *intra muros* views.

18   Stanton, *Gospel*, 124.

19   D. Hare has recently called this position 'the growing consensus' ('How Jewish Is the Gospel of Matthew?', *CBQ* 62 [2000]: 264–77).

20   G. Bornkamm, 'End-Expectation and Church in Matthew', in G. Bornkamm, G. Barth, and H. Held, *Tradition and Interpretation in Matthew*, trans. P. Scott (London: SCM, 1963), 22.

21   Bornkamm, however, later migrated from this position to the other view; see Bornkamm, 'The Authority to "Bind" and "Loose", in the Church in Matthew's Gospel', in *The Interpretation of Matthew*, ed. G. Stanton (Philadelphia: Fortress Press, 1983), 85–97.

muros'), G. Kilpatrick,[22] and W. D. Davies,[23] the latter claiming that Matthew's Gospel was composed in response to the so-called Council of Javne following the destruction of the temple in 70 CE.

The *intra muros* view does not display uniformity among its proponents.[24] One of the mistakes scholars often make in this debate is to equate socio-religious location with 'ethnic' identity.[25] The two, however, should not be confused. It is quite possible, on the one hand, for a Jew to become acculturated and assimilated to Gentile thought and practice. Two examples of this would be Dositheos son of Drimylos, a priest in the royal cult of Alexander in the third century BCE, and Philo's nephew, Tiberius Julius Alexander.[26] It is equally possible, on the other hand, for a Gentile to embrace thoroughly Jewish thought and practice.[27] This study does not focus directly on the question of ethnic identity (which would be the corollary to socio-religious orientation) but rather, on the issue of socio-religious location.

Discussions concerning Matthew's socio-religious location, moreover, suffer significantly from the inadequate and historically inaccurate categorization of false opposites. Scholars who believe that Matthew and his community decisively broke away from Judaism and no longer participated in the public synagogue environment refer to the Mattheans as *extra muros*; those who assert that they still existed within Judaism and the public synagogue refer to them as being *intra muros*. While *extra muros*/*intra muros* has long been the standard language for the debate, it greatly oversimplifies what would doubtless have been a highly complex situation.[28] Consequently, this language stunts the advancement of the debate.

22   G. Kilpatrick, *The Origins of the Gospel According to St. Matthew* (Oxford: Clarendon Press, 1946).

23   W. D. Davies, *The Setting of the Sermon on the Mount* (Cambridge: Cambridge University Press, 1966).

24   See, for example, A.-J. Levine, *The Social and Ethnic Dimension of Matthean Social History* (Lewiston: Edwin Mellen Press, 1988), Saldarini, *Christian-Jewish*, and D. Sim, *The Gospel of Matthew and Christian Judaism: The History and Social Setting of the Matthean Community*, SNTW, ed. J. Barclay, J. Marcus, and J. Riches (Edinburgh: T&T Clark, 1998).

25   See, for example, Stanton's review of Matthean scholarship in 'Origin', especially.

26   See J. Barclay, *Jews in the Mediterranean Diaspora: From Alexander to Trajan 323 BCE–117 CE* (Edinburgh: T&T Clark, 1996), 104–105.

27   An example of this phenomenon can be observed in Paul's letter to the Galatians.

28   Hence, A. Chester remarks that 'the theological, historical, social, economic and political issues involved [in comparing the eschatology of Jews and Christ-believers] are much more complex ... hence I am dubious about setting up so simple a contrast and critical of attempts to do so' ('The Parting of the Ways: Eschatology and Messianic Hope', in *Jews and Christians: The Parting of the Ways AD 70 to 135*, ed. J. Dunn [Tübingen: J. C. B. Mohr Paul Siebeck, 1992], 303).

This type of either/or configuration fails to describe adequately or accurately the historical picture of the social interactions between Jews and Christ-believers.[29] Even scholars who embrace the terms *intra muros* and *extra muros* recognize the complexity of social interactions between the groups. For example, while Foster freely adopts the *intra muros/extra muros* language, he notes, in speaking of Sim's categories of antinomistic Gentile Christ-believers and rigorist Jewish non-Christ-believers, 'there is a range of possibilities between these extremes, and it appears more plausible to argue that [the Matthean] group was in a period of flux'.[30] Similarly, R. Brown disputes the frequent characterization of the Jesus movement as 'Jewish Christian' and 'Gentile Christian', insisting that '*one can discern from the NT at least four different types of Jewish/Gentile Christianity*'.[31] The language of *intra muros* and *extra muros*, then, needs to be nuanced (as others have done) if indeed it is to be used at all.

D. Boyarin provides a more sophisticated way of conceptualizing socio-religious interactions between early NCB Jews and Christ-believers.[32] In his examination of accounts of martyrdom in the bavli and in contemporaneous writings of Christ-believers, Boyarin persuasively demonstrates that the relationships between Jews and Christ-believers could be intertwined at times. Consequently, scholars should not think of Judaism and Christ-belief as circles – separate, intersecting, concentric, or otherwise.[33] Rather, interactions between the two groups are better configured as points on a continuum, with one end perhaps representing a highly nationalistic, stringently Torah-observant, form of Judaism that is hostile towards Christ-belief,[34] and the other end indicative of an equally polar form of Torah-free, anti-Judaistic Christ-belief

---

29   While commentators tend to homogenize the different CB groups in the New Testament, a close look can reveal something of a religious spectrum among Christ-believers: Hellenists like Stephen for whom the Temple cult held little practical relevance (Acts 7; cf. Hebrews); Jews like Paul who, according to his letters advocated a Law-free mission to the Gentiles, but who still participated in the Temple cult according to Acts 21.18-26; and James, who led a compromise between the Law-free position of Paul and the CB Pharisees (Acts 15.5) – who would represent yet another point on the spectrum.

30   Foster, *Community*, 257.

31   R. Brown, 'Not Jewish Christianity and Gentile Christianity but Types of Jewish/Gentile Christianity', *CBQ* 45 (1983), 74 (his emphasis). Hagner ('*Sitz im Leben*') approvingly takes up Brown's categories. The complexity of the situation can also be seen in some of the more incidental comments of scholars. J. Cousland concludes his study: 'Thus, to answer the time-honoured question of whether Matthew's situation is *intra-* or *extra-muros*, one would have to reply that it is *extra-muros* but very much focussed on those who are still *intra-muros*' (*The Crowds in the Gospel of Matthew*, NTS, vol. 102 [Brill: Leiden, 2002], 304).

32   D. Boyarin, *Dying for God: Martyrdom and the Making of Christianity and Judaism* (Stanford: Stanford University Press, 1999), 1–21 (especially).

33   Contra, for example, Alexander, 'Partings'.

34   E.g. Saul of Tarsus (cf. Acts 8.1-3; Gal. 1.13-14; Phil. 3.4-6).

that rejected Jewish-national restoration.[35] There would, thus, have been many permutations between these two end points and the boundaries between these sub-groups would have been quite blurred, with the exchange of beliefs and customs moving in both directions.[36] Some of the factors that would determine an author or a group's place on this Judaism–Christ-belief spectrum would include, for example, the degree to which Torah is observed, the level of participation in the Temple cult, and attitudes towards Gentiles.[37] Boyarin's continuum ('wave theory') illustration provides a much more nuanced and historically plausible depiction of the social-historical realities of Matthew's time.

Thus, in describing Matthew's socio-religious orientation, rather than labelling the author as *intra muros* or *extra muros*, a better approach would be to locate him on a socio-religious spectrum. Because of the common custom among scholars of describing early NCB Jews and Christ-believers in terms of false opposites, however, a Judaism–Christ-belief spectrum like Boyarin's (with one pole devoted to Judaism and the other to Christ-belief) might still be perceived as perpetuating this practice. Hence, in view of the blurred boundaries between sub-groups, and in view of the numerous issues that can be involved in locating a group on a socio-religious continuum, the spectrum used in this study will relate specifically to belief in Jewish nationalism or Jewish-national restoration.

Historians and biblical scholars regularly use 'Jewish nationalism', 'Jewish national identity', and other related expressions, and all such terms have their own weaknesses.[38] A full-blown discussion of ancient

---

35   Boyarin writes, 'On one end [of the continuum] were the Marcionites, the followers of the second-century Marcion, who believed that the Hebrew Bible had been written by an inferior God and had no standing for Christians and who completely denied the "Jewishness" of Christianity. On the other were the many Jews for whom Jesus meant nothing. In the middle, however, were many gradations that provided social and cultural mobility from one end of this spectrum to the other' (*Dying*, 8). Boyarin's configuration of interactions between Jews and Christ-believers illustratively expands some of the observations of S. Wilson, who notes that some groups of Christ-believers 'found themselves straddling, and thus inevitably blurring, the dividing lines between the Jewish and Christian communities' (*Related Strangers: Jews and Christians 70–170 CE* [Minneapolis: Fortress Press, 1995], 143).

36   Consequently, Saldarini writes, 'Thus a sharp division between the postdestruction Jewish community and Matthew's Christian-Jewish group is unnecessary and unlikely. The Jewish and Christian communities in the eastern Roman Empire were varied in their practice and thought as they responded to a variety of local situations. This fluid situation provides the contexts for Matthew's Christian-Jewish group' (*Christian-Jewish*, 26).

37   E.g. were Gentiles proselytized? Were they considered ritually impure? Were they expected to adhere fully to the Mosaic Law?

38   For an informative discussion of frequently used terms, see D. Goodblatt, *Elements of Ancient Jewish Nationalism* (Cambridge: Cambridge University Press, 2006), 1–27.

Jewish nationalism is far from necessary for the present investigation;[39] what remains most germane, however, is its overall character or spirit. While Jewish nationalism in antiquity consisted of numerous aspects like Temple, Land, and kingship, the various components symbolize or express hopes for the physical and/or moral restoration of the Jewish people, particularly (though not exclusively) during the time of Matthew.[40]

On a socio-religious spectrum mapping belief in Jewish nationalism, one end would represent a zealous, nationalistic concern for the moral well-being and political-national restoration of the nation of Israel; groups at the other end would have no desire whatsoever for Israel's restoration.[41] There are several reasons for this particular choice of spectrum for the present study. First and foremost, as will be observed, overtones of Jewish-national restoration are regularly associated with the shepherd metaphor; hence, because the metaphor often conveys sentiments of Jewish nationalism, this kind of spectrum would be most appropriate for an analysis devoted to that metaphor. Second, Jewish nationalism represents a central theme in the writings of ancient NCB Jews. Third, Jewish nationalism is broadly applicable; that is, while not as major a theme for Christ-believers, the future of Israel does nevertheless factor into their theology in different ways.[42]

If Matthew's socio-religious orientation can be described in terms of occupying a particular position on a socio-religious spectrum rather than simply as either *intra muros* or *extra muros*, the debate over Matthew's social location can not only move forward in fresh terms, but the description of his socio-religious orientation will correspond more closely with the complex social-historical situation of the first century. While there are various ways of achieving this aim of locating Matthew on this socio-religious spectrum, this study will use the shepherd metaphor as a means of accessing and comparing the patterns of thought (reflected by its appropriation) between Matthew and other early writers, and then analyse the implications of the results from a social-historical perspective.

---

39   For some recent examinations of ancient Jewish nationalism, see Goodblatt, *Elements*, S. Schwartz, *Imperialism and Jewish Society 200 BCE to 640 CE* (Princeton: Princeton University Press, 2001), and D. Mendels, *The Rise and Fall of Jewish Nationalism* (New York: Doubleday, 1992).

40   Despite the overall shape of Jewish nationalism, aspirations for national restoration would not have been exactly uniform. Perhaps the clearest example of this would be in the re-establishing of the rule of the Mosaic Law for the nation. Whose interpretation should be followed: the Pharisees', the Sadducees', the Essenes', or those of another group?

41   Besides numerous non-Jews and Christ-believers, some highly acculturated NCB Jews would probably also be found at this end (perhaps, for example, Dositheos the priest and Tiberius Julius Alexander; cf. discussion above).

42   See, for example, Paul's deliberations about Israel in Romans 11.

1.2.2 *The shepherd metaphor*

Because Matthew shows himself to be steeped in the worldview, thought, and language of the texts included in the Hebrew Bible (= HB), an examination of the metaphor in the HB would prove beneficial for understanding its use in his Gospel. Numerous commentators have studied the shepherd metaphor in the HB and related literature.[43] For most of the twentieth century, few scholars devoted significant attention to the shepherd motif in Matthew largely because historical-critical studies concentrated on the more obvious titles for Jesus featured in all four canonical Gospels.[44] While these scholars understand the important role that titles play in the presentation of Christology, their overemphasis on some titles causes them to miss the significance of the shepherd motif in Matthew's thought.[45]

Because Matthew, implicitly but plainly, links the 'Son of David' and shepherd motifs (cf. the analyses of sections 4.2.1 and 4.2.2 below),[46] a brief review of 'Son of David' studies can provide additional insight for understanding the place of the shepherd motif in the history of scholarship. 'Son of David' studies began to burgeon after the important study of J. Gibbs, who traces the Son of David motif through the First Gospel to determine the purpose it held for Matthew.[47] The first monograph devoted to this title was the influential dissertation of C. Burger.[48] Gibbs highlights the lowly nature of those healed by the Son of David, but Burger is the first to recognize that Matthew most frequently associates the 'Son of David' title with Jesus' acts of healing. While Burger

43   E.g. P. de Robert, *Le Berger D'Israël: Essai sur le Thème Pastoral dans l'Ancien Testament*, CT, ed. J.-J. von Allmen, vol. 57 (Neuchâtel: Delachaux et Niestlé, 1968); P. Porter, *Metaphors and Monsters: A Literary-Critical Study of Daniel 7 and 8* (Lund: CWK Gleerup, 1983), 61–120 (especially); E. Hoffmann, 'Das Hirtenbild im alten Testament', *Fundamentum* 4 (1987): 33–50; R. Hunziker-Rodewald, *Hirt und Herde: Ein Beitrag zum alttestamentlichen Gottesverständnis*, BWANT 155 (Stuttgart: Kohlhammer, 2001); and J. Vancil, 'The Symbolism of the Shepherd in Biblical, Intertestamental, and New Testament Material' (PhD Dissertation, Dropsie University, 1975). For a more detailed list, see W. Baxter, 'Matthew's Shepherd Motif and its Socio-Religious Implications' (PhD Dissertation, McMaster University, 2007), 14.

44   E.g. F. Hahn, *Christologische Hoheitstitel: Ihre Geschichte im frühen Christentum* (Göttingen: Vandenhoeck & Ruprecht, 1966) and O. Cullmann, *Christologie du Nouveau Testament* (Neuchâtel: Delachaux & Niestlé, 1958).

45   For example, while J. Kingsbury (*Matthew: Structure, Christology, Kingdom* [Philadelphia: Fortress Press, 1975]) uses forty-four pages to discuss the Christological title Son of God, he devotes the same number of pages to cover twelve other Christological motifs, only one of which he reserves for 'Shepherd'.

46   Cf. also the discussions (later in this section) of the contributions of F. Martin concerning 'thematic clusters', in Matthew, and Y. Chae's study on the Davidic shepherd.

47   J. Gibbs, 'Purpose and Pattern in Matthew's Use of the Title "Son of David"', *NTS* 10 (1964): 446–64.

48   C. Burger, *Jesus als Davidssohn: Eine traditionsgeschichtliche Untersuchung*, FRLANT 98 (Göttingen: Vandenhoeck & Ruprecht, 1970).

believes that this association was unexpected in early Jewish circles, L. Novakovic more recently argued that, in view of the Evangelist's citations of Isaiah and Deutero-Isaiah in relation to Jesus' healings, because Jesus was the messiah, his acts of healing represent the fulfilment of scripture.[49] All of these studies rightly draw attention to the significance of the Son of David title for Matthew, particularly as it relates to the question of Jesus' messianic acts of healing. However, they illegitimately downplay the extensive Jewish overtones of the title as well as the socio-religious implications that it may have held for the Evangelist.

Although scholars duly note Matthew's references to Davidic mes-siahship, they nevertheless tend to minimize or even expunge the Jewish, political-national implications of the title.[50] In his perceptive article on Matthew's understanding of the Davidic messiah motif, D. Verseput per-suasively demonstrates that Matthew never subverts traditional Jewish expectations associated with Davidic hope.[51] He traces the development of the Evangelist's Davidic messiah theme, beginning with the opening chapters of the narrative. According to Verseput, the Davidic genealogy, coupled with the 'key position of [the] angelic revelation at the outset of the story' in Mt. 1.21 ('and he will save his people from their sins'), dem-onstrates on the part of Matthew 'surprisingly little reticence in associat-ing Jesus' Davidic right with an earthly political agenda'.[52] Similarly, the so-called Miracle Chapters (i.e. Matthew 8–9) depict a Davidic messiah concerned with alleviating the suffering of his people sorely afflicted because of their sins; and when Jerusalem becomes the setting of the narrative, the crowds that follow Jesus closely identify with the Davidic hope he offers,[53] although the city of Jerusalem does not.

Thus, whereas the interpretation of the Gospel of Matthew frequently falls prey to the a-political and non-Jewish-national tendencies of NT scholars, Verseput correctly understands that Matthew's use of the Son of David title fits easily within and does not undermine traditional Jewish, Davidic expectation. In other words, the Evangelist does not shy away from the 'earthly political agenda' associated with the Son

---

49   L. Novakovic, *Messiah, the Healer of the Sick: A Study of Jesus as the Son of David in the Gospel of Matthew*, WUNT 2/170 (Tübingen: Mohr Siebeck, 2003).

50   For example, I. Broer ('Versuch zur Christologie des ersten Evangeliums', in *The Four Gospels: Festschrift Frans Neirynck*, ed. F. van Segbroeck et al., 3 vols [Leuven: Leuven University Press, 1992], 2.125–82) asserts that Matthew's use of the title is simply explained by his Markan source and not early Jewish expectation.

51   D. Verseput, 'The Davidic Messiah and Matthew's Jewish Christianity', *SBLSP* (1995): 102–16.

52   Verseput, 'Davidic Messiah', 108. Verseput argues that the interruption of the Davidic dynasty caused by the Babylonian exile (Mt. 1.17) is taken up again by the John the Baptist narrative, with its quotation from Isaiah 40 and the pronouncement of the mes-siah's imminent coming, which in turn sets the stage, narratively speaking, for Matthew's initial description of Jesus' messianic acts in Matthew 4–9.

53   Cf. Mt. 20.29-34; 21.9; and 21.15.

of David title, but adopts the 'Davidic agenda' embraced by so many other segments of Second Temple Judaism. But because Verseput's narrative-critical approach focuses narrowly on Matthew's use of 'Son of David', he overlooks how the Evangelist's closely related shepherd motif contributes to the discussion. The present study takes this next step and examines how the shepherd motif adds to the understanding of the Gospel's political-national expectations of Jesus as Israel's messiah.

Probably the first scholar to give significant attention to Matthew's shepherd motif was F. Martin.[54] Martin recognizes that although the motif is not the central preoccupation of the author, 'Mt, more than any of the other NT authors, has a consistent and well-developed message which he develops around the theme of shepherd.'[55] Because an image can be evoked in various ways, Martin examines the image of the shepherd by focusing on the Evangelist's 'overt allusions' to the metaphor in the biblical tradition, on the one hand, and his 'interior allusions' to other motifs, on the other. With respect to these interior allusions, Martin notes that 'an image may be the bearer of a theme and may become the vehicle by which two themes interpenetrate and mutually modify one another'.[56] Consequently, Martin looks for clusters and 'constellations of thematic image words', recognizing that Matthew forges a thematic constellation between the images of Shepherd, Son of David, healing, and King of the Jews. In Martin's view, then, the more pronounced Son of David theme would receive further development by the shepherd motif, and the shepherd motif would be expanded by the Son of David theme.

Martin makes the important narrative connection between the Son of David and the shepherd motifs. Additionally, his more literary approach to Matthew allows him to discern the literary skill and sophistication of the author, and the biblical literacy of the audience. His literary-critical approach, however, does not enable him to explore adequately the theological intentions that lay behind the Evangelist's deployment of these motifs, nor of course, any socio-religious implications – both of which occupy Part II of this study.

J. P. Heil also recognizes the prominence of the shepherd imagery in Matthew.[57] In particular, he believes that Ezekiel 34 serves as the basis of a narrative strategy for the Gospel writer: 'Matthew's shepherd metaphor is guided and unified by Ezekiel 34, which supplies the reader with some of its terms and with all of its concepts and images.'[58]

---

54   F. Martin, 'The Image of the Shepherd in the Gospel of Sant [sic] Matthew', *Science et Esprit* 27 (1975): 261–301.

55   Martin, 'Image', 271.

56   Martin, 'Image', 264.

57   J. P. Heil, 'Ezekiel 34 and the Narrative Strategy of the Shepherd and Sheep Metaphor in Matthew', *CBQ* 55 (1993): 698–708.

58   Heil, 'Ezekiel 34', 708.

Consequently, Heil focuses on the explicit references to 'sheep' and 'shepherd' in the narrative and their correlation to Ezekiel 34. In asserting the influence of Ezekiel 34 on Matthew, Heil (like Martin) assumes that the implied reader would be familiar with scriptural imagery and that this familiarity would inform the readers' understanding of the Gospel narrative.[59] Heil correctly underscores the subtle yet prominent place that Ezekiel 34 occupies in Matthew's thought;[60] and he also understands that Matthew likely wrote for an audience that would have been familiar with his scriptural imagery. However, in seeking to justify Ezekiel 34 as the terminological source for the Evangelist's shepherd motif, Heil fails to discuss how Matthew understands and integrates the theology of Ezekiel 34 into his Gospel. In addition, his emphasis on Ezekiel 34 obscures the significant contribution of other key 'shepherd' passages which Matthew employs: Mic. 5.1 (= 5.2 in English translations),[61] 2 Sam. 5.2, and Zech. 13.7 – three texts which are analysed in detail in chapter 4 below. Furthermore, there is no place in Heil's narrative-critical approach to explore the social implications of Matthew's use of Ezekiel and the shepherd metaphor.

More recently, C. A. Ham has investigated the thematic and theological function of Zechariah in Matthew through a literary and exegetical analysis of themes derived from and related to Zechariah, as they relate to Jesus and his mission.[62] According to Ham, not only does Matthew's use of Deutero-Zechariah demonstrate coherence between their respective theologies, it also shows the influence of the theology of Deutero-Zechariah on Matthew's theology: 'the presentation of the Davidic king and the rejection of the divinely appointed shepherd in Zechariah has influenced the theology of Matthew and its presentation of Jesus as coming king and rejected shepherd'.[63] Ham thus views the Evangelist's use of Deutero-Zechariah as mediating the Gospel writer's motifs of kingship and the shepherd, whereby Matthew presents Jesus as the humble king. He rightly recognizes the link between the shepherd motif and kingship: the shepherd motif emphasizes the rejection (from the standpoint of the narrative) of Jesus' kingship. Furthermore, in identifying this connection, his study corroborates the Jewish-national outlook of the Evangelist; however, Ham does not develop this point. Nor, despite the monograph's title, is Ham's focus the shepherd metaphor: he is

---

59   Heil, 'Ezekiel 34', 699, n. 3.

60   Cf. the observations of B. B. Scott, *Hear Then the Parable: A Commentary on the Parables of Jesus* (Minneapolis: Fortress Press, 1989), 413.

61   There is a one verse discrepancy between the Massoretic Text (= MT) and the English versions: 4.14 (the final verse of chapter five in the MT) = 5.1 in the English versions. The MT enumeration for Micah will be followed in this study.

62   C. A. Ham, *The Coming King and the Rejected Shepherd: Matthew's Reading of Zechariah's Messianic Hope* (Sheffield: Sheffield Phoenix Press, 2005).

63   Ham, *Coming King*, 125.

much more concerned with Matthew's use of Zechariah. Consequently, his study of the 'Rejected Shepherd' suffers from significant omissions (e.g. Mic. 5.1 and 2 Sam. 5.2 in Mt. 2.6, and Ezek. 34.17 in Mt. 25.32) that would have helped to inform his study of the shepherd-king motif.

In his dissertation, *Der Hirte Israels*, G. Garbe explores the question of Israel's salvific status in Matthew's Gospel in light of the nation's rejection of Jesus.[64] Garbe ultimately seeks to answer the question of whether God, in Matthew's view, has abandoned the Jewish nation and replaced them with Gentile Christ-believers. To address this question he examines Matthew's understanding of the destruction of Jerusalem and whether the Evangelist continued the mission to Israel after it had rejected Jesus and Jerusalem was destroyed. Garbe employs redaction, narrative, and reader response criticism, concentrating largely on the introduction (Matthew 1–2), the conflict narratives (particularly Matthew 21–23), and the eschatological passages of Matthew 24–25.[65] He assumes as a starting point a salvation-historical perspective for his analysis,[66] and believes that 'In jeder dieser drei Phasen hat Israel einen besonderen Ort.'[67] Garbe contends that Matthew has a theology of Israel ('Israeltheologie'): although the nation had rejected Jesus as the messiah and Jerusalem was destroyed, the mission to Israel continues, and God will ultimately restore the nation as his people in the Final Judgment.

Garbe correctly perceives the important function that Matthew's Gospel has in the 'Partings' debate.[68] In terms of his analysis, he rightly recognizes the significance that the first two chapters of the Gospel hold for understanding how the rest of Matthew should be read. In his estimation, the introduction does not simply reveal the Jewish character of the Gospel, it represents an Israel-oriented reading expectation ('Israelorientierte Leseerwartung') that begs for some kind of resolution in the narrative. In other words, right from the Gospel's outset, Matthew's missional concern is the nation of Israel. Ultimately, however, the monograph – despite its main title (*Der Hirte Israels*) – is much less concerned with Matthew's portrayal of Jesus as Israel's Shepherd, and concentrates far more on examining Israel as God's flock ('Israeltheologie'). Consequently, the study does little overall to advance the discussion of Matthew's shepherd motif.[69]

---

64   G. Garbe, *Der Hirte Israels: Eine Untersuchung zur Israeltheologie des Matthäusevangeliums*, WMANT 106 (Neukirchen-Vluyn: Neukirchener Verlag, 2005).

65   His primary focus here is the Final Judgment pericope of 25.31-46.

66   For Garbe salvation history consists of three phases: the time of the earthly Jesus and his works in Israel ('Reich des Menschensohnes'); the time of Matthew (i.e. the time between the earthly Jesus and his Parousia); and Jesus' Parousia, which features the eschatological Final Judgment.

67   Garbe, *Hirte*, 18.

68   See Garbe, *Hirte*, 2.

69   Thus, for example, in its analysis of the Gospel, only the use of 'shepherd', in 2.6 and 25.32 are examined with any depth – only insofar as they relate to determining

In a work more focused on investigating the Evangelist's shepherd motif, Y. Chae explores the association of Jesus' healing miracles with Davidic Christology (i.e. the Son of David title).[70] In order to illuminate this association, he explores the Davidic shepherd tradition in biblical and post-biblical literature, and then analyses Matthew's use of this tradition against this background. He demonstrates that this tradition exhibits common features among those authors who employ it, and that Matthew interacts with this tradition in detail. Chae concludes that in the Gospel, the Son of David heals through the mediating image of the shepherd motif. Chae rightly recognizes that to understand fully Matthew's use of the shepherd metaphor, it must not only be compared with HB texts, but also with Second Temple Jewish texts.

Still, some of Chae's observations and conclusions, although thought-provoking, must be challenged. When he discusses the role of the eschatological shepherd in texts such as Ezekiel 34 and *Psalms of Solomon* 17, he far too easily merges the activity of teaching into shepherding, when in fact, as chapter 2 of this study will show, teaching was a later and somewhat unexpected association of the shepherd metaphor. Not surprisingly, while Chae can acknowledge the 'nationalistic' outlook of the shepherd's mission, he nevertheless tends to mute the political-national overtones in his analysis. Similarly, he asserts that Matthew associates the activity of teaching with his portrayal of Jesus as the Shepherd.[71] Not only is this association between shepherding and teaching lacking in the major deployments of the metaphor in the Gospel, viz. in 2.6; 9.36; 10.6; 15.24; 18.12-14; 25.32; and 26.31, but other activities are actually correlated with shepherding: ruling (2.6), healing (9.36; 10.6; 15.24), searching for/gathering the lost (18.12-14), judging (25.32), and offering an atoning sacrifice (26.31). Moreover, Chae's work suffers from ignoring the use of the tradition in the texts of Christ-believers.[72] By contrast, in addition to analysing the shepherd metaphor in Second Temple Jewish texts (including the ones Chae overlooks), the present inquiry examines the appropriation of the metaphor by Christ-believers and compares Matthew's shepherd motif with both sets of authors.

Israel's salvific status – but not with an eye to discussing any Christological implications of these texts.

70   Y. Chae, *Jesus as the Eschatological Davidic Shepherd: Studies in the Old Testament, Second Temple Judaism, and in the Gospel of Matthew*, WUNT 216 (Tübingen: Mohr Siebeck, 2006).

71   He writes that 'as the Davidic Shepherd-Appointee [Jesus] is the Teacher *par excellence* for the eschatological flock, i.e., first, the lost house of Israel (10:1-6; 15:24), then the restored Israel, and finally the enjoined nations (28:16-20)' (*Davidic Shepherd*, 379).

72   He includes *4 Ezra* 2, but mistakenly under the guise of a Second Temple Jewish text.

J. Willitts sets out in his dissertation to identify the 'lost sheep of the House of Israel' (Mt. 10.6; 15.24).[73] Willitts argues that this phrase should be understood against the backdrop of eschatological Messianic Shepherd-King expectation, and consequently, he investigates the use and trajectory of this motif in the HB and Second Temple Judaism. He concludes that because this 'trajectory of eschatological expectation within Judaism maintains the original shape of a concrete eschatological expectation of political-national restoration', the lost sheep logion refers to 'remnants of the former Northern Kingdom of Israel who continued to reside in the northern region of the Land of Israel'.[74] According to Willitts, the Jewish inhabitants of this territory would represent the focus of Jesus' mission.

Willitts explicitly reinforces and develops Verseput's earlier insight about the 'political-national' dimension of Second Temple Jewish expectation concerning the messianic Son of David, demonstrating that 'Son of David' expectation included the idea of the shepherd-king. He perceptively shows how the shepherd-king motif bears stark national overtones in the HB, as well as in certain Second Temple texts. In particular, his detailed examination of the motif in *Psalms of Solomon* 17 reveals how pronounced the political-national component of Davidic shepherd expectation could be, and the significant bearing this text has for the study of the Davidic shepherd tradition in Matthew's Gospel. Furthermore, Willitts is the first scholar to use the shepherd motif to identify the flock that the Matthean Jesus sought to reach.

Although Willitts focuses on a particular use of the shepherd image (viz. non-YHWH shepherd-kingship), his review of Second Temple works ignores the important Dream Visions section of *1 Enoch*, which would affect the picture of the image's development that Willitts seeks to trace in his study. In addition, Willitts (like Chae) takes an unnecessarily one-sided approach to the question. The Davidic shepherd-king tradition is appropriated – albeit to a lesser degree – by Christ-believers other than Matthew. Would not these uses also constitute part of the tradition's historical development, and as such require comparison with Matthew? Further, in his analysis of Matthew he omits the shepherd-king motif's use in the Parable of Final Judgment (25.31-46), despite the fact that it fits his criteria for inclusion in his study of Matthew. How would the inclusion of this more eschatological and universally oriented text have affected his judgements? As mentioned earlier, the present study will cover the important ground of the Davidic shepherd tradition's appropriation by the Second Temple Jewish and CB authors that the studies of Chae and Willitts neglect.

---

73   J. Willitts, *Matthew's Messianic Shepherd-King: In Search of 'the Lost Sheep of the House of Israel'*, BZNW 147 (Berlin: Walter de Gruyter, 2007).

74   Willitts, *Shepherd-King*, 31.

Moreover, none of these authors address the question of Matthew's socio-religious orientation. Because of their literary-critical or narrative-critical approaches, most of these studies concentrate on text-oriented questions. While Willitts is more focused on the significance of Jesus' messianic mission for Matthew's own mission, he does speak explicitly (albeit in part) on the question of the Evangelist's socio-religious location: 'There are plenty of indications within the Gospel that the authorial audience is a mid to late first-century law-observing Jewish populace.'[75] However, because the focus of Willitts's thesis lies elsewhere, he simply assumes this orientation as the starting point for his inquiry. By contrast, the present investigation seeks to address this question directly – by means of examining Matthew's Shepherd Christology.

1.2.3 Strategies for determining social location

Besides the misleading *intra muros/extra muros* terminology that commentators employ in the debate over Matthew's socio-religious orientation, a second factor that impedes the discussion concerns methodology. Exegetical explorations into Matthew's socio-religious location tend to focus on the same body of evidence. Scholars typically investigate the Evangelist's portrayal of different groups in the Gospel, viz. the scribes, Pharisees, and Sadducees.[76] Within these sorts of studies Matthew's harsh 'anti-Jewish' polemic is often highlighted.[77]

More recently, scholars such as Stanton have sought to analyse this polemic using a social-scientific approach.[78] Other studies have sought to analyse Matthew's view of the Mosaic Law,[79] the place of Gentiles in the Gospel,[80] or the so-called 'church–synagogue' distinction.[81] Some scholars like Saldarini and Foster combine these elements.[82] Certainly, each of these strategies has merit and provides an essential piece to solving the puzzle of Matthew's socio-religious orientation. But as Hagner notes, these types of study merely '[emphasize] one side of the data in the Gospel to the neglect, if not the exclusion, of data on the other

75   Willitts, *Shepherd-King*, 40.
76   E.g. Saldarini, *Christian-Jewish*, 44–67.
77   E.g. D. Hare, *The Theme of Jewish Persecution of Christians in the Gospel According to St. Matthew*, SNTSMS 6 (Cambridge: Cambridge University Press, 1967) and Clark, 'Gentile Bias'.
78   Stanton (*Gospel*, 85–107) draws comparisons with the Qumran community (specifically, the Damascus Document); cf. B. Malina and J. Neyrey, *Calling Jesus Names: The Social Value of Labels in Matthew* (Sonoma: Polebridge, 1988), and their application of social conflict theory.
79   E.g. Davies, *Setting*.
80   E.g. D. Hare, 'The Rejection of the Jews in the Synoptic Gospels and Acts', in *Antisemitism and the Foundations of Christianity* (New York: Paulist Press, 1979), 38–39, and D. Sim, 'The Gospel of Matthew and the Gentiles', *JSNT* 57 (1995), 19–48.
81   E.g. Stanton, *Gospel*, 113–45.
82   Saldarini, *Christian-Jewish* and Foster, *Community*.

side'.[83] Additionally, while re-cultivating previously ploughed lines of argumentation in NT studies can sometimes prove to be fruitful, it can also result in crystallizing untested assumptions, thereby impeding the advancement of the debate. Sometimes a fresh approach is called for to further a debate. One such approach – the present study – offers a new puzzle piece by bringing Matthew's Christology to bear on the problem.

Few inquiries into Matthew's socio-religious orientation consider the Evangelist's Christology. The studies of Malina and Neyrey[84] and Stanton (who follows them)[85] do consider Matthew's Christology, by primarily focusing on the names that Jesus' opponents call him in the conflict narratives.[86] Malina and Neyrey, for their part, focus on the process – how Christology generally is shaped by social location – but do not consider particular elements of the social setting. Although Stanton makes specific correlations between the two, he examines Matthew's Christology having explicitly already made up his mind on the matter. Thus he analyses the Evangelist's Christology as a way to confirm his position and not as a means of determining it.

While the names that Jesus' (Matthew's) opponents call him have value for discerning Matthew's socio-religious location, the names that Matthew himself calls Jesus also have important bearing on the question. For reasons discussed more fully in section 1.4.5 below, among Matthew's various descriptions of Jesus, 'Shepherd' offers significant potential for assessing the Evangelist's socio-religious orientation because its usage by Second Temple Jews and Christ-believers reveals specific tendencies or patterns of thought by which to map and compare Matthew's own deployment of the metaphor.

1.3 Materials[87]

While the most detailed exegesis of this study will focus on the Gospel of Matthew, in order to understand the socio-religious and cultural environment in which Matthew composed his Gospel – and hence better comprehend Matthew – several groups of primary texts must be analysed. Not unlike other Christ-believers, the Evangelist was clearly immersed in the worldview and language of the Jewish scriptures, the HB. A formalized 'canon' likely did not exist in Matthew's day; nevertheless, the Evangelist considered these texts sacred, and religiously authoritative

---

83   Hagner, '*Sitz im Leben*', 36.
84   Malina and Neyrey, *Calling Jesus*.
85   Stanton, *Gospel*, 169–91.
86   These two works will be discussed further in section 1.4.3 below.
87   For a list of the specific texts analysed representing NCB Jews and Christ-believers, see sections 3.2.1 and 3.4.1 below, respectively.

and binding.[88] Hence, to comprehend the Evangelist's shepherd motif the metaphor must be carefully examined in the HB, for Matthew uses it explicitly and implicitly to develop his motif. Further, when Matthew employs a HB text for his Gospel, the text takes on additional meanings according to the literary context in which he places it. This new meaning in the Gospel can be compared with the meaning of the text that the Evangelist cites in its original, literary context.

The second group of primary texts that must be included in this study are the writings of early NCB Jews.[89] Because NCB Jews considered the HB texts to be sacred, and because they too adopted the shepherd metaphor from HB texts (explicitly and implicitly), analysing their appropriations can shed light on the Evangelist's deployment of the metaphor in his Gospel. Matthew will at times use the metaphor in ways consonant with NCB Jewish authors; at other times, his appropriation of the metaphor will differ considerably. It will be possible to determine points of continuity and discontinuity between Matthew and Second Temple Jews by examining the use of the shepherd metaphor by NCB Jews, and discerning the patterns of thought behind its appropriation, which will aid in situating Matthew's use of the metaphor. The date of Second Temple Jewish texts examined in chapter 3 of the study ranges from the second century BCE to the Bar Kokhba Revolt of 132–35 CE. The earlier date boundary would approximate a chronological continuation with the HB texts investigated in chapter 2. The upper date limit allows for a chronological overlap with Matthew. In this way, a fuller picture will be provided of how the metaphor was used by NCB Jews in and around the time of Matthew.

One body of texts written by NCB Jews that the present study will not include for several reasons is rabbinic literature. First, this study ultimately focuses on Matthew, a first-century figure, while rabbinic literature exceeds his time period by a substantial margin. Although much of this corpus likely contains earlier material, discerning which sayings and assigning dates is notoriously difficult. Second, even if this enormous sub-task was assumed, the payoff would be marginal at best, for these texts merely confirm how Second-Temple NCB Jewish authors employ the shepherd metaphor. Thus, the Targumim frequently translate 'shepherd' literally (e.g. Num. 27.17; 1 Kgs 22.17; Isa. 63.11; Zech. 11.5); and their non-literal interpretations of 'shepherd' (רעה) adhere to the pattern that is seen elsewhere in the writings of earlier NCB Jews.[90]

---

88   E.g. Mt. 5.17-18; 15.3; 22.29.

89   At times these writings will be referred to throughout the study as 'Second Temple' Jewish texts, or their authors as 'Second Temple Jews', merely for the sake of stylistic variation. Clearly, Jewish texts like *4 Ezra* and *2 Baruch* were written after the destruction of the Second Temple.

90   For a preliminary description of these patterns of usage, see the discussion of the רעה metaphor in section 1.4.6 below. The Targumim interpret רעה as 'king' (e.g. Jer.

For reasons similar to those discussed above, another set of primary texts that must be included in this kind of study of Matthew is the writings of the Evangelist's fellow Christ-believers. Most Christ-believers regarded the Jewish Scriptures as sacred, and adopted the shepherd metaphor from these texts. It will be possible to determine points of continuity and discontinuity between Matthew and other Christ-believers by examining the use of the shepherd metaphor by early Christ-believers, and by discerning the patterns of thought reflected in their appropriation of it to help to locate Matthew's deployment of the metaphor.

Of non-Jewish, NCB writings, Roman texts would possess the most impact for any study of Matthew because of the strong social and political influence the Roman Empire would have had upon its Jewish and CB constituents.[91] While earlier non-Jewish cultures, e.g. Babylonian, Persian, and Hellenistic, clearly affected the thought and writings of Jews living within those particular eras, the respective bonds of influence of these cultures would naturally have weakened over time, and the generation of Jews furthest away from a given era would have been impacted the least by that era.[92] This lessening of cultural sway would have especially been the rule after one nation conquered and replaced another in Palestine.

Besides Roman, the only other culture that may possibly have had significant influence with the Mattheans would have been Hellenistic. The New Testament offers clear evidence of the interplay between Greeks, on the one hand, and Jews and followers of Jesus, on the other.[93] But despite embracing the Greek language and appropriating, at times, various Hellenistic traditions, because the Roman Empire had replaced Hellenistic rule of Palestine over a hundred years before Matthew's Gospel, many of the remnants of Hellenistic influence would have been mediated through the dominant host culture of Rome, which embraced and took over large swathes of Hellenistic culture. A. Berlin, for example, notes: '[In the eastern Empire] Greek culture, in the form of language,

---

2.8; 6.2-3; 10.21; Zech. 10.2; 13.7; cf. Ps. 78.71-72), 'ruler' (e.g. Zech. 11.4-7; cf. y. *Sanh.* 10.2; *Gen. Rab.* 48.15), 'leader' (e.g. Ezekiel 34 passim), 'administrator' or 'governor' (e.g. Jer. 3.15; 23.1-4; Ps. 80.1), 'mighty men' (Nah. 3.18), 'sustain' or 'care for' (e.g. Gen. 48.15; 49.24; 2 Sam. 5.2; 7.7; Pss 23.1; 28.9; cf. b. *Pes.* 118a); they employ the metaphor to depict God protecting his people (e.g. *Exod. Rab.* 13.18; 14.15). Moses, too, is viewed as a faithful shepherd of God's people (e.g. *Ruth Rab.* 1.1; *Num. Rab.* 25.19). Even when the scribe in Eccl. 12.11 translates 'one shepherd' as 'Moses the Prophet', his interpretative translation is consonant with the pattern of appropriating the shepherd metaphor for pre-monarchical rulers like Moses (e.g. Num. 27.17; Isa. 63.11; cf. *Eccl. Rab.* 12.11).

91 For a more detailed discussion of this influence, see section 3.3.1 below.

92 This is not to deny that remnants of earlier cultures remained in Jewish culture. Clearly some would have, but their impact would have been felt much less by generations of Jews further removed from a given culture; and in some cases cultural remnants may have been mediated through the dominant culture of the time.

93 E.g. the LXX, Jn 12.20-23; Acts 6.1; Rom. 1.13-14; 1 Cor. 1.21-24.

literature, and philosophical schooling, was used by and under Romans as "a universally intelligible code" . . . [such that] Greek styles were one manifestation of Roman control.'[94] Moreover, Hellenistic appropriation of the shepherd metaphor largely parallels its use in Ancient Near Eastern literature.[95] Hence, an analysis of the writings of NCB Greeks would add little of import to the discussion at hand.

W. Carter has drawn attention to the relationship between Matthew's Gospel and the Roman Empire.[96] While Carter overstates his thesis at times, his general question must be taken into account: what role did the author's and audience's experience of Roman Imperial power play in understanding how the Gospel was framed?[97] Matthew would thus represent – at least in part – a response to this context of Roman political, economic, ideological, and social domination in which the Jesus movement sought to carve out a place for itself. Possible cultural influences on Matthew, then, need to be investigated: how Matthew's deployment of 'shepherd' compares with its use in Roman texts may have a bearing on pinpointing his socio-religious location.

Among Roman sources, only those authors whose dates would have at least partially overlapped with those of Matthew will be examined. That is, people belonging to the earliest Matthean communities, including the author of the Gospel, would likely have been born in the early part of the first century CE and probably would have died either at the end of the first century or early into the second century; hence, the authors of Roman texts surveyed in chapter 3 of the study chronologically overlap with the first century.

Roman authors predating Matthew do use 'shepherd';[98] but these texts need not be examined for the present investigation. Although earlier Jewish traditions like the Jewish scriptures very obviously influenced Matthew's thought, it neither follows nor is all that probable that earlier Gentile writings or traditions had much sway with the Evangelist. On the one hand, there is simply very little evidence to support the view that early Greek or Roman traditions had an impact on the Gospel.[99] While

---

94   A. Berlin, 'Romanization and anti-Romanization', in *The First Jewish Revolt: Archaeology, History, and Ideology*, ed. A. Berlin and J. A. Overman (London: Routledge, 2002), 69.

95   See Vancil, 'Shepherd', 99–127, and G. Alders, *Political Thought in Hellenistic Times* (Amsterdam: Adolf M. Hakkert, 1975), 17–27.

96   Carter has written extensively on this topic; for a list of some of these works, see W. Carter, *Matthew and Empire: Initial Explorations* (Harrisburg: Trinity Press, 2001), 2–3; cf. J. Riches and D. Sim (eds), *The Gospel of Matthew in its Roman Imperial Context*, JSNTSS 276 (New York: T&T Clark International, 2005).

97   The starting point for Carter's method is the historical context of Matthew: 'the Gospel comes from and addresses a world dominated by the Roman Empire' (*Empire*, 1).

98   E.g. the Italian poet Virgil (c. 70–19 BCE) deploys pastoral themes featuring literal shepherds in his poems.

99   E.g. D. Balch finds parallels for Matthew's use of περὶ νόμων ('concerning

Philo, for example, was a Jew devoted to Judaism and consequently much of his writings focused on the Jewish scriptures and certain elements of the Jewish religion, his commitment to Greek philosophy is readily apparent in all of his treatises. The same cannot be said for the author of Matthew: ancient Greek or Roman writings find no place in his story of Jesus. On the other hand, Roman authors typically avoid using 'shepherd' metaphorically for rulers (as will be observed in section 3.3 below) – quite unlike Matthew. This discrepancy also suggests that Matthew was not influenced by earlier Roman traditions. Conversely, given the overall insignificance the nascent Jesus movement held for the culturally dominant Roman Empire – its inconsequentiality evidenced by the paucity of and only passing references to the movement by first-to-second-century Roman authors – it seems highly unlikely that Matthew ever influenced Roman writers.

Earlier Roman writings could possibly have had some sway with Matthew if he was a converted non-Jew, or a Jew who was strongly attracted to Roman thought and culture (the way, for example, Philo was clearly drawn to Greek and Hellenistic thought), but it remains highly unlikely that early Gentile authors would have had much play with a CB Jew like Matthew, whose text exhibits, by all accounts, very obvious Jewish rather than Roman affinities. If some measure of influence existed it would come about for Matthew, as a member of the Roman Empire, through regular social interactions with non-Jewish Romans: i.e. through general cultural influence.[100]

1.4 Methodological Issues

1.4.1 Using texts for determining social location

New Testament scholars have long recognized the complexities involved in moving from the world of or within a text to the historical events to which a text refers. S. Byrskog summarizes the objection of scholars who advocate the separation of story and history: 'To read narrative texts both as "mirrors" reflecting self-contained worlds and as "windows" opening up to extrafictional and diachronic levels of history is often considered to be a violation of proper hermeneutical conduct.'[101]

---

laws') in the writings of Dio Chrysostom and Dionysius of Halicarnassus ('The Greek Political Topos περί νόμων and Matthew 5:17, 19, and 16:19', in *Social History of the Matthean Community: Cross-Disciplinary Approaches*, ed. D. Balch [Minneapolis: Fortress Press, 1991], 68–84), but he fails to prove that Matthew owes his deployment of this phrase to the Hellenistic thought represented by Dio and Dionysius.

100 For further discussion, see section 3.3.1 below.

101 S. Byrskog, *Story as History – History as Story: The Gospel Tradition in the Context of Ancient Oral History*, repr. (Boston: Brill, 2002), 1. For a helpful review of scholarship addressing the question of the relationship between text and history, see Byrskog, *Story*, 1–17.

Further, beyond the problems of correlating text with historical refer-ent is the difficult enterprise of deriving social-historical realities from a text. B. Holmberg cautions scholars who consider the text as purely 'transparent':[102]

> A text can just as well be standing in a negative correlation to the situation of the receivers, i.e., challenge or try to change it. In practice this means that one should at least ask oneself if the correlation between the analyzed text and its social situation is complete or partial, positive or negative.[103]

In other words, even if transparency is assumed, in what way is the text being transparent: wholly, partially, directly, indirectly, inversely? Scholars should not assume a uniform, straightforward transparent reading of the text.

Although a few commentators reject all degrees of transparency,[104] social theorists have long recognized the interwoven nature of the individual–society relationship. In his discussion of religion and world-construction, P. Berger recognizes that re-appropriating or discussing the outside world is dependent upon (i.e. is possible because of) the realities that comprise that world, and informed and shaped by those realities.[105] In other words, a narrative text presents, on the one hand, a story of historical or historical-like events, which is shaped by the diverse social-historical factors influencing the author.[106] Thus, as

---

102   A 'transparent' text means that the situations described within the narrative are a direct reflection of the situations faced by the original audience addressed by that text. Thus, for example, contentious quarrels between the Pharisees and Jesus in Matthew's Gospel would be more a reflection of the ongoing, harsh disputes between Matthew's audience and the Pharisees than of controversies between Jesus and the Pharisees.

103   B. Holmberg, *Sociology and the New Testament: An Appraisal* (Minneapolis: Fortress Press, 1990), 125.

104   E.g. F. Watson, 'Toward a Literal Reading of the Gospels', in *The Gospels for All Christians: Rethinking the Gospel Audiences*, ed. R. Bauckham (Grand Rapids: Eerdmans, 1998), 195–217.

105   P. Berger, *The Sacred Canopy: Elements of a Sociological Theory of Religion* (New York: Random House, 1990). He notes that society, as a dialectic process, consists of three moments or steps: 'externalization' (humans acting upon the world outside of them), 'objectivation' (the formation of a world resulting from externalization), and 'internalization' (the re-appropriation of what has been formed). In regards to the latter step, Berger comments, 'The process of internalization must always be understood as but one moment of the larger dialectic process that also includes the moments of externaliza-tion and objectivation. ... Not only is internalization part of the latter's larger dialectic, but the socialization of the individual also occurs in a dialectic manner. The individual is not molded as a passive, inert thing. Rather, he is formed in the course of protracted con-versation (a dialectic in the literal sense of the word) in which he is a *participant*' (*Sacred Canopy*, 18, his emphasis).

106   E. Wainwright (*Shall We Look for Another? A Feminist Rereading of the Matthean Jesus*, BLS, gen. ed. N. Gottwald and R. Horsley [Maryknoll: Orbis Books, 1998], 36) speaks of this text–context interaction as the 'inseparability of text, reader, and context'.

Byrskog notes, '[Gospel] narratives inevitably contain stories about the past history as well as the present existence. Interpretation [by the author] was the bridge between them, bringing the two worlds of history and story together.'[107] Similarly, the author's audience, on the other hand, is affected by their own social-historical factors (often but not always overlapping with the author's), as well as by the text itself, which can frequently diverge from their version of oral tradition of the events of which they read. Within the interconnectedness of text and social-historical context, the narrative world of the text and the social location of the world behind the text intersect; and insofar as they intersect, the text world can offer insight into the social location represented by the text. This region of overlap, then, enables scholars to do more than explain what a text means. Exegetes can also deduce some of the social-historical realities surrounding the author and the intended audience. But to what extent do these realities reflect the circumstances of the author and to what degree those of the audience?

1.4.2 Whose social location is it anyways?

R. Bauckham has called into question the consensus view that each Gospel was written for a specific community, asserting that 'the Gospels were written for general circulation around the churches and so envisaged a very general Christian audience. Their implied readership is not specific but indefinite: any and every Christian community in the late-first-century Roman Empire.'[108] In his very suggestive essay ('For Whom Were Gospels Written?') Bauckham demonstrates in an overview of New Testament scholarship that the case for community was merely assumed from the beginning,[109] and that scholars, in effect, take a Pauline approach to interpreting a Gospel's social setting. Bauckham, however, contrasts the genre and purpose of Gospels with (those of the Pauline) letters: letters explicitly identify the readers and the situation(s) addressed; hence, subsequent readers of Paul's letters remain entirely cognizant of the fact that Paul – in the first instance – wrote to someone else.[110] Also, letters were written as a stand-in for the author who was separated from the readers by distance and unable to communicate with them in person. A Gospel, on the other hand, is a βίος, a form of ancient

107 Byrskog, *Story*, 265.
108 Bauckham, 'Introduction', in *The Gospels for All Christians: Rethinking the Gospel Audiences*, ed. R. Bauckham (Grand Rapids: Eerdmans, 1998), 1.
109 Bauckham, 'For Whom Were the Gospels Written?', in *The Gospels for All Christians: Rethinking the Gospel Audiences*, ed. R. Bauckham (Grand Rapids: Eerdmans, 1998), 13–22.
110 However, based on the subsequent collection of Paul's letters, historical specificity and general application are not mutually exclusive. Evidence for this complementary perspective comes from the letters themselves: Paul can remind the Corinthians that the things he shares with them he shares 'everywhere in every church' (1 Cor. 4.17; 14.33).

biography; hence, like other ancient biographies it was intended to circulate widely, not locally.[111] Further, a βίος was never meant to be a stand-in for its author – it was literature intended to inspire its readers and apply to them generally.

Despite inconsistencies in his argument, Bauckham's thesis remains convincing at some points. He demonstrates the need to reject a wholesale transparent reading of the Gospels in favour of a more measured transparency: i.e. not every element within the narrative need correspond to the social situation of the audience.[112] Bauckham also shows the importance of distinguishing between the social context of the author and that of the readers.[113] Hence, the Gospel's theological distinctives would be more representative of the author than of his audience.[114] That said, there remains a sense in which the author's views could represent those immediately around him, i.e. an inner circle of associates, to be distinguished from his (or perhaps 'their') audience.[115] In this way, the views of Matthew would, technically, represent a 'community': his inner circle of associates.

Bauckham forcefully argues that the original audience of a Gospel probably extended beyond the local community of which the Evangelist was a part. As his critics rightly contend, however, a 'universal' audience seems

111   See R. Burridge, *What are the Gospels? A Comparison with Graeco-Roman Biography*, 2nd edn (Grand Rapids: Eerdmans, 2004), and Stanton, *Gospel*, 50–51.

112   Within the Two-Source Hypothesis this would especially be true since Matthew incorporates much of Mark and Q – both directed to different audiences – as is.

113   Bauckham notes, 'Certainly it may be argued that the community in which a Gospel was written is likely to have influenced the writing of the Gospel even though it is not addressed by the Gospel' ('For Whom', 44); cf. the critical remarks of Holmberg, *Sociology*, 140–41.

114   In his response to Bauckham, D. Sim insists that 'the Evangelists shaped their Gospels in the light of their prospective readers, the communities in which they lived' (Sim, 'The Gospels for All Christians? A Response to Richard Bauckham', *JSNT* 84 [2001], 25). Consequently, Sim asserts that the opposing views of Torah represented in Mark and Matthew represent the views of their respective audiences. While this obviously would have been the case to some degree – the two would certainly not be mutually exclusive – exactly to what degree can never be answered, never mind assumed. That, generally speaking, the theology of a text represents that of the author more than his readers' can be observed even in other forms of theological writing. For example, with Paul, did the Corinthian community – an assembly started by Paul – mirror the theology reflected by him in his letters to them? It would seem at a number of points that they did not, which is precisely why Paul instructs them: e.g. his discussions of head coverings (1 Cor. 11.2-16) and glossolalia (1 Corinthians 12–14).

115   Social theorists, for example, recognize that not only are individual beliefs and values not formed in a vacuum, they are not maintained in isolation – others equally share and embrace them. Thus, Berger writes, 'While it may be possible, perhaps for heuristic purposes, to analyse man's relationship to his world in purely individual terms, the empirical reality of human world-building is aways a social one. Men *together* shape tools, invent languages, adhere to values, devise institutions, and so on' (*Sacred Canopy*, 7, his emphasis).

unlikely.[116] Hence, while the Gospels were intended to circulate widely and were not bound to one specific locale,[117] they were probably not written for a universal audience, as Bauckham supposes. In view of the preceding discussion, then, the socio-religious orientation determined by this present inquiry will correspond more to that of Matthew (and his inner circle of associates) than that of his audience; that is to say, a distinction should be maintained between Matthew's views and those of his audience – although these would not necessarily be mutually exclusive. How, then, can Matthew's socio-religious location be derived from his Christology?

1.4.3 Using Christology for determining socio-religious orientation

Christological studies tend to be theologically or historically focused, and hence do not typically consider questions of social location. Moreover, with the advent of literary criticism in the 1970s, social questions became completely overshadowed by literary ones or ignored altogether,[118] thus crystallizing the separation of Christology and social location. As mentioned in section 1.2.3 above, social location inquiries have largely ignored the significant piece that Christology brings to the puzzle of Matthew's socio-religious orientation. Malina and Neyrey first recognized the inadequacy of viewing Christology in purely philosophical, metaphysical, or historical terms, because of its intrinsic social dimension: '[A biblical historian must] describe and explain the behaviour of group members, not disembodied ideas or concepts. Christology, if truly "historical", will be Christology "from the side". It must take into account the human evaluative process.'[119]

In taking a 'from the side' approach, Malina and Neyrey examine the conflict in Matthew 12 and 26–27 by focusing on the negative labels given to Jesus by his opponents and the positive titles given to him by his followers. Thus, the interest of these two authors lies more in the process in which Jesus receives these titles than the result, i.e. the titles themselves:

> The *historical* significance of those titles will not stand apart from the *cultural* and *social* underpinnings those titles were meant to maintain. The titles

116   See the critical reviews of M. Mitchell, 'Patristic Counter-Evidence to the Claim that the Gospels were Written for All Christians', *NTS* 51 (2005): 36–79; T. Kazen, 'Sectarian Gospels for Some Christians: Intention and Mirror Reading in the Light of Extra-Canonical Texts', *NTS* 51 (2005): 561–78; Sim, 'Response'; and P. Esler, 'Community and Gospel in Early Christianity: A Response to Richard Bauckham's *Gospels for All Christians*', *SJT* 51 (1998): 235–48.

117   Sim is willing to concede this point, adding, 'This concession would entail only a slight revision of the consensus position. We would need to broaden the definition of any given Gospel community and view it not as a single church, but as a cluster of churches linked by geographical proximity and a shared theological perspective' ('Response', 24).

118   E.g. Kingsbury, *Matthew*.

119   Malina and Neyrey, *Calling Jesus*, xii.

were not ideas or concepts meant to define some abstract divine being but
social labels endowed with meaning and feeling meant to mark off the inter-
ests of contending groups.[120]

Although their study rightly recognizes the 'inseparability of text,
reader, and context',[121] Malina and Neyrey do not take the next step:
to identify specific aspects of the social context of the Christ-believers
represented by Matthew's Gospel.

Stanton takes this step.[122] He acknowledges that 'most of Matthew's
major Christological emphases are a development or a modification
of themes which were already prominent in the sources on which
the evangelist drew, and hence not directly related to the "parting of
the ways"'.[123] Nevertheless, he also maintains, 'Some of Matthew's
Christological themes are clearly related *indirectly* to the parting.'[124]
Stanton focuses on the accusations against Jesus of being a magician
(an implicit charge) and a deceiver (an explicit charge), as well as on
the disputes involving the 'Son of David' title. Like Malina and Neyrey,
Stanton asserts that these passages reveal counterclaims of Matthew
against these accusations (originally levelled by Jesus' opponents),[125]
and argues that these counterclaims reveal Matthew's socio-religious
orientation, which Stanton understands as the Mattheans recently separating from Judaism and from Jewish synagogue. The obvious problem
in Stanton's attempt to employ Christology to determine social location,
however, is that the matter has been settled before beginning his investigation.[126] Consequently, he examines Matthew's Christology simply
to confirm his view and not to establish it – unlike the present study.[127]

Although the approach of using the labels of Jesus' (Matthew's)
opponents offers insight into Matthew's socio-religious location, additional (and in some ways, more direct) insight can be gleaned from
the names used for Jesus by Matthew himself because his names for
Jesus are bound to his own social-historical context. One such name is
'Shepherd'.

---

120   Malina and Neyrey, *Calling Jesus*, 135–36 (their emphasis).
121   So Wainwright, *Shall We*, 36.
122   Stanton, *Gospel*, 169–91.
123   Stanton, *Gospel*, 189.
124   Stanton, *Gospel*, 189 (his emphasis).
125   Matthew would have used these counterclaims to equip his audience to respond
to the same accusations made some fifty years later by their own opponents.
126   He begins his analysis by writing, 'In the preceding chapters of this book I have
argued that Matthew has written his gospel to a cluster of Christian communities which
have recently parted company painfully with Judaism' (*Gospel*, 169).
127   Thus, while Stanton's analysis plainly demonstrates conflict between the
Mattheans and Jewish leaders, it does not necessarily follow that this conflict spells
separation from Judaism, anymore than conflict between the Sadducees and the Pharisees
means that the former group had separated from Judaism.

1.4.4 *Using metaphor for accessing social location*

As the previous section shows, scholars have recently come to recognize the usefulness of Christology in the debate over Matthew's social location. The antecedent question to the discussion of how the shepherd metaphor in particular can contribute to determining social location would be: can metaphors, being linguistic or literary constructions, be used to glean social history?[128]

Simply put, metaphors function to enhance understanding. Linguists have long realized that a gap exists between words and the referents they attempt to describe.[129] Metaphors help bridge this word–referent divide variously. They provide ways of expressing ideas or phenomena which could otherwise not be described in literal terms. They simplify or compact communication. They also vivify language. The frequency and significance of metaphors in language and communication have led G. Lakoff and M. Johnson to the conclusion that metaphor is more than a matter of language – it is a matter of thought: it governs reasoning and constitutes understanding.[130] Despite flaws to their theory of the metaphor,[131] Lakoff and Johnson correctly draw attention to the fact that metaphor is fundamental to how people think. Metaphors are not simply language ornaments: they are thought essentials. C. Tilley comments that metaphor cannot function merely as word substitution and nothing more, since '[t]his perspective is inadequate because it is incapable of providing an account of the processes by means of which novel metaphors get produced'.[132]

---

128   J. Fernandez, who readily recognizes the importance of metaphors for anthropological analysis, quaintly captures the reluctance of some scholars in his field: 'One always feels a bit sheepish of course about bringing the metaphor concept into the social sciences and perhaps this is because one always feels there is something soft and woolly about it' (Fernandez, *Persuasions and Performances: The Play of Tropes in Culture* [Bloomington: Indiana University Press, 1986], 6).

129   For a brief but helpful discussion of this point, see C. Tilley, *Metaphor and Material Culture* (Oxford: Blackwell Publishers, 1999), 6–8.

130   G. Lakoff and M. Johnson, *Metaphors We Live By* (Chicago: University of Chicago Press, 1980), and also Lakoff and M. Turner, *More Than Cool Reason: A Field Guide to Poetic Metaphor* (Chicago: University of Chicago Press, 1989).

131   For a critique of Lakoff and Johnson, particularly as their work relates to biblical studies, see D. Aaron, *Biblical Ambiguities: Metaphor, Semantics, and Divine Imagery* (Leiden: Brill, 2002), 10–15, 101–11.

132   Tilley, *Metaphor*, 12. Similarly, J. Culler ('The Turns in Metaphor', in *The Pursuit of Signs* [London: Routledge, 1981], 55), notes how the universal act of grouping distinct things under a common heading based on perceived resemblances – the classical definition of a metaphor (describing one thing in terms of another) – reveals how intrinsic metaphor is to the way people think.

Given the primary nature of metaphors in human thought, scholars have begun to make the connection between metaphor and culture. T. Fitzgerald, for example, states, 'More than merely figurative speech – always rooted in cultural and social experiences – metaphors carry culture-bound assumptions about our everyday lives. What a culture values, then, will frequently be metaphorically expressed.'[133] Similarly, Tilley remarks how '[metaphor] can also be conceived as a quality which links together individuals and groups'.[134] Consequently, he writes, 'Learning metaphor becomes part and parcel of the process of the acquisition of cultural knowledges and the authority residing in their acquisition.'[135]

This metaphor–culture connection has been taken up recently in biblical studies. Drawing upon the insights of Lakoff and Johnson, and P. Ricoeur,[136] G. Anderson considers metaphors vehicles for the deeper understanding of one's place in the world.[137] He agrees with Ricoeur that metaphors possess intrinsic meaning in their own right (hence, Ricoeur's adage: 'the symbol gives rise to the thought'), but he parts company with him in recognizing that the ultimate significance of the metaphor comes from the context in which the user employs it. Anderson writes:

> Rather, it is within the foundation myths of a given culture that these primary symbols [metaphors] are deployed in a more robust and profound manner. In such narratives a culture takes up the larger issue of the fundamental grammar of these symbolic lexemes and articulates in story form how one can understand one's place in the world because of them.[138]

Similarly, in his discussion of the semantic importance of metaphors, Porter notes that 'a correct understanding of a metaphor can be reconstructed only from its social or extralinguistic context ... [including] the historical background'.[139] The meaning of a metaphor, then, is tied to the social-historical context in which it is used. Thus, a metaphor has

---

133   Fitzgerald, *Metaphors of Identity: A Culture-Communication Dialogue* (New York: State University of New York Press, 1993), 160.

134   Tilley, *Metaphor*, 9.

135   Tilley, *Metaphor*, 9.

136   P. Ricoeur, *The Symbolism of Evil*, trans. E. Buchanan (New York: Harper & Row, 1967).

137   G. Anderson, 'From Israel's Burden to Israel's Debt: Towards a Theology of Sin in Biblical and Early Second Temple Sources', in *Reworking the Bible: Apocryphal and Related Texts at Qumran*, ed. E. Chazon, D. Dimant, and R. Clements, STDJ 58 (Leiden: Brill, 2005), 1–30.

138   Anderson, 'Israel's Debt', 2–3.

139   Porter, *Monsters*, 5; cf. the discussion of Huntzinger, 'End of Exile', 23–54.

intrinsic meaning but it is closely tied to the social-historical context of the one who appropriates it, whereby the metaphor's meaning is developed further. Huntzinger underscores these two observations:

> [Later authors] did not merely 'borrow' the metaphor – careful not to ply or mold it in any way – but they made it theirs by taking it and asking what the metaphor was saying to them. The reality depicted by the metaphor had significance for them which is why they used it. By taking ownership of the metaphor they were able to shape it for themselves and make it useful just as it had been useful to the previous community from whom they had inherited it.[140]

According to Huntzinger (et al.), metaphor users recognize the intrinsic meaning that a metaphor possesses – which is why they use it – and they seek to develop that meaning for those with whom they communicate. Thus, given the primary nature of metaphor with respect to thought and communication, and given the close connection between metaphor and culture,[141] the appropriations of metaphors should reflect something of the borrower's thoughts or patterns of thought, according to the way in which a writer 'shapes' or uses it.

Patterns of thought represent part of what E. P. Sanders calls 'patterns of religion'. He defines a pattern of religion as 'the description of how a religion is perceived by its adherents to *function*'.[142] The key, he notes, is not what adherents do (i.e. their religious practices), but how they understand what these practices accomplish for them in their religion. Consequently, a pattern of religion '*does* have to do with *thought*, with the *understanding* that lies behind religious behaviour, not just with the externals of religious behaviour'.[143] In other words, a pattern of religion is comprised of patterns of ritual (behaviour) and patterns of thought (theology), the latter of which, according to Sanders, consists of separate motifs.[144] Of these two constituent elements comprising a pattern of religion, this study focuses on patterns of thought – concerning the shepherd metaphor.

---

140   Huntzinger, 'End of Exile', 54.
141   'Culture' meaning a set of shared beliefs, values, and practices.
142   E. P. Sanders, *Paul and Palestinian Judaism: A Comparison of Patterns of Religion* (Philadelphia: Fortress Press, 1977), 17 (his emphasis).
143   Sanders, *Paul*, 18 (his emphasis).
144   Sanders, *Paul*, 18. While many of the conclusions which Sanders draws from his work remain flawed – something his numerous detractors point out – his *stated* method of examining the context and function of a motif on its own terms, first and foremost, before moving on to compare the motif's use in two religions, is not simply valid but wise.

1.4.5 Using the shepherd metaphor for assessing socio-religious orientation

Of Matthew's various Christological strands, 'Shepherd' offers significant potential for exploring his socio-religious orientation because of its use by NCB Jewish, NCB Roman, and CB authors. Because the metaphor is a core leadership symbol for early Jews and Christ-believers, it would represent a central thought pattern for these authors. As chapters 2 and 3 of this study will show, 'shepherd' is employed as a metaphor for pre-monarchical rulers of Israel, the Jewish monarchy, members of the ruling class, as well as authoritative NCB Jewish teachers, on the one hand, and for assembly leaders in CB circles, on the other. The shepherd metaphor, then, relates to the hierarchical realities of a community, and the way in which it is appropriated can provide a window into how a community might structure itself socially.[145]

Not only is the metaphor an important symbol for leadership, but it represents one of a handful of terms that is used in a distinctive way by these different groups of ancient authors. As will be demonstrated in chapter 3 below, there are characteristic tendencies in its usage by these authors, reflecting specific patterns of thought. One distinctive use of the metaphor, for example, that sets its appropriation by NCB Jews apart from the other two groups of authors is the frequent overtones of Jewish nationalism. Similarly, a frequent characteristic of Jewish eschatology over and against the eschatology of Christ-believers is the concern for the restoration of national Israel.[146] These types of distinctive patterns of thought reflected in the use of the metaphor by the different groups of authors analysed in this study provide essential points of comparison with Matthew: With which group does the Evangelist's shepherd motif reflect continuity? The answer to this question provides a small but still essential piece to the puzzle of Matthew's socio-religious orientation.

At this point it should be emphasized that although this study is concerned with comparing a particular metaphor in different bodies of literature, it avoids what Sanders considers the key mistake often made by NT scholars engaged in comparative research with early Jewish writings.[147] Of special relevance for this inquiry is his criticism of studies that compare 'individual motifs'. He regards these types of comparison

---

145 For a discussion of hierarchical social structures and religious experiences reflected in the roles of 'Steward', 'Prophet', and 'Keeper of the Word', see R. Williams, *Stewards, Prophets, Keepers of the Word: Leadership in the Early Church* (Peabody: Hendrickson, 2006).

146 Cf. the analysis of Chester, 'Eschatology and Messianic Hope', 239–313. According to Dunn, it was this 'Jewish national particularism' that 'came into ever sharper confrontation [with 'Christian christological particularism'] until a decisive parting of the ways was unavoidable' ('Preface', in *Jews and Christians: The Parting of the Ways AD 70 to 135*, ed. J. Dunn [Tübingen: J. C. B. Mohr Paul Siebeck, 1992], viii).

147 See Sanders, *Paul*, 1–29.

as 'inadequate for the true comparison of religions' because scholars tend to prefer one religion over another, and they also ignore the historical context of a given motif.[148] The present investigation differentiates itself from those that Sanders et al. criticize in that it adopts a more even-handed and holistic approach to examining a motif. 'Shepherd' represents a significant metaphor both for Jews and Christ-believers – not just one group. Additionally, the study is not concerned with the question of origins but with differences in thought patterns reflected by the patterns of usage of the metaphor. In other words, unlike many other studies, the focus of this investigation is not on an 'individual motif' but on the use of a motif. Thus, it is crucial that the appropriation of the metaphor by each group of authors be understood in its own right and on its own terms. Consequently, a good deal of attention in this study is devoted to considering the function and the context of every appropriation of the shepherd metaphor. By discerning the respective functions and contexts of the metaphor's use by Second Temple Jews, Romans, Matthew, and other Christ-believers, patterns or tendencies in thought can be properly mapped and accurately assessed for areas of continuity and discontinuity between Matthew and writers from these other groups.

1.4.6 Matthew's 'shepherd': signficant and serviceable?

In view of the subsequent discussion, some preliminary matters concerning the shepherd metaphor's usage must be addressed. First, can Matthew's shepherd motif be considered significant? Unlike other Christological titles which (at times) reflect Matthean invention or redaction, the same cannot be said about 'shepherd': in Mt. 2.6 the metaphor is simply embedded in a scripture citation; 9.36 merely takes over a Markan allusion to scripture; in 25.32 Matthew compares the Son of Man's acts to a shepherd and not the Son of Man himself; and 26.31 represents another Markan citation of scripture. Can this type of employment of the metaphor represent a significant interest in the metaphor on the part of the Evangelist?

From a redaction-critical perspective, which concentrates on changes to the sources, these occurrences of the metaphor could perhaps be deemed insignificant. A composition-critical approach, however, recognizes that when scripture citations and Markan sayings are transferred to a new narrative context, these citations are given new meanings, since meaning is dependent upon literary context. But something more could perhaps be said about Matthew's 'incidental' use of the shepherd metaphor.

---

148   See Sanders, *Paul*, 13. J. Z. Smith is much more overt in his criticism of these studies arguing that their (sometimes hidden) motivation is highly apologetic: to '[protect] the privileged position of early Christianity' (*Drudgery Divine: On the Comparison of Early Christianities and the Religions of Late Antiquity* [Chicago: University of Chicago Press, 1990], 48).

In each of these texts, Matthew had other options from which to choose to make his particular point in the narrative – options which would have excluded the metaphor. The thrust of Matthew's citation in 2.6 is the justification of the messiah's place of origin. Micah 5.1 satisfies this point by itself. Additionally, had the Evangelist wanted to emphasize the ruling aspect of Jesus by blending Mic. 5.1 with another scripture text – without invoking the shepherd metaphor – 'shepherd'-less texts were available to him. For example, a mixed citation of Mic. 5.1 and Ps. 130.8 would have accomplished this nicely: 'And you Bethlehem, land of Judah, by no means are you least among the rulers of Judah, for out of you will come a ruler [Mic. 5.1], *and he will redeem Israel from all their sins* [Ps. 130.8].' In view of Mt. 1.21b ('and he will save his people from their sins'), the shepherd-less text of Ps. 130.8 would make even better sense than 2 Sam 5.2.[149] That Matthew opts for the latter text – which employs 'shepherd' – suggests an interest on his part explicitly to link the metaphor with Jesus through prophetic/scriptural citation.[150]

Although two of Matthew's appropriations of the metaphor come straight out of his Markan source, it would be unwise to assume that there would, therefore, be no significance to these uses, as Davies and Allison comment:

> Our author's compositional habits were not like those of a sea-bottom scavenger which picks up everything without discrimination. Matthew, as his treatment of Mark demonstrates, felt quite free to drop what did not impress him as valuable. So it is very hazardous to dismiss any verse in Matthew as without meaning because traditional.[151]

Thus, in the case of Mt. 26.31, had Mark's citation of the shepherd text (Zech. 13.7) not suited Matthew, the Evangelist could very well have crafted a betrayal scene without it, as Luke and John did (Lk. 22.31-38; Jn 13.21-38). Moreover, in Mt. 9.36, the logion of Mk 6.34 appears in a very different literary context in Matthew than it does in Mark, thereby revealing Matthew's strong interest in Mark's allusion here to the HB.[152]

---

149   Other possibilities would include, for example, Isa. 32.1a; 49.7b; and Jer. 23.5b.

150   While 2 Sam. 5.2 links Jesus to David's lineage, the Evangelist has already made the case for this in his genealogy. Something else prompted his use of 2 Sam. 5.2: 'shepherd'.

151   W. D. Davies and D. Allison, *The Gospel According to Saint Matthew*, 3 vols, ICC (Edinburgh: T&T Clark 1988–97), 2.192.

152   See the discussion of these texts in sections 3.4.2 (Mark) and 4.2.2 (Matthew) below.

In the pericope of Final Judgment in 25.31-46, again the question could be asked, did Matthew have metaphorical options from which to choose other than the shepherd-sheep metaphor? The answer is yes. Matthew appropriates the metaphor to describe the manner by which Jesus will judge all the nations that gather before him in the Eschaton. Of the various metaphors from which to choose,[153] the Evangelist could have chosen the harvest metaphor, first introduced by the words of John the Baptist: 'Whose winnowing fork is in his hand and he will clean out his threshing floor and gather his wheat into his barn, but the chaff he will burn up with unquenchable fire' (Mt. 3.12). This harvest judgement picture is filled out further in the parable of the tares (13.24-30, 36-43), which speaks of the 'angels gathering' the people of the 'world' before the 'Son of Man' and separating the people into wheat (the righteous) and tares (the wicked), with the former group shining in the 'Father's kingdom'. Matthew uses all of these ideas in his scene of Final Judgement. The Evangelist, then, was anything but boxed into using the shepherd metaphor in 25.31-46. That he chose it, however, would suggest – particularly in view of its other occurrences in his Gospel – that its deployment in his scene of Final Judgment was consonant with his concern to depict Jesus as Israel's Shepherd.[154]

Thus, the Evangelist' choice of 2 Sam. 5.2 over and against other suitable scripture texts, his handling of Mk 6.34, his adopting of Mk 14.27, and his choice of the shepherd-sheep metaphor over other equally appropriate metaphors in his scene of Final Judgment demonstrate the significance that the shepherd metaphor held for Matthew. The importance of the metaphor receives further corroboration from Matthew's unique citation of the shepherd narrative of Zechariah 11 in 27.9-10 (see section 4.2.5 below), the references to Jesus being sent to the 'lost sheep of the house of Israel' in 10.6 and 15.24, as well as the interconnectedness between the shepherd and the Son of David motifs (see sections 1.2.2 above and 4.2.2 below).

The second preliminary matter concerns the specific methodological focus of the analysis. The investigation of the shepherd metaphor will concentrate on explicit uses of 'shepherd' and 'shepherding' (רעה in Hebrew,[155] ποιμήν or ποιμαίνω in Greek). This focus, however, does not mean that shepherding imagery without the use of 'shepherd' has been overlooked in this study – it has not. The imagery associated with the shepherd metaphor in the HB can be quite broad;[156] but when the

153   E.g. the warrior-judge imagery of Isa. 11.1-5 and Ezekiel 21, and the dragnet in Mt. 13.47-50.

154   Cf. Chae (*Davidic Shepherd*, 220–21), who argues for the importance of this metaphor on completely different grounds.

155   The Qal participle form of the verb רעה also serves as the substantive 'shepherd'.

156   Shepherding imagery can be evoked by the mention of 'sheep' (e.g. 2 Sam. 24.17; Ps. 95.7; Mic. 2.12), a shepherd's duties of leading, feeding, guiding, and gathering the flock

shepherd metaphor is invoked without using רעה, it does not appreciably add to the use of the רעה-metaphor but merely follows the pattern
of usage outlined in chapter 2 below.

Thus, for example, parallel to רעה, biblical writers use 'rod' (שבט)
metaphorically to signify rulers: Jewish monarchs or members of the
ruling class,[157] Gentile kings or leaders,[158] or YHWH.[159] Likewise,
'staff' (משען/משענת) is employed metaphorically for Jewish monarchs
or members of the ruling class,[160] Gentile rulers,[161] and for YHWH.[162]
At times judgement is associated with these terms, but this, too, follows
the pattern of רעה. Porter notes that herd leader language, i.e. 'he-goat'
(עתוד), 'ram' (איל), and 'bull' (פר, ראם), can evoke the shepherd metaphor. Thus, these animals symbolize (Gentile) monarchs[163] and military leaders.[164] Verbs with pastoral connotations are often employed
for YHWH: e.g. נחה ('lead', 'guide'),[165] נהל ('lead', 'guide'),[166] אסף
('gather'),[167] יצא ('go out'),[168] and בוא ('lead out').[169]

Similarly, shepherd imagery without the use of 'shepherd' in Second
Temple Jewish texts adds little to the discussion of the metaphor.[170]
Although צאן ('sheep') can conjure up the image of a shepherd, the
focus of צאן metaphors tends to be on the sheep not the shepherd, as

---

(e.g. Ps. 68.7; Isa. 49.10), as well as by his accoutrements (e.g. Isa. 10.5, 24; Ezek. 37.19).
For a survey of shepherding imagery in the HB beyond the use of 'shepherd', see Hunziker-
Rodewald, *Hirt*, 39–204, Fikes, 'Shepherd-King' and Huntzinger, 'End of Exile'. Wild
beast imagery can also presuppose the protection of a shepherd (e.g. 1 Sam. 17.34-35;
Mic. 5.7). For an investigation of shepherding imagery that includes this type of broader
pastoral imagery, see Porter, *Monsters*, 61–120.

157   Genesis 49.10; Num. 21.17; Ps. 2.9; 125.3; Isa. 11.4; Ezek. 19.11, 14.
158   Second Samuel 7.14; Isa. 10.5-8; 14.5, 29; 19.13; Amos 1.5; Zech. 10.11.
159   Job 9.34; 21.9; Ps. 23.4; 45.7; Isa. 30.31; Lam. 3.1; Ezek. 20.37; Mic. 7.14.
160   Isaiah 3.1-4.
161   Numbers 21.18; 2 Kgs 18.21/Isa. 36.6; Ezek. 29.6.
162   Psalm 23.4; i.e. as the psalmist's Shepherd, YHWH's staff offers him comfort.
163   Isaiah 14.9; Dan 8.4-8.
164   Isaiah 34.2-7; Ps. 22.12, 20; Zech. 10.3-5.
165   Exodus 13.17-21; 15.13; Deut. 32.12; Neh. 9.12, 19; Job 12.23; Pss 5.9; 23.3;
27.11; 43.3.
166   Exodus 15.13; 2 Chron. 32.22; Pss 23.2; 31.4; Isa. 40.11; 49.10.
167   Isaiah 49.5; Mic. 2.12; 4.6.
168   Isaiah 37.32; 40.26; 49.9; Ezek. 20.38; 34.13; Mic. 2.13; 7.15.
169   Numbers 27.17; Ps. 78.54; Jer. 30.3; 31.8-9; Ezek. 34.13; Zech. 10.10.
170   Some examples may prove helpful. Ram/bull imagery is used as a stand-in for
'shepherd', in *T. Jos.* 19.6 and *1 Enoch* 89.45-50. In the former text, the bull represents
the (possibly messianic) protector of the flock; in the latter text, the rams represent King
David and King Solomon. In *1 Enoch* 89.28-45, 'sheep' signify Israel's pre-monarchical
rulers: Moses, Joshua, and the Judges. Philo uses the shepherd's rod to symbolize the
imparting of discipline or self-control to rule the mind (e.g. *Leg.* 2.88-93; 1.77-78) or
sharing in God's shepherding activity (e.g. *Mut.* 135). When he employs 'sheep', his focus
takes an entirely different order: the efficacy of the sacrificial system (e.g. *Spec.* 1.257-58;
202-203); cf. Seibel, 'Shepherd & Sheep', 110–50.

is frequently the case in the HB. צאן is used metaphorically by itself (i.e. without רעה) twenty-two times of its 248 occurrences: it can refer to the special relationship between the nation Israel and YHWH,[171] the recipients (typically Israel) of YHWH's intervention,[172] victims of another nation's military advance,[173] subjects of a king/ruler,[174] objects of reproach,[175] and Israel's straying from YHWH.[176]

Of the two words in the HB used for 'shepherd', viz. רעה and בקר, focusing on the former term yields more fruitful results because בקר is almost never used metaphorically, while רעה is frequently employed in this way.[177] רעה then would correspond most closely to ποιμαίνω (and ποιμήν) the standard verb (and noun) used in Greek sources like Matthew for 'shepherd'.[178] By concentrating on רעה, the comparisons that are drawn between Hebrew texts and Greek texts will correspond more precisely. Thus, in texts which either have a Hebrew *Vorlage*[179] or in texts written by authors who knew Hebrew,[180] רעה would represent the Hebrew term standing behind the use of ποιμήν or ποιμαίνω in the texts which appropriate HB 'shepherd' passages.

In addition to these observations, the primary focus of this study deals with one strand of Matthew's Christology, Shepherd, and Matthew most frequently employs 'shepherd' (ποιμήν/ποιμαίνω) to deploy his Shepherd Christology (see chapter 4 below). Admittedly, Shepherd

171   Psalms 74.1; 79.13; 95.7; 100.3.
172   Psalms 77.21; 78.52; Mic. 2.12; Zech. 9.16.
173   Psalm 44.23; Mic. 5.7.
174   Second Samuel 24.17; Jer. 13.20.
175   Psalm 44.12; Jer. 12.3.
176   Isaiah 53.6. T. Slater (*Christ and Community: A Socio-Historical Study of the Christology of Revelation*, JSNTSS 178 [Sheffield: Sheffield Academic Press, 1999], 165–66) divides the above usages of 'sheep' (and also 'ram') into two categories: generic references and sacrificial references which, he notes, are maintained in Second Temple literature. In each of these categories, the emphasis is on the state of the sheep, not the nature or activity of the shepherd. Hence, when an author uses 'sheep' metaphorically, he is more interested in saying something about the sheep/people. When he uses 'shepherd' metaphorically, however, his interest lies in the shepherd/leader.
177   Of the 183 instances of בקר in the HB, the noun form never appears metaphorically, while the verb is used metaphorically twice in Ezekiel: 34.11, 12. By contrast, of the 167 occurrences of רעה, almost half (eighty-two) are metaphorical.
178   The LXX employs ποιμήν/ποιμαίνω for רעה ninety-two times, βόσκω for רעה seventeen times, and νέμω seven times. Of the latter two terms, νέμω never appears in the New Testament. While βόσκω appears nine times in the New Testament, it is never used for Jesus and only twice (Jn 21.15, 17) does it refer to leaders in CB communities, in contrast to ποιμαίνω/ποιμήν.
179   Of the Second Temple Jewish texts to be examined section 3.2 below, most scholars maintain that Judith, *Psalms of Solomon*, *Apocryphon of Ezekiel*, Pseudo-Philo, *2 Baruch*, and perhaps parts of *1 Enoch* were originally written in Hebrew.
180   Among the New Testament texts examined in this study, it seems probable that the authors of Matthew, John, Jude, and Revelation knew Hebrew.

Christology can be conveyed apart from the explicit use of 'shepherd', i.e. by using 'sheep'. But while Bracewell claims that focusing on 'shepherd' to the exclusion of 'sheep' would produce a biased study,[181] this is not actually the case. As discussed above, in the instances in the HB and Second Temple Jewish literature in which 'sheep' is used metaphorically without 'shepherd', they do not change in any appreciable way the portrait of the shepherd that is otherwise produced. In addition, the focus of 'sheep' metaphors is the sheep not the shepherd. As for the NT, 'sheep' is never employed metaphorically without 'shepherd' in Mark, John, Hebrews, and 1 Peter.[182] In Luke's metaphorical uses of 'sheep' in 12.32 and 15.4-6, the concern in the former is the sheep, while the latter relates to Jesus' inclusive mission;[183] he also uses 'sheep' for Jesus in Acts 8.32 (in a citation of Isa. 53.7-8) to describe the messiah's scripture-predicted, sacrificial death. All of these points are explicitly made by the 'shepherd' metaphor.[184] As will be observed in chapter 4 below, the metaphorical uses of 'sheep' in Matthew's Gospel do not alter in any way his Shepherd Christology.[185] Thus, metaphorical uses of 'sheep' do not affect the results of this study. Therefore, in chapters 2 to 4 below, concentrating on passages which employ 'shepherd' (רעה or ποιμαίνω/ποιμήν) will suffice for achieving the purposes of the study.

1.4.7 Methodological approach[186]

The first aim of this study is to investigate how Matthew presents Jesus as Israel's Shepherd and to examine how this motif contributes to the overall theological framework of the Gospel. The second aim is to assess the motif's implications for Matthew's socio-religious orientation and to outline some of the social-historical realities related to his socio-religious location. An effective and appropriate means to achieve these objectives will involve a literary analysis of the pertinent texts. Any discussion of social history must begin with closely reading and understanding the primary texts, for in the case of Matthew especially, this is the only arte-fact relating to him and his community that exists for academic study. Thus, any debate over the social location of Matthew must begin with understanding the Evangelist's message on its own terms, which offers a window into his theology and socio-religious location.

---

181   Bracewell, 'Shepherd Imagery', 4.
182   See Mk 6.34; 14.27; Jn 10; 21.15-17; Heb. 13.20; 1 Pet. 2.25; 5.2-3; cf. Acts 20.28-29).
183   See the discussion of these texts in section 3.4.5 below.
184   Paul, for his part, employs 'sheep' metaphorically in Rom. 8.36 (in a citation of Ps. 44.22) to describe the sometimes perilous circumstances of Christ-believers.
185   See the discussion of 'sheep' passages without 'shepherd', in Matthew in section 4.1 below.
186   For a more detailed discussion of the respective methologies employed here, see Baxter, 'Shepherd', 53–56.

There are several distinct but integrated components of the literary analysis employed in the present study, which commend themselves for Gospel study and which, when applied in concert, can produce a clearer picture than if used in isolation: composition criticism which, by concentrating on the final form of the text as a whole can allow for the type of contextual literary dissection needed to analyse the shepherd motif;[187] redaction criticism which, by focusing on the differences in the Synoptic tradition (between Matthew and Mark especially) can offer insights into Matthew's thought and emphases; intertextuality, i.e. the (re-)use of the Jewish scriptures by New Testament authors, since a close comparison between the scripture passage and Matthew's appropriation of it can shed additional light on the Evangelist's thought and emphases;[188] and narrative criticism to analyse the narrative flow of Matthew to capture the meaning conveyed by his story of Jesus. Since texts are the product of social history, the study will seek to explore the social-historical implications of the results of this composite methodological approach using the Gospel as a window into the social and religious history surrounding the text.[189] The social-historical implications will come to the fore in Part II of the study.

1.4.8 Mode of procedure

In view of discussing the implications of Matthew's shepherd motif for his socio-religious orientation, it will be necessary to map how the metaphor is employed by the different groups of authors. This map of uses will demonstrate the diversity of understandings that existed for the metaphor between these groups. Moreover, from this map, patterns of usage that reflect distinctive patterns of thought for each group of authors can be traced, and it is against these patterns that Matthew's own usage and thought concerning the metaphor can be compared. While some measure of overlap may be inevitable, the differences will be crucial for understanding Matthew. Whose literary and cultural world does the Evangelist's thought patterns most closely resemble? This type of agreement would

---

187   Cf. the discussions of composition criticism by B. Charette, *The Theme of Recompense in Matthew's Gospel*, JSNTSS 79 (Sheffield: Sheffield Academic Press, 1992), 16–19, and Willitts, *Shepherd-King*, 38–39. This study thus assumes authorial intent. For a discussion of authorial intent within the context of metaphor usage, see Aaron, *Biblical Ambiguities*, 5–7, 79–83.

188   For a discussion of this complex issue, see S. Porter, 'The Use of the Old Testament in the New Testament: A Brief Comment on Method and Terminology', in *Early Christian Interpretation of the Scriptures of Israel: Investigations and Proposals*, ed. C. A. Evans and J. A. Sanders, JSNTS 148 (Sheffield: Sheffield Academic Press, 1997), 79–96.

189   For a useful summary of social-historical methodology, see P. Harland, *Associations, Synagogue, and Congregations: Claiming a Place in Ancient Mediterranean Society* (Minneapolis: Fortress Press, 2003), 14–18.

suggest a measure of socio-religious continuity between Matthew and the group in question, and thus, represents one means of ascertaining the Evangelist's socio-religious orientation, which can then be described in terms of its location on a socio-religious spectrum.[190]

It should be emphasized that, because the interaction between NCB Jews and Christ-believers was complex and involved diverse spheres of engagement, more than one type of spectrum could be generated reflecting socio-religious location. For example, Matthew's socio-religious orientation could be discussed in terms of ritual practices: the Temple cult, the Sabbath, purity laws; how does Matthew's attitude towards these types of rituals compare with the attitudes of NCB Jews and Christ-believers (Fig. 1.1 below).[191] Alternatively, it could be examined in terms of attitudes towards Gentiles: how does Matthew's view of Gentiles compare with the views of other Christ-believers and NCB Jews (Fig. 1.2 below)?[192]

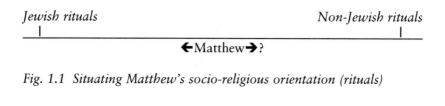

Fig. 1.1 *Situating Matthew's socio-religious orientation (rituals)*

Fig. 1.2. *Situating Matthew's socio-religious orientation (Gentiles)*

190   Smith is surely correct in his critique of scholars comparing religions when he notes that 'the statement of comparison is never dyadic, but always triadic; there is always an implicit "more than", and there is always a "with respect to"' (*Drudgery*, 51). In other words, comparisons cannot be absolutized, but rather, are best plotted on a spectrum.

191   Cf. Saldarini, *Christian-Jewish*, 124–64.

192   For other spheres of engagement between groups, see Barclay, *Jews*, 88–102. Smith echoes the need for comparing specific attributes only: 'For the purposes of comparison [traditional categories like "Jewish" and "Gentile"] must be disaggregated and each component compared with respect to some larger topic of scholarly interest. That is to say, with respect to this or that feature, modes of Christianity may differ more significantly between themselves than between some mode of one or another Late Antique religion' (*Drudgery*, 117–18).

This investigation is concerned primarily with locating Matthew along a spectrum based on patterns of thought concerning the leadership symbol of the shepherd metaphor (Fig. 1.3).

Fig. 1.3. Situating Matthew's socio-religious orientation (other)

There are diverse ways of ascertaining patterns of thought – of conceptualizing or comprehending different aspects of religious life. The shepherd metaphor provides one effective means of doing this because of its primary nature – it represents a core leadership symbol for both early NCB Jews and Christ-believers – and because it is used in characteristic fashion by NCB Jews, Romans, and Christ-believers.

With this in mind, the study shall proceed as follows. The shepherd metaphor will first be analysed in the HB and its uses mapped. 'Shepherd' passages from the HB which Matthew cites in relation to Jesus will receive particular emphasis since these texts will provide a more specific base of comparison with Matthew's appropriation of them. After analysing the metaphor in the HB, the appropriation of the shepherd metaphor by NCB Jewish, Roman, and CB authors will be investigated. The thrust of this analysis will be to map patterns of usage in order to discern distinct patterns of thought or of tendencies in these groups of authors. It must be stated that the reason for treating these texts in this order and under these three headings is simply heuristic. These classifications have no bearing on the conclusions of the study and are used only for the sake of convenience and clarity.

In Part II of the study, Matthew's shepherd motif will be examined and its theological contributions to the Gospel discussed. Finally, Matthew's motif will be compared with the metaphor's use by the groups of authors analysed in chapter 3 to determine with which group Matthew's motif best aligns. That is, Matthew's appropriation of the shepherd metaphor will reflect patterns of thought with regard to the metaphor that will place him on a socio-religious spectrum mapping belief in Jewish-national restoration either in closer proximity to belief in Jewish nationalism or closer to a rejection of Jewish-national restoration. After determining Matthew's location on this spectrum, some of the social-historical implications of his position will be outlined in order to show how Matthew's socio-religious orientation would have influenced some of the institutional realities of the Mattheans.

Part I

The Shepherd Metaphor in Literature
Related to Matthew

Chapter 2

THE HEBREW BIBLE

2.1 Introduction

Because Matthew shows himself to be steeped in the worldview, thought and language of the HB, an examination of the shepherd metaphor in it is an essential prerequisite for understanding the Evangelist's shepherd motif. Matthew's literary and theological concerns can be more clearly discerned, points of continuity and discontinuity between Matthew and the HB identified, and any social implications for the Gospel better assessed by comparing his deployment of a 'shepherd' text with the corresponding HB passage.[1] Although this book will consider Matthew's social setting, the same cannot be said for the numerous social settings of HB texts examined. While the texts included in the HB consist of overlapping worldviews, originating in diverse time periods and social situations, when these texts began to be put together in a collection, they represented yet another time period and social setting. Matthew's contact with the texts would be limited to the latter situation; hence, the social settings of HB texts will generally not be discussed except when especially appropriate.

This chapter will proceed by presenting a thematic survey of the metaphorical use of רעה in the HB.[2] In the HB the metaphor of the shepherd typically refers either to rulers or to YHWH. In what follows, the various ways that the metaphor is used for these two referents shall be examined: what types of rulers are likened to shepherds and how does YHWH serve as a shepherd for his people? Special emphasis will be given to 'shepherd' texts specifically employed by Matthew, viz. Mic. 5.1, 2 Sam. 5.2, Ezek. 34.5, 17, Zech. 11.13, and Zech. 13.7, to provide a base of comparison for Matthew's appropriation of these texts. The analysis of these particular texts will centre on the identity and

---

1   B. Peckham's observation applies here: '[Hebrew Scripture texts were composed] by authors with training and skill who meant what they said. They were read and redone by others who knew what they said but meant something different' (*History and Prophecy: The Development of Late Judean Literary Traditions*, ABRL [New York: Doubleday, 1993], viii).

2   In almost half of its 167 occurrences, רעה is used metaphorically. For a discussion of shepherds and sheep in ancient Israel, see Huntzinger, 'End of Exile', 56–62.

activity of the shepherd.[3] These categories will provide significant points of comparisons with Matthew's deployment of these texts.

2.2 Thematic Survey of the Shepherd Metaphor

2.2.1 Rulers as shepherds

The biblical authors employ the shepherd metaphor for leaders in Israel's early (pre-monarchical) past.[4] Thus, Joshua and Moses are implicitly considered shepherds (Num. 27.17;[5] cf. Isa. 63.11) as are Israel's judges (2 Sam. 7.7/1 Chron. 17.6). It is not unexpected, then, that with the advent of the monarchy, Israel's kings are depicted as shepherds,[6] such as Ahab (1 Kgs 22.17/2 Chron. 18.16) and especially, David: 'And he chose David his servant ... to shepherd Jacob his people and Israel his inheritance. And he shepherded them with integrity of heart; with the skills of his hands he led them' (Ps. 78.70a, 71b-72).

One text within this category of 'rulers as shepherds' that Matthew appropriates is 2 Sam. 5.2b: 'You will shepherd my people Israel' (cf. Mt. 2.6b). Of particular relevance for the later discussion of Matthew's use of this text is the identity of the shepherd, the activity of the shepherd, and the identity of the shepherd's sheep. The shepherd in question is David, who ascends to the throne in place of Saul by the divine appointment of YHWH.[7] To shepherd Israel means to rule the nation as its king.[8] Hunziker-Rodewald maintains that רעה in 2 Sam. 5.2bα

---

3   The identity of the shepherd's sheep may also be discussed when it sheds additional light on the shepherd.

4   Psalm 49.15a presents one instance in the HB where the shepherd-sheep metaphor does not represent the king-subject relationship, but rather, death and the disobedient: 'Like sheep they are appointed for Sheol; death shall be their shepherd' (NRSV). That the next strophe speaks of the upright 'ruling' over them, however, reinforces the meaning of 'shepherd' here: death rules over the disobedient.

5   De Robert lists ANE parallels for the Num. 27.17 phrase 'like sheep without a shepherd', calling this expression a 'véritable cliché de la terminologie royale de l'ancien Orient: on la retrouve en Egypte et en Mésopatamie, ainsi que dans l'Ancien Testament' (*Berger*, 46).

6   Cf. the use of שבט ('rod') to signify Jewish monarchs in, for example, Gen. 49.10, Ps. 2.9, and Isa. 11.4.

7   The point of David's replacement of Saul is variously underscored in the text by the double use of the pronoun אתה ('you'): 'you will shepherd' and 'you will lead'. De Robert comments, 'Il semble donc que dans ces traditions sur David le titre de berger comme celui de *nagid* représentent la vocation du roi voulu de Dieu, et soient liés à l'élection par YHWH' (*Berger*, 55).

8   There is a clear parallelism between the two strophes in 5.2b:

אתה תרעה את־עמי את־ישראל

ואתה תהיה לנגיד על־ישראל

You will shepherd my people Israel,

And you will be a leader over Israel.

possesses definite military connotations because of its close association with נָגִיד ('leader') in 5.2bβ – an overtly military term (cf. its use in 1 Sam. 9.16; 10.1; 2 Sam. 7.7-9).[9] The scope of David's shepherding (i.e. the identity of his sheep) is the entire kingdom of Israel;[10] the Jewish-national outlook of the text (i.e. its concern for the moral renewal, or in this case the political-national restoration of Israel), then, is obvious. As section 4.2.1 below will show, Matthew's deployment of 2 Sam. 5.2b closely corresponds to these characteristics of the HB text.

The prophets depict not only pre-monarchical rulers but frequently Israel's monarchs as shepherds within the context of negative judgement. Jeremiah, for example, condemns Judah's monarchy for its role in bringing about the Babylonian exile (Jer. 23.1-2;[11] cf. 10.21; 50.6). Similarly, Ezekiel offers an even more severe and explicit critique of the monarchy: 'Woe to the shepherds of Israel who are shepherding themselves! Should the shepherds not shepherd the flock? The curds you eat, with the wool you clothe yourselves, and the fat animals you slaughter – but the flock you do not shepherd' (Ezek. 34.2b-3; cf. 34.8-9, 15-17).

The prophets apply רָעָה not only to Israel's monarchs but to Gentile kings, as well.[12] They, too, are usually judged: 'Weep, shepherds, and wail! Roll in the dust, leaders of the flock, for your days for slaughter have come. You will fall and be scattered like fine pottery' (Jer. 25.34; cf. 25.35-36; 49.19; 50.44; Zech. 11.15-17). Occasionally they are viewed more positively: '[YHWH] says of Cyrus, "My shepherd. Every delight of mine he will accomplish. And he will say to Jerusalem, 'Let

---

Thus to shepherd Israel is to be their leader (נָגִיד) which, in conjunction with the threefold repetition of 'king' for David in v. 3, would mean 'monarch' (cf. נָגִיד in 1 Sam. 9.16; 10.1; 13.14; 25.30; 2 Sam. 6.21; 7.8; see G. Hasel, 'נָגִיד', *TDOT* 9 (Grand Rapids: Eerdmans, 1998), 187–202.

9   Hunziker-Rodewald, *Hirt*, 47–49; cf. Willitts (*Shepherd-King*, 56), who similarly asserts that the echo of 2 Sam. 5.2 with 1 Sam. 18.5, 13, 16 shows that David's ruling activity is both political and military.

10   The comprehensive scope of David's reign is underscored by the repetition of 'all' and 'Israel': 'all the tribes of Israel' came to David (v. 1a), 'all the elders of Israel' came to David (v. 3a); David will shepherd God's people 'Israel', be the leader over 'Israel' (v. 2b); he was anointed king over 'Israel' (v. 3c). Two other factors within the narrative emphasize David's reign over the entire nation of Israel. On the one hand, he had already been anointed as 'king over the house of Judah' (2 Sam. 2.4). Hence, his anointing over Israel in 5.3 signifies the uniting of the kingdoms under David. The transitional phrase in v. 5, on the other hand, states that he reigned thirty-three years in Jerusalem over 'all Israel and Judah'.

11   The larger literary context of Jeremiah 21 and 22, which deal with King Zedekiah's request for deliverance and the eventual end of his and of his successors' reigns, as well as the promise of a future Davidic king in counterpoint to Israel's careless shepherds, would suggest that the monarchy is specifically in view in 23.1-2.

12   Cf. the use of שֵׁבֶט ('rod'), מִשְׁעֶנֶת/מַשְׁעֵנָה ('staff'), and animals to signify Gentile rulers: e.g. 'rod' in Isa. 14.5; Amos 1.5; Zech. 10.11; 'staff' in 2 Kgs 18.21/Isa. 36.6; Ezek. 29.6; and animals in Isa. 14.9 and Dan. 8.4-8.

it be built,' and to the temple, 'Let it be established'"' (Isa. 44.28; cf. Jer. 43.12). The extent of shepherding can range from the large scale of ruling nations to the much smaller scale of commanding field troops.[13] In describing the Babylonian siege, for example, Jeremiah writes, 'The beautiful and delicate one I [= God] will destroy: the Daughter of Zion. Against her shepherds will come with their flocks; and upon her they will pitch their tents, each will shepherd his own portion' (Jer. 6.2-3; cf. 12.10; 22.22; Mic. 5.5b-6; Nah. 3.18).

The shepherd metaphor frequently extends beyond the monarchy to include other members of Israel's leadership.[14] Thus, Jeremiah the prophet defends himself against his accusers by asserting that he never shirked his duties as a shepherd of God's people (17.16).[15] Similarly Deutero-Isaiah includes prophets as members of Israel's leadership: 'Those watching Israel are blind! All of them do not know ... they are shepherds who do not know how to discern' (Isa. 56.10a, 11b;[16] cf. Zech. 10.2-3). Deutero-Zechariah chastises the ruling class because of its illegitimate wealth: 'Those who buy them will slaughter them but will not be free from guilt. And those who sell them will say, "Blessed be the Lord, for I am rich!" And those who shepherd them will not have compassion on them' (Zech. 11.5). That the buyers and sellers here should be identified with the shepherds/leaders – i.e. those who exercise some measure of control over the flock – is suggested by the structure of the verse.[17] Thus, when YHWH commissions the prophet to shepherd the flock, the prophet assumes (figuratively speaking) the responsibilities of Israel's ruling class and not the monarchy.[18]

Along with kings past and present, Israel's future rulers are also likened to shepherds (e.g. Jer. 3.15; 23.3-4). Several HB texts that

---

13   Cf. the use of animals to symbolize military leaders in Isa. 34.2-7; Ps. 22.12, 20; and Zech. 10.3-5.

14   Cf. the use of שׁבט ('rod') and משׁענת/משׁע ('staff') to symbolize members of the ruling class in, for example, Num. 21.17; Ezek. 19.11 and Isa. 3.1-4, respectively.

15   Elsewhere, however, Jeremiah distinguishes between prophets and shepherds: 'The priests did not say, "Where is the LORD?" Those who handle the law did not know me; the rulers (רעה) transgressed against me; the prophets prophesied by Baal, and went after things that do not profit' (Jer. 2.8, NRSV).

16   In the prophets, Israel's 'watchers' typically refer to God's prophets, e.g. Jer. 6.17; Ezek. 3.17; 33.2-7; Hos. 9.8; Mic. 7.4, 7; Hab. 2.1.

17   That is, קניהן יהרגן ('those buying them slaughter them') is parallel with ורעיהם לא יחמול עליהן ('and those shepherding them do not have mercy on them'). In other words, the buyers (and sellers) represent the shepherds. Additionally, the nature of the metaphor, viz. the use of 'buyers and sellers' – i.e. those controlling the flock – would also point in this direction.

18   P. Hanson concurs: '[The prophet] is commissioned to shepherd Yahweh's flock; this shepherding is the actual responsibility of the nation's leaders ... [as 'shepherd'] came in post-exilic times to designate the civil leaders of the people' (*The Dawn of Apocalyptic: The Historical and Sociological Roots of Jewish Apocalyptic Eschatology*, rev. edn [Philadelphia: Fortress Press, 1979], 342).

Matthew cites fall within this subcategory of usage, viz. Mic. 5.1, Ezek. 34.23-24, and Zech. 13.7. In Mic. 5.1 the prophet predicts: 'And you, Bethlehem Ephrathah, are insignificant among the clans of Judah. From you one will go forth for me who will rule Israel.' According to Micah's oracle, the future shepherd will be an exalted ruler, whose greatness is reflected in the renown that will become associated with his place of origin, Bethlehem Ephrathah.[19] His ancestry stems from the lineage of David;[20] and he possesses a unique relationship with YHWH: YHWH is called, 'the Lord his God' (יהוה אלהין [v. 3bβ]),[21] in whose authority 'he will stand and shepherd (רעה) his flock' (v. 3aα). The future Davidide's shepherding activity is characterized as kingly rule over his people: he 'will be a ruler (מושל) over Israel' (v. 1bβ).[22] In addition to the obvious military and Jewish-national restoration connotations (similar to 2 Sam. 5.2), there are eschatological overtones with this Davidic ruler: he will deliver the Israelites from the Assyrian invaders who storm their land by leading his own army of shepherds against them in battle (cf. 5.4b-5).[23] The sheep are Jews living in the land of Israel: those who survived in the land during the exile, as well as those Jews who returned to the land after it was over – this latter segment of the flock is specifically identified as 'the rest of his brothers, those returning to the sons of Israel' (v. 2b). As will be shown in the discussion of Matthew, these features of a Davidide

---

19   The coming figure's greatness is also expressed by a contrast of associated terms: Judah's exilic king is called a שפט ('judge' [4.14b]), while the future shepherd is called a מושל ('ruler'), a term with a much closer semantic range to מלך ('king'). When used in this Qal active participle form (only in the historical writings), מושל refers exclusively to God (2 Sam. 23.3; 1 Chron. 29.12; 2 Chron. 20.6) or to David's successors (2 Chron. 7.18; 9.26).

20   The Davidic ancestry of this future ruler is emphasized in the final clause of v. 1c: 'and his origins are from of old, from days of antiquity' (ומוצאתיו מקדם מימי עולם). מוצאת reinforces יצא (v. 1bα): יצא does not refer to the Davidic ruler's earthly affairs but his ancestral descent, underscored by the double reference to ancientness in v. 1c. The grammatical construction of ימי + עולם appears six times in the HB. The phrase is used with a sense of exaltation with reference to the earlier, joyful days of Israel's history, e.g. the Exodus or the Conquest. This sense is conveyed once by Amos with respect to the Davidic monarchy which God promises to restore (Amos 9.11). Hence, here in v. 1 the phrase would likely connote the glorious days of the Davidic era, which will be renewed, according to Micah, with the advent of this future ruler.

21   Here again, Davidic ancestry is underscored: of Israel's kings, only David, according to the biblical tradition, spoke of YHWH as being 'my God'.

22   In ruling Israel he will 'stand and shepherd' them in the strength and majesty of YHWH (v. 3a). 'Standing' often conveys the idea of someone serving in a particular position by divine appointment, e.g. Num. 27.19-22 (Joshua), Isa. 11.10 (the root of Jesse), Jer. 23.18, 22 (prophets of YHWH), and Zech. 3.1 (Joshua the high priest).

23   If 'Assyria' typologically represents the totality of forces that have oppressed Israel (not just Assyria), then this verse would have an eschatological sense to it: Israel's ultimate victory over its foes lies in the indeterminate future; cf. T. McComiskey, *Micah*, EBC 7 (Grand Rapids: Eerdmans, 1985), 429–30.

closely aligned with God and appointed as king over the entire nation of Israel resemble Matthew's appropriation of this text.

In the second passage Matthew deploys, Ezekiel 34,[24] the prophet declares YHWH's promise to the exiles:

> So I will save my flock and they will no longer be plundered, and I will judge between sheep and sheep. And I will place over them one shepherd and he will shepherd them – my servant David – he will shepherd them, and he will be their shepherd. And I, the Lord, will be their God, and my servant David will be prince in their midst. I the Lord have spoken.
>
> (Ezek. 34.22-24)

Here, the coming shepherd is a king from the Davidic line: twice he is referred to as 'David' in Ezekiel 34 (and twice more in the closely related passage, Ezek. 37.24-25); he ascends to the throne by divine appointment;[25] and his shepherding activity consists of reigning over the people of God as their ruler – in contrast to Israel's failed shepherds, who are responsible for bringing about the exile.[26] The Jewish-national perspective of the passages is clear: if the establishing of 'one shepherd' over the people (v. 23a) is understood in light of the related oracle of the joining of the sticks in Ezek. 37.15-28, then the people of God would be comprised of the reunified northern and southern kingdoms.[27] When the fuller picture of the 'shepherd' in Ezekiel 34 is taken into account,[28] it will be observed in chapter 4 of this study that Matthew substantially patterns his shepherd motif after Ezekiel.

The third passage cited by Matthew which likens a future ruler of Israel to a shepherd is Zech. 13.7: "'O sword, awake against my shepherd and against the person next to me," declares the Lord of Hosts. "Strike the shepherd and the flock will be scattered and I will turn

---

24   As section 4.2.2 below will demonstrate, Matthew alludes to Ezekiel 34 in the eighth and ninth chapters of his Gospel, as well as in Mt. 25.32.

25   David is identified in the oracle as 'my servant' (cf. 37.24-25); 'my servant' refers to David seventeen times in the HB (three times more often than the second most frequent referent for this expression, Moses), and would underscore David's special role in the history of Israel as a divinely sanctioned agent to bring about the purposes and the glory of YHWH's rule.

26   YHWH promises to appoint the Davidic shepherd to be 'prince' or 'king' over Israel (34.24 and 37.24a, respectively). I. Duguid notes that Ezekiel prefers to use 'prince' (i.e. נשׂיא rather than מלך) for Israelite kings, and that he employs the term quite differently from the way it is typically used in the HB (*Ezekiel and the Leaders of Israel*, VTS 56 [Leiden: Brill, 1994], 12–33), suggesting that, because of the abuses of power by past kings, נשׂיא [conveys] a ruler with limited authority, genuinely representative of the people'.

27   According to the prophecy of 37.15-28, Israel and Judah will reunite under one (Davidic) monarch.

28   That is to say, not simply the portion dealing with a future Davidic king, but the metaphor as it relates to YHWH and his shepherding activities.

my hand against the little ones"' (cf. Mt. 26.31). The shepherd comes from the line of David. That the Davidic line is specifically in view is suggested by 13.1, which singles out the 'house of David'. He also possesses a close relationship with YHWH: YHWH refers to the shepherd as 'my shepherd', [29] and as 'the person next to me'. The striking down of the shepherd should be understood as an act of divine judgement by YHWH (likely executed by the ruler's opponents).[30] Ultimately, this act of judgement brings about the cleansing of the people.[31] The recipients of this purification through the striking down of the shepherd are those who dwell (or who survive) in the land of Israel after the exile, i.e. the 'one-third' who are not struck down in judgement (v. 8).[32] The strong concern for the people of the land reveals the Jewish-national outlook of the text. Matthew's appropriation of this text will mirror Deutero-Zechariah's notion of a Davidide closely related to God, who is struck down by God to purify his people.

2.2.2 *YHWH as a shepherd*

In addition to employing the metaphor for rulers, a number of texts included in the HB liken YHWH to a shepherd,[33] whose care for his people embodies the ideal shepherd. In four instances רעה is used as a title or in near titular fashion for YHWH.[34] In the blessing Jacob offers his son Joseph, it occurs within a series of titles for God: 'because the hand of the Mighty One of Jacob, because of the Shepherd, the Rock of Israel, because of the God of your fathers ... and the Almighty'

29   The only other instance in the HB where רעה bears the 1CS suffix י is in Isa. 44.28, where it refers to King Cyrus, whom YHWH appoints to rebuild Jerusalem and the temple.

30   When YHWH is the subject of 'turn a hand against' (either שוב יד על or על נטה יד), it is always in the context of judgement: e.g. in the case of נטה יד על, it is judgement against Israel or Judah (Isa. 5.25a; Jer. 6.12; Ezek. 6.14; 14.13 [cf. 14.9, where the recipients are false prophets]; 16.27; Zeph. 1.4; 2.13), or against other nations (Jer. 51.25; Ezek. 25.7; 13.16). In the case of שוב יד על, it is judgement against Israel (Isa. 1.25), or against foreign nations (Ezek. 38.12; Amos 1.8).

31   So Zech. 13.8c-9a: 'But one-third will remain in it [= the land]. I will bring the one-third into the fire and I will refine them like the refining of silver, and I will test them like the testing of gold'. Cf. P. Larmarche, *Zecharie IX–XIV: Structure littéraire et messianisme* (Paris: Gabalda, 1961), 107–108, and S. Cook, 'The Metamorphosis of a Shepherd: The Tradition History of Zechariah 11.17 + 13.7–9', *CBQ* 55 (1993), 462.

32   The geographical focus of the oracle is the land of Israel. From the post-exilic perspective of Deutero-Zechariah there are two groups of people: the majority ('two-thirds') who perished at the hands of the Babylonians during the siege (v. 8a) and the remnant ('one-third') who were left in the land (v. 8b).

33   Cf. the use of שבט ('rod') for YHWH in Job 9.34; 21.9; Pss 23.4; 45.7; Isa. 30.31; Lam. 3.1; Ezek. 20.37; Mic. 7.14.

34   Vancil, Wallis et al. note how this particular usage is extensively paralleled in ANE literature, e.g. Vancil, 'Sheep, Shepherd', 1188; Wallis, 'רעה', 548–49, and J. Jeremias, 'Ποιμήν', *TDNT* 6 (Grand Rapids: Eerdmans Publishing, 1968), 486–87.

(Gen. 49.24b-25a). Here רֹעֶה is paralleled by the more common titles for YHWH, אֵל ('God') and שַׁדַּי ('Almighty'). The author of Psalm 23 declares, 'The Lord is my shepherd' (v. 1aα); consequently, the psalmist testifies in the rest of the psalm how YHWH provides for, guides and protects him.[35] In a psalm attributed to Asaph, the author writes, 'O Shepherd of Israel, listen. You who lead Joseph like a flock, who sits between the cherubim, shine forth. Before Ephraim and Benjamin and Manasseh, awaken your might and come to our salvation' (80.1-2). What was perhaps implicit in Psalm 23 is made explicit in Psalm 80: YHWH's royal rule is often conjoined to his pastoral care of Israel.[36]

The fourth text appears in the epilogue of Ecclesiastes. After a lauda-tory description of Qoheleth (12.9-10), the redactor of the epilogue[37] writes, 'The words of the wise are like goads, and like embedded nails are their collected sayings – given by one Shepherd' (12.11). Scholars have offered different views for the identity of 'one Shepherd' (רֹעֶה אֶחָד).[38] The reasons for believing that 'one Shepherd' refers to YHWH are sev-eral. Most commentators agree that the most obvious or natural refer-ent for 'shepherd' here is God, given the metaphor's usage in the HB.[39] Additionally, the only other references to 'one shepherd' in the HB are found in Ezek. 34.23 (רֹעֶה אֶחָד) and Ezek. 37.24 (רוֹעֶה אֶחָד), which refer to a future Davidic monarch, whose shepherding of the nation is explicitly co-extensive with YHWH's, i.e. YHWH is the one who shepherds. Lastly, the text draws a distinction between the 'upright and faithful words' of Qoheleth the 'wise one' (חָכָם [sg.]) in vv. 9-10 and the words of 'the wise ones' (חֲכָמִים [pl.]) in v. 11a, i.e. wise sayings that do not originate with Qoheleth.[40] This would seem to suggest that

---

35   The psalmist also uses a staff to symbolize the comfort that YHWH offers him (v. 4).

36   E.g. Mic. 2.13; cf. J. Thomson, 'The Shepherd-Ruler Concept in the OT and Its Application in the NT', *SJT* 8 (1955): 407–408.

37   Scholars agree that the epilogue (12.9-14) represents a later addition to the rest of the book. For a summary of the arguments, see G. Wilson, '"The Words of the Wise": The Intent and Significance of Qohelet 12.9-14', *JBL* 103/2 (1984), 175–78.

38   For a review and refutation of the major alternatives, see Baxter, 'Shepherd', 71–74.

39   E.g. G. Barton, *The Book of Ecclesiastes* (Edinburgh: T&T Clark, 1908), 198; Zimmermann, *Inner World*, 163; R. Murphy, *Ecclesiastes*, WBC 23a (Dallas: Word Books, 1992), 125; E. Christianson, *A Time to Tell: Narrative Strategies in Ecclesiastes*, JSOTSS 280 (Sheffield: Sheffield Academic Press, 1998), 105–106; and Fox, *Ecclesiastes*, 84; for a list of scholars, see Krüger, *Qoheleth*, 211 n. 14.

40   Wilson concludes from his literary analysis of the epilogue that '(1) the epilogist refers here to a select collection of carefully arranged wisdom sayings; and (2) that col-lection is *not* coextensive with Qohelet' ('Intent', 177, his emphasis). Similarly Sheppard notes, 'If בַּעֲלֵי אֲסֻפּוֹת is taken to signify "overseers of the collections," then the anteced-ent to "these" must be those same collections or "the words of the wise," that is, a refer-ence to a set of existent collections or books inclusive of, but larger than, Qoheleth' ('The Epilogue to Qoheleth as Theological Commentary', *CBQ* 39 [1977], 188).

each of these subjects received their particular teaching from the same source, viz. 'one shepherd'. The easiest way to explain how diverse but authoritative wisdom teachings can come from the pens of different scribes would be if the author believed that God was the ultimate author of wisdom.[41] While it is possible that the words of the wise are being likened to a shepherd, it seems more likely, based on grammatical, theological, and contextual grounds, that their source of origin, viz. YHWH, is the focus of the comparison.[42]

This usage in Eccl. 12.11, then, would represent a unique deployment of the shepherd metaphor. Earlier HB texts describe the activity of YHWH as a Shepherd using very pastoral imagery: in terms especially appropriate for describing the duties of literal shepherds. Thus YHWH is portrayed as providing for the material needs of the flock, delivering them from enemies, resettling his people in their land, providing watchful leadership, and the like. In Ecclesiastes 12, however, the pasture that YHWH offers his flock is wisdom. Further, within the immediate context of the epilogue, the flock (i.e. the receiver of YHWH's wisdom) should probably be identified as Qoheleth and other sages, who would, in turn, transmit these teachings to the people. This type of extended and non-pastoral use of the metaphor will be observed more frequently in the writings of other Second Temple Jews and Christ-believers, including Matthew.[43]

In most of the texts in which YHWH is likened to a shepherd, the focus of the comparison is his activity as it relates to his people. Thus, in the blessing Jacob bestows on Joseph's sons, רעה is used to describe implicitly God's role in Jacob's life: 'May the God before whom my fathers walked ... the God who shepherds me all my life to this day, the angel who has delivered me from all harm . . .' (Gen. 48.15b-16a).[44] The passage characterizes God's saving of Jacob from his brother Esau's

---

41   This would be especially true if, as numerous scholars assert, the redactor(s) of the epilogue represented a competing wisdom tradition and sought to correct Qoheleth's teaching; cf. F. Zimmermann, *The Inner World of Qohelet* (New York: KTAV Publishing, 1973); Sheppard, 'Epilogue'; Wilson, 'Intent'; Krüger, *Qoheleth*; et al. This view of God being the ultimate source of wisdom would stand behind b. Hag. 3b, which explains the sometimes contradictory views that rabbis held of Torah, by appealing to Eccl. 12.11c.

42   Grammatically, the use of אחד points in this direction: if 'words of the wise' is the focus of the comparison, then the presence of אחד (as an indefinite marker) would be superfluous, even confusing. Theologically, YHWH is the Shepherd for his followers in the HB. Contextually, the warning of 12.12 seems to make better sense if God is in view: to reject the words of the wise is to reject their ultimate source, God, who is to be feared (v. 13) because he will judge everyone accordingly (v. 14).

43   Bracewell observes a similar kind of development in Greek literature, noting that Epictetus uses the sheep-shepherd metaphor to depict Greek philosophers (in *Enchir.* 46). Here, however, the focus is on the 'sheep': philosophers are likened to sheep, while the 'shepherd', although mentioned, is more or less incidental in the passage.

44   In v. 15, אלהים ('God'), מלאך ('angel'), and גאל ('deliverer') appear in parallel with רעה, as each term has the definite article ה.

vengeful wrath and the guile of his father-in-law Laban, and his leading him back to the land promised to Abraham as the activity of a shepherd. In the prophetic texts, YHWH's shepherding activity refers to his rescuing, gathering, and protecting his people. Hence, Jeremiah declares:

> Behold, I am bringing them from the land of the north and I gather them from the ends of the earth ... 'he who scatters Israel will gather them and will watch over his flock like a shepherd. For the Lord will ransom Jacob and redeem them from the hand of those stronger than they.'
>
> (Jer. 31.8a, 10b-11; cf. Ps. 28.9; Isa. 40.11; Mic. 7.14)[45]

The prophet promises that YHWH will rescue the captives from their Babylonian bondage, gather them together, and watch over them once again as their shepherd.[46]

Two texts that Matthew appropriates fall within the 'YHWH as a Shepherd' classification. One is Ezekiel 34, which is the most detailed text depicting YHWH as a shepherd. The prophet declares:

> For thus says the Sovereign Lord, 'Behold, I myself will seek after my flock and look after them. As a shepherd looks after his flock on the day he is in the midst of his flock which is scattered, so I will look after my sheep and rescue them from all the places where they were scattered, there on a day of clouds and darkness. ... 'I myself will shepherd my sheep and I myself will cause them to lie down,' declares the Sovereign Lord. 'Those that are perishing I will seek after, those that stray I will bring back, those that are injured I will bind up and those that are weak I will strengthen. But the fat and the strong I will destroy; I will shepherd the flock with justice.
>
> (Ezek. 34.11-12a, 15-16)

Of special interest here is the nature of YHWH's shepherding activity and the recipients of his shepherding. According to Ezekiel 34, YHWH's activity as shepherd consists of three elements. First, against the backdrop of Israel's failed leadership,[47] in assuming the reins as Israel's

---

45   Cf. the employment of verbs with pastoral connotations used to evoke the image of YHWH as shepherd, without using רעה: e.g. נחה ('lead', 'guide') in Exod. 13.17-21; Deut. 32.12; Neh. 9.12; נהל ('lead', 'guide') in Exod. 15.13; 2 Chron. 32.22; Isa. 49.10; אסף ('gather') in Isa. 49.5; Mic. 2.12; 4.6; יצא ('go out') in Isa. 37.32; Ezek. 20.38; and בוא ('lead out') in Jer. 30.3; Zech. 10.10.

46   According to Chae, the Davidic shepherd traditions present a consistent pattern of Israel's restoration: Davidic expectation–shepherd imagery–end of exile (*Davidic Shepherd*, 93).

47   The first section of Ezekiel's oracle (vv. 2-6) represents an indictment of Israel's shepherds. These shepherds are denounced because they care only for themselves to the complete neglect of the flock. Duguid convincingly argues that the condemned shepherds, strictly speaking, should be taken as referring to the previous kings (Jehoiakim and Zedekiah) rather than the entire ruling class (*Ezekiel*, 39–40).

Shepherd, YHWH will do what the evil shepherds should have done but did not do by attending to the lost, the strays, the injured, and the weak: his shepherding activity closely echoes – but in the reverse – the charge in v. 4 brought against the condemned shepherds: 'You have not strengthened the weak or healed the sick or bound up the injured. You have not brought back the strays or searched for the lost.'[48] Second, he will save his people from the consequences of bad shepherding: 'I will rescue them from all the places where they were scattered, there on a day of clouds and darkness. And I will bring them out from the nations and gather them from the lands, and I will bring them into their own land' (34.12b-13a).

Finally, YHWH promises to judge 'the fat and the strong' (34.16bα). Duguid identifies these judged herd leaders, i.e. 'the fat and the strong' (v. 16bα)/'the rams and the goats' (v. 17bβ), as the ruling class,[49] since the 'strong' (חזק) have already been given a negative connotation in 34.4,[50] and because the strong sheep have already been judged in connection with the indictment of the shepherds.[51] The judgement upon the shepherds is comprised, negatively, of removing them from the flock, on the one hand,[52] and positively, of providing a just and true Davidic shepherd to lead the flock, on the other. As will be seen later, Matthew will apply these attributes of YHWH as Israel's Shepherd to Jesus: Jesus is the true Davidic Shepherd who replaces Israel's evil shepherds. The recipient of YHWH's shepherding according to the oracle is the entire nation of Israel, i.e. the reunified northern and southern kingdoms.

In addition to Ezekiel 34, the other text Matthew cites within the 'YHWH as a shepherd' category is Zech. 11.13a: 'And the Lord said to me, "Throw [the 30 pieces of silver] to the potter, the majestic price [for being their shepherd] at which I was priced by them."'[53] Here, the

---

48   The reverse order of the recipients, 'the sick'/'the injured'/'the straying'/'the lost' in v. 4, compared with 'the lost'/'the straying'/'the injured'/'the sick' in v. 16, would serve both to heighten the contrast between the evil shepherds and YHWH (i.e. they are the opposite) as well as the reversal of fortune that YHWH shall effect: he shall do what they did not.

49   Duguid, *Ezekiel*, 121–22.

50   I.e. the evil shepherds have ruled the sheep with 'harshness (חזק) and with brutality'.

51   Additionally, in light of the close parallel concerns (of seeking, healing, and the like) between vv. 4 and 16, the herd leaders should be identified with the shepherds; cf. Porter, *Monsters*, 70–72.

52   For a more detailed discussion of this point, see Baxter, 'Shepherd', 77.

53   In the narrative oracle of 11.4-17, the prophet had been divinely commissioned to shepherd the people only to be relieved of his duties by the flock (vv. 4-12). While the prophet receives a severance pay of thirty pieces of silver (v. 12), according to the wording of v. 13a, 'the majestic price at which I [i.e. YHWH] was priced' (אשר יקרתי אדר היקר), it was actually YHWH whose shepherding had been appraised. Thus, when the prophet is sent to shepherd the people he serves as a stand-in for YHWH, their true Shepherd (cf. Mark Boda, 'Reading Between the Lines: Zechariah 11.4-16 in Its Literary

leaders of the flock of Israel reject YHWH as their shepherd.[54] While C. and E. Meyers consider this shepherd oracle to be a retrospective commentary on the Babylonian exile (i.e. its causes and consequences),[55] in view of Deutero-Zechariah's obvious appropriation and reversal of Ezekiel 34 and 37,[56] it would seem better to understand this prophecy as referring to the post-exilic circumstances of the redactor. Because the nation rejects YHWH, he revokes his covenant with them. While both the flock at large and the leaders are addressed in the oracle, the burden of the guilt over the breaking of the covenant falls at the feet of the latter group: they are singled out for abusing the flock (resulting in the exile

Contexts', in *Bringing out the Treasure: Inner Biblical Allusion in Zechariah 9–14*, ed. M. Boda and M. Floyd, JSOTSS 370 [Sheffield: Sheffield Academic Press, 2003], 281; also A. van der Woude, 'Die Hirtenallegorie von Sacharja XI', *JNSL* 12 [1984], 144). The conceptual parallels between Zech. 11.16 and Ezek. 34.4, 16 (where the prophet accuses Israel's shepherds of shirking their duties and YHWH promises to do what they failed to do, respectively) would also support this position:

Zech. 11.16	*Ezek. 34.4*	*Ezek. 34.16*
הנכחדות לא־יפקד	את־הנחלות לא חזקתם	את־האבדת אבקש
הנער לא יבקש	ואת־החולה לא־רפאתם	ואת־הנדחת אשיב
והנשברת לא ירפא	ולא־שברת לא חבשתם	ולא־שברת אחבש
הנצבה לא יכלכל	ואת־הנדחת לא השבתם	ואת־החולה אחזק
	ואת־האבדת לא בקשתם	

Zech. 11.16 / Ezek. 34.4 / Ezek. 34.16

Those who perish he will not visit / The weak you did not strengthen / Those who perish I will seek after

The young he will not seek / The sick you did not heal / Those who strayed I will bring back

The injured he will not heal / The injured you did not bind up / The injured I will bind up

The healthy he will not feed / Those who strayed you did not bring back and those who perish you did not search for / The weak I will strengthen

Differences in grammar and vocabulary aside, virtually all scholars recognize that Deutero-Zechariah has been influenced here by Ezekiel 34 (for a list of some of these scholars, see Boda, 'Reading', 284). The foolish shepherd will not do for the people what their true Shepherd YHWH had done for them in the past. Some scholars (e.g. Hanson) try to identify the shepherd of this oracle with the one struck down in 13.7, but van der Woude's arguments to the contrary ('Hirtenallegorie', 142–43), particularly in light of the probable parallel between 12.10–13.2 and 13.7-9, seem to carry more weight.

54 This rejection of YHWH as Israel's shepherd is somewhat similar to Hos. 4.16: 'The Israelites are stubborn, like a stubborn heifer. How then can the Lord pasture (רעה) them like lambs in a meadow?' The stubbornness of the people causes them to act more like cows than sheep, consequently making it difficult for YHWH to shepherd them.

55 C. Meyers and E. Meyers, *Zechariah 9–14*, AB 25C (New York: Doubleday, 1993), 281. Of the possibility of a prophetic sign pointing to a past event, however, van der Woude rightly insists, 'dass eine Zeichenhandlung nicht Erlebtes, sondern Bevorstehendes zum Ausdruck bringt' ('Hirtenallegorie', 144).

56 Cf. the analyses of Boda, 'Reading', 284–88 and Hanson, *Dawn*, 343–53.

[vv. 4-6]), for acknowledging yet ignoring the veracity of the prophet's word to them (vv. 10-11), and for pricing and paying off the prophet, and relieving him of his shepherding duties (vv. 12-13).[57] As chapter 4 of this study will reveal, Matthew transposes this theme of YHWH's rejection as Israel's Shepherd to Jesus, whose rejection by the Jewish leaders climaxes in his passion.

2.3 Summary and Conclusions

A thematic survey of 'shepherd' in the HB reveals that רעה as a metaphor most frequently stands for earthly rulers. As summarized by Table 2.1, prior to the monarchy, Israel's leaders like Moses and Joshua are likened to shepherds, as are Israel's kings. The term also applies to Gentile monarchs, military leaders, and to members of Israel's leadership, including prophets and civic leaders.

Table 2.1 Rulers as shepherds

Pre-Monarchical Jewish leaders	Jewish monarchs	Jewish leaders	Future Jewish rulers	Gentile monarchs	Military commanders
Num. 27.17	2 Sam. 5.2	Jer. 17.16	Jer. 3.15	Jer. 22.22	Jer. 6.2-3
2 Sam. 7.7	1 Kgs 22.17/2	Isa. 56.10-11	Jer. 23.3-4	Jer. 25.34-36	Jer. 12.10
1 Chron. 17.6	Chron. 18.16	Zech. 10.2-3	Mic. 5.3	Jer. 43.12	Mic. 5.4-5
Isa. 63.11	Ps. 78.71-72	Zech. 11.5	Ezek. 34	Jer. 49.19	Nah. 3.18
	Jer. 2.8		Zech. 13.7	Jer. 50.44	
	Jer. 10.21			Isa. 44.28	
	Jer. 23.1-2			Zech. 11.15-17	
	Jer. 50.6				
	Ezek. 34				

Overtones of Jewish-national restoration are clearly present in texts dealing with Jewish leaders, and in a few instances (Jer. 23.3-6; Ezekiel 34; Mic. 5.3-5; Zech. 13.7) they are given an eschatological slant. This concern for Jewish nationalism will be regularly taken up by Second Temple Jewish authors who appropriate the shepherd metaphor.

In addition to earthly rulers, YHWH is commonly depicted as a shepherd: see Table 2.2. YHWH's shepherding is frequently linked to his

---

57   Hanson comments on the sign in v. 13: 'The message is shocking but seems unmistakable: by this act the shepherd identifies the ultimate source of the corruption and the exploitation which are destroying the community: the temple and its leaders are to blame!' (*Dawn*, 347).

royal rule. For the biblical authors YHWH embodies the ideal shepherd: he gathers his lost flock, leads them to abundant pasture, and carefully watches over them to protect them from danger. A Jewish-national restoration outlook also undergirds a number of 'YHWH as a Shepherd' passages (e.g. Ps. 80.1-2; Ezekiel 34).

Table 2.2 YHWH as a shepherd

YHWH as deliverer	YHWH as general caregiver	YHWH as a provider of wisdom
Gen. 48.15	Ps. 23.1	Eccl. 12.11
Gen. 49.24	Jer. 31.10	
Ps. 28.9	Ezek. 34	
Ps. 80.1	Hos 4.16	
Isa. 40.11	Mic. 7.14	
	Zech. 11.13	

Of some importance is the type of imagery that the biblical authors typically employ to depict the shepherding acts of YHWH: the language of, for example, 'leading', 'guiding', 'gathering', 'protecting', 'pasturing' his flock, represents very pastoral or earthy imagery that would be commonly used to describe the duties of literal shepherds. This pastoral description of shepherding or the lack thereof will prove to be a significant characteristic of Second Temple Jewish and some CB authors who take up the metaphor later.

While YHWH's shepherding activity prior to and including the exile is described in very pastoral terms, during the post-exilic era, the metaphor becomes extended to include the giving of wisdom to the nation's wisdom teachers responsible for disseminating wisdom and knowledge to the rest of the nation. As previously mentioned, this new use of the shepherd metaphor does not replace its more typical usages – it merely adds to them. As the next chapter will demonstrate, this extension of the metaphor will continue in the writings of NCB Jews and Christ-believers.[58]

58   For a more focused discussion of the extending of the metaphor, see W. Baxter, 'From Ruler to Teacher: The Extending of the Shepherd Metaphor in Early Jewish and Christian Writings', in *Early Christian Literature and Intertextuality*, ed. C. A. Evans and D. Zacharias, vol. 1, Studies in Scripture in Early Judaism and Christianity 14, ed. C. A. Evans, LNTS 391 (London: T&T Clark, 2009), 208–24.

Also of note in this thematic study is the common contextual pattern for רעה. When referring to earthly rulers, in approximately two-thirds of its occurrences judgement is implicit to the literary context in which רעה is used: someone is either being judged, is about to be judged, or is executing a sentence of judgement on another. In fact, in most of these instances the shepherds or leaders are the objects of judgement.[59] By comparison, when 'sheep' (צאן), for example, is used metaphorically, judgement is involved only about one-third of the time.[60] This would seem to suggest that when the biblical authors invoke the shepherd metaphor with רעה, an implicit negative critique of the ruling establishment may be involved. Since judgement is an important theme for Matthew,[61] one that intersects with his shepherd motif (most explicitly in 25.32; see section 4.2.3 below), this observation will play a valuable role in evaluating Matthew's stance towards the nation of Israel with respect to the question of whether he believes God has rejected it.

Additionally, some common traits seem to emerge from the particular HB texts that Matthew appropriates to develop his shepherd motif. First, each of these texts can be used to produce a messianic interpretation and as such, some common messianic contours can be observed: all of these texts (if the two passages from Deutero-Zechariah are taken together) deployed by Matthew feature a figure embodying Davidic ancestry, and this Davidide possesses a unique relationship with YHWH whereby YHWH works coextensively through the agency of this figure, to gather together his dispersed people in order to rule over them. Second, the people who are gathered together in the Land and over whom this Davidic figure rules make up the reunified kingdom of Israel. Third, within the literary context of each of these passages what

---

59   See 1 Kgs 22.17/2 Chron. 18.16; Jer. 2.8; 22.22; 23.1-4; 25.34-36; 49.19; 50.44; Ezekiel 34; Zech. 10.2-3; 11.5-8; 13.7; Nah. 3.18. Jeremiah 3.15 describes the coming of future kings, against the backdrop of the nation's failed leadership (most specifically, 2.8, 26-28, passim). Only twice is the nation Israel judged within the wider literary context (in Isa. 56.11; Jer. 10.21). At other times, the shepherd serves (in the broader context) as an agent for divine judgement: Isa. 44.28; Jer. 6.3; 12.10; 17.16; 43.12; Mic. 5.3-5; Zech. 11.9. While not involving judgement per se, Num. 27.17 describes a dangerous situation for the nation in the wake of Moses' impending departure, viz. to be without a shepherd. Similarly, Jer. 50.6 describes the appalling situation of the shepherds having caused their sheep to stray and roam aimlessly. The lack of a tone of judgement in the remaining 'shepherd' texts can be explained by their retrospective orientations: 2 Sam. 5.1-4/1 Chron. 11.1-3 describes David's coronation over a kingdom that had been divided through war; 2 Sam. 7.5-7/1 Chron. 17.4-6 describes God's dealing with his people prior to the construction of the temple; Psalm 78 is an historical psalm whose retelling of Israel's history climaxes with the reign of David; Isa. 63.11-14 represents a brief retrospective of how God delivered his people from Egypt through agency of Moses.

60   צאן is used metaphorically by itself (i.e. without רעה) twenty-two times in the HB; only six involve judgement.

61   See D. Marguerat, *Le Jugement dans l'évangile de Matthieu* (Geneva: Labor et Fides, 1981).

Matthew appropriates is the idea of failed leadership: the Davidide comes to replace Israel's leaders who have failed to execute their duties faithfully as shepherds of God's flock and who, consequently, have brought the people of God into disastrous circumstances from which they need rescuing. The notion of YHWH raising up a Davidic shepherd to replace Israel's unfaithful leadership in order to tend his people bears significant implications for Matthew.

These basic characteristics of the shepherd metaphor observed in the HB would have been standard fare for subsequent NCB Jewish and CB commentators who appropriated the metaphor in their own religious writings to communicate something of import to their respective audiences; and indeed, as the next chapter shall show, their use of the metaphor – particularly, among the former group – often mirrors the patterns observed in the HB. Points of departure from these patterns, however, will be significant, and variations will offer comparisons with Matthew, in determining whether the patterns of thought of the Evangelist concerning the shepherd metaphor more closely resemble those of NCB Jews or those of other Christ-believers. The focus of this study shall now turn to the writings of NCB Jews, NCB Romans, and Christ-believers, and their employment of the shepherd metaphor.

Chapter 3

THE TEXTS OF NCB JEWS, NCB ROMANS, AND CHRIST-BELIEVERS

3.1 Introduction

The importance of exploring the shepherd metaphor in the writings of NCB Jews, NCB Romans, and Christ-believers in preparation for a study of the motif in the Gospel of Matthew and its implications for Matthew's socio-religious orientation cannot be overstated. Since NCB Jews adopted, like Matthew, the shepherd metaphor from HB texts, analysing their appropriations can shed light on the Evangelist's deployment of the metaphor in his Gospel. Matthew will sometimes use the metaphor in ways consonant with NCB Jews, and at other times with other Christ-believers. By examining the use of the shepherd metaphor by these authors and discerning the patterns of thought of each group, it will be possible to determine where Matthew's thought patterns concerning the metaphor fit among these authors. Hence, attention will be paid particularly to questions concerning the social setting of the Jewish texts as a means of setting in greater relief the socio-religious orientation of the author and/or the group addressed, and of showing the kinds of Second Temple Jewish groups that used the metaphor.[1]

This chapter will begin by presenting a thematic survey of the metaphorical use of 'shepherd'[2] in the writings of NCB Jews. Next, the use of 'shepherd' in Roman writings will be analysed, followed by an examination of the texts of Christ-believers contemporaneous with the Gospel of Matthew.[3] As in the previous chapter, the focus will be on metaphorical

---

1   When discussing the social setting of the different early Jewish texts, caution must be exercised. The present study does not assume that every text (e.g. *1 Enoch*) was the product of a tightly organized and highly coordinated community; rather, a text most likely reflects the ideology of various groups of people; cf. G. Nickelsburg, 'Response: Context, Text, and Social Setting of the Apocalypse of Weeks', in *Enoch and Qumran Origins: New Light on a Forgotten Connection*, ed. G. Boccaccini (Grand Rapids: Eerdmans, 2005), 241.

2   In early Jewish texts with a Hebrew *Vorlage*, 'shepherd' would (as in the HB) translate רעה, while ποιμήν and ποιμαίνω would likely underlie 'shepherd' in texts with a Greek *Vorlage*; see the discussion in section 1.4.5 above.

3   Hence, the Christian additions of *4 Ezra*, which are substantially later, will not be assessed; cf. T. Bergren, *Fifth Ezra: The Text, Origin and Early History*, SCSS 25, ed.

deployments of 'shepherd' rather than 'sheep',[4] and the exegesis of texts will concentrate on the shepherd metaphor, without being especially concerned with other elements in a passage, unless they possess particular bearing for understanding the metaphor. Apart from Roman texts (section 3.3 below), literal usages of 'shepherd' will be ignored, except when they offer additional insight into its metaphorical deployment.

3.2 The Use of the Shepherd Metaphor in the Writings of NCB Jews

3.2.1 Introduction

To ascertain Matthew's socio-religious orientation, his shepherd motif must be compared with the employment of the metaphor by Second Temple Jewish authors in order to compare their respective patterns of thought. This section will examine the shepherd metaphor as it is appropriated in the following texts: Festival Prayers, 4QWords of the Luminaries, the Damascus Document, *1 Enoch*, Ben Sira, Judith, *Psalms of Solomon*, Pseudo-Philo, *4 Ezra*, *2 Baruch*, *Apocryphon of Ezekiel*, as well as the relevant works of Philo of Alexandria and Flavius Josephus. This analysis will seek to identify the patterns of thought which characterize the use of the metaphor by Second Temple Jewish authors. These patterns of thought will then provide a useful point of comparison for Matthew's shepherd motif in Part II of the study.

3.2.2 Rulers as shepherds

As in the HB, NCB Jews such as Josephus use 'shepherd' as a metaphor most frequently for rulers. Born in 37/38 CE, Josephus came from an upper-class, priestly, Jerusalem family, but was granted Roman citizenship by Emperor Vespasian and lived the second half of his life in Rome.[5]

C. Cox and W. Adler (Atlanta: Scholars Press, 1990), 24–26, and B. Metzger, 'The Fourth Book of Ezra', *OTP*, 1.520.

4   This is because shepherd imagery without the use of 'shepherd' neither adds appreciably to nor changes the basic pattern observed for the usage of the metaphor; see the discussion of this point in section 1.4.5 above. Consequently, the writings of Christ-believers from the period subsequent to Matthew are excluded from this study because, on the one hand, the shepherding imagery of these documents revolves around the use of 'flock' rather than 'shepherd' (e.g. *1 Clem.* 16.1; 54.2; 57.2); and on the other hand, when 'shepherd', is appropriated (e.g. Ign. *Phld.* 2.1) it merely (and without substantial insight) reflects the use of the term for assembly leaders already found in the New Testament, which will be discussed in section 3.4.3 below.

5   While some scholars believe that Josephus (i.e. by the time of *AJ*) became a Pharisee, S. Schwartz (*Josephus and Judaean Politics*, CSCT 18 [New York: Brill, 1990]) offers a more nuanced position, noting that 'Josephus moved close to Pharisaism without actually adhering to it, or promoting adherence among others. The leadership he pro-

That Palestinian-born Josephus became a 'Diaspora Jew by adoption'[6] is evidenced (at least in part) by his extensive use of the Hellenistic style of writing he learned in Rome.[7] Of significance for properly understanding Josephus' use of 'shepherd' in *AJ* 17.278 (discussed in section 3.2.5 below) is the purpose of *AJ* and its intended audience. This text emphasizes the crucial importance for the Jews to observe the Mosaic Law correctly. Because of its centrality for Jews, Josephus claims that the Law possesses fundamental relevance for the Gentile nations who govern them: Gentile rulers will be punished by God if they do not permit the Jews to follow their laws, and will also incite widespread Jewish revolt against their government. *AJ*, then, seems primarily to have been written for Greek and Roman authorities, with the aim of securing their continued support for the Jews and their leaders.[8]

In one of the two instances that Josephus employs 'shepherd' metaphorically,[9] he uses it for King Ahab: in recalling the history of Israel's monarchy Josephus implicitly cites Micaiah's prophecy against King Ahab that Israel would be 'just like sheep without a shepherd' [*AJ* 8.404]). The use of 'shepherd' in the text Josephus cites presupposes Jewish-national sentiments: if Ahab goes to war he will die in battle; thus without its king, 'all Israel' will be scattered on the mountains – rather than remain as a nation under its monarchy. Because Josephus simply recounts Israel's history using the story of Kings, this perspective is also reflected in his account. In the second metaphorical use of

motes likewise must have been close to Pharisaism, but refrained from actual adherence to the party' (*Josephus*, 200).

6   So Barclay, *Jews*, 346. For further discussion of his social context, see Barclay, *Jews*, 346–68.

7   E.g. his use of characterization through speeches, emotion and pathos, eroticism, Hellenistic vocabulary in ethics and philosophy; cf. Barclay, *Jews*, 357–58. Additionally, Josephus adopts a 'classical pattern' of a historical account comprised primarily of political and military history, which demonstrates a high level of Roman influence; see Schwartz, *Josephus*, 47–57, for a list of Greek and Graeco-Oriental influences.

8   Josephus's style in *AJ* may suggest an attempt by Josephus to write in a stylistically pleasing manner for Gentiles. By contrast, the audience for *BJ* – which does not mention 'shepherd' in the parallel for *AJ* 17.278 – would most likely be primarily Jewish: on the one hand, *BJ* was originally in Aramaic and only later translated into Greek; thus, it would have originally been intended for Jewish readers (and only later would the audience have expanded to non-Jews – hence, the translation into Greek). On the other hand, it is more supportive of the priestly traditions (unlike *AJ*), and it seeks to absolve the Romans from culpability in regards to the destruction of Jerusalem, thereby implicitly promoting the acceptance of Rome by Jews. These factors would support a primarily Jewish audience for *BJ* (cf. Barclay, *Jews*, 351–56).

9   Josephus employs ποιμήν/ποιμαίνω literally over forty times in his writings. Usually he uses the term for the vocation (e.g. he refers to Abel as a shepherd [*AJ* 1.53], Jacob [*AJ* 1.309], Joseph's brothers [*AJ* 2.186–88], Moses [*AJ* 2.265], David [*AJ* 6.163], and Israel's ancient ancestors [*Ap.* 1.82-103; 1.230-66]), or more generally (*AJ* 1.169, 219, 260–61, 285–87, 258–64; 6.185, 297).

'shepherd', he employs the term for David: in recounting God's plague against Israel described in 2 Samuel 24, he cites the LXX version of 2 Sam. 24.17, where King David explicitly refers to himself as Israel's 'shepherd' (*AJ* 7.328).[10]

Philo of Alexandria, whose social setting most closely resembles Josephus's (of all the authors examined in this section), employs the metaphor much more frequently than Josephus. As a Hellenistic Jewish commentator of the Jewish scriptures,[11] Philo (born c. 30–20 BCE) draws freely from Platonic, Stoic, and Pythagorean philosophy[12] to extol the Jewish religion and important Jewish figures such as Moses and the Patriarchs,[13] and to demonstrate the significance and relevance of the Jewish scriptures.[14] Since some of Philo's treatises attest to criticisms of Jews by non-Jews,[15] some of what he writes must be considered an apologetic for Judaism,[16] extensively addressing questions of polytheistic worship, participation in non-Jewish traditions, associations and activities, and matters of table fellowship, thereby suggesting that these were serious issues for Jews in his community.[17] Sandmel suggests that Philo's expositions of the Law targeted Jews on the verge of apostasy.[18] It would seem, then, that Philo's audience would have been Diaspora

---

10   The LXX version of 2 Sam. 24.17 differs from the MT in that David's plea begins, 'Behold, I am the one who has sinned; and I am the shepherd (ὁ ποιμήν), I have done wrong. And these are sheep' (v. 17bα). The MT, however, reads, 'Behold, I have sinned and I have done wrong, and these are sheep' (v. 17bα), thus omitting 'the shepherd' (הרעה).

11   For a helpful discussion of the views of Philo's profile (exegete, philosopher, etc.), see P. Borgen, *Philo of Alexandria: An Exegete for His Time*, New Testament S 86 (Leiden: Brill, 1997), 1–13.

12   Of his very obvious incorporation of Greek philosophy, J. Barclay writes, '[His] integration of Judaism into Hellenistic culture was exceptionally profound, but [he] ultimately turned that synthesis to the advantage and defence of the Jewish community' (*Jews*, 180). For further discussion of Philo's social context, see Barclay, *Jews*, 158–63.

13   Thus (as S. Sandmel notes), Philo did not write treatises on Pythagoras, Plato, or Aristotle; he wrote on Abraham, Joseph; and Moses: for Philo, Hellenism ultimately served Judaism.

14   While Sandmel considers most similarities between Philo's exegetical method and the early rabbis overdrawn, he nevertheless acknowledges some measure of overlap, owing to a communication between Alexandria and Palestine (*Philo of Alexandria: An Introduction* [Oxford: Oxford University Press, 1979], 132–34).

15   E.g. *Legatio ad Gaium*, *De specialibus legibus*, and *De virtutibus*.

16   Sometimes he does this explicitly (e.g. *Hypothetica*), sometimes implicitly; cf. R. Hecht, 'The Exegetical Context of Philo's Interpretation of Circumcision', in *Nourished with Peace*, ed. F. Greenspahn, E. Hilgert, and B. Mack (Chico: Scholars Press, 1984), 52–79.

17   Cf. Borgen, *Philo*, 158–75.

18   Sandmel writes: 'If in Alexandria [Jews were] nearly on the verge of leaving the Jewish community, as did Philo's nephew, *The Exposition* [*of the Law*] might well have been addressed to them ... there would conceivably be very little difference in actuality in the tone of a writing whether it was aimed at friendly Gentiles or at uninformed Jews on the threshold of apostasy' (*Philo*, 47; cf. Barclay, *Jews*, 174–80).

– specifically, Alexandrian – Jews but with perhaps some interested Gentiles.

Philo applies the metaphor to kings,[19] three times referring to monarchs generally as 'shepherds of people' (*Mos.* 41, 61; *Prob.* 31; cf. *Agric.* 50), and specifically to Emperor Gaius (*Leg.* 44). He also uses the term for Israel's pre-monarchical rulers, implicitly for Moses (whom Philo regards as a king)[20] and explicitly for his successor Joshua in *Virt.* 58: Philo states that Moses asked God to 'find a man to set over the multitude to guard and protect it, a shepherd who shall lead it blamelessly that the nation may not decay like a flock scattered about without one to guide it', thus reflecting Jewish-national concerns.[21] Philo depicts the activity of a shepherd-ruler with fairly pronounced pastoral imagery, suitable for describing the activities of the shepherding vocation: the shepherd guards, protects, leads and guides the flock.

Like Philo, the author of *Liber Antiquitatum Biblicarum* (*LAB*), viz. Pseudo-Philo, also employs the metaphor for Moses. Virtually all scholars agree that *LAB* dates between 30 and 100 CE, with a date in or around 70 CE probably advocated by most.[22] A Palestinian origin is suggested by the author's interest in stock Palestinian traditions,[23] his concern for Palestinian geography,[24] the likelihood of a Hebrew *Vorlage*,[25] and the numerous verbal parallels with the (probably) Palestinian texts of *4 Ezra* and *2 Baruch*.[26]

19   For a detailed exposition of shepherd and sheep imagery in the works of Philo, see Seibel, 'Shepherd & Sheep', 48–161.

20   Insofar as Moses is a 'shepherd' he represents a king, saviour, legislator, teacher of virtue (who produces virtue in his flock), revealer of divine truth, and agent of Logos (cf. Seibel's detailed discussion of Moses as a shepherd in Philo in 'Shepherd & Sheep', 62–84).

21   Philo here cites Num. 27.16-17, equating shepherding Israel to guarding and protecting it to ensure that the flock would not become morally corrupt in their scattered state. Seibel suggests that this prayer represents an extended application of the verse by Philo: 'This is no longer a prayer for the election of Joshua, however, but an intercession of the shepherd Moses on behalf of his flock that they may continue to be led by right reason' ('Shepherd & Sheep', 82).

22   See S. Olyan, 'The Israelites Debate Their Options at the Sea of Reeds: *LAB* 10.3, Its Parallels, and Pseudo-Philo's Ideology and Background', *JBL* 110/1 (1991), 87, especially n. 40.

23   E.g. the location of the cult, the rules for sacrifice, the Law and the covenant, eschatology, and angelology.

24   See D. Harrington, 'Biblical Geography in Pseudo-Philo's *Liber Antiquitatum Biblicarum*', *BASOR* 220 (1975): 67–71.

25   See H. Jacobson, *A Commentary on Pseudo-Philo's Liber Antiquitatum Biblicarum*, 2 vols (Leiden: Brill, 1996), 1.215–24; also D. Harrington, 'Pseudo-Philo', *OTP*, 2.298–99.

26   If Olyan ('Debate') is correct, then *LAB* 10.3 would also suggest a Palestinian provenance; cf. the judgement of Jacobson, *Pseudo-Philo*, 1.210–11.

When applying the metaphor to Moses, Pseudo-Philo explicitly underlines Moses' role as Israel's intercessor. He writes, 'Who will give us another shepherd[27] like Moses or such a judge for the sons of Israel to pray always for our sins and to be heard for our iniquities?' (19.3b; cf. v. 9a).[28] According to Pseudo-Philo: Moses, as Israel's shepherd, was responsible both to lead and to intercede with God on behalf of the nation. Thus, the text reflects a concern for Israel's well-being.

King David is a referent for the metaphor in the Dead Sea Scrolls.[29] There is nearly unanimous agreement that the general period of the Qumran community extended from the second century BCE to the first century CE.[30] The consensus theory regarding the social origins and history of the Qumran community identifies the community in some manner with the Essenes.[31] The assumption for this study, however, is that the Qumran community was a subgroup of Essenes.[32] The Essenes were probably part of a larger, broad-based coalition of Palestinian Jewish religious conservatives, the Hasidim.[33] If the Essenes, the parent group

27   Although the text of Pseudo-Philo exists in Latin, if *LAB* was originally composed in Hebrew, then רעה would stand behind the Latin term for 'shepherd', *pastor*.

28   The use of 'judge' in v. 3, since it is paired with 'shepherd', likely refers to the leadership position (e.g. the judges that appear in the story, beginning with the election of Kenaz in ch. 25), rather than the act of executing judgement.

29   In addition to the five instances where רעה appears metaphorically in the Scrolls, it also occurs in the highly fragmentary 4Q254 (*4QCommGen. C*) vii 1-5, where it seems to appear in a direct quote from Gen. 49.24-25. In 11Q5 (11QPsalms^a) רעה is used literally for David in Psalm 151A, referring to his humble beginnings as a shepherd of his father's flocks (in XXVIII, 4). The parallelism between l. 3b-4a, 'he appointed me a shepherd for his flock and a ruler over his young goats' (רועה לצונו ומושל בגדיותיו ישימני), and l. 12a, 'and he appointed me leader over his people and ruler over the sons of his covenant' (וישימני נגיד לעמו ומשל בבני בריתו), might suggest a subtle metaphorical sense to 'shepherd' here: in which case, 'shepherd' would refer here to David's ruling over Israel.

30   See J. Magness, *The Archaeology of Qumran and the Dead Sea Scrolls* (Grand Rapids: Eerdmans, 2002), 47–71; S. Talmon, 'The "Dead Sea Scrolls" or "The Community of the Renewed Covenant?"', in *The Echoes of Many Texts: Reflections on Jewish and Christian Traditions*, ed. W. Dever and J. Wright (Atlanta: Scholars Press, 1997), 129, and L. Schiffman, *Reclaiming the Dead Sea Scrolls* (New York: Doubleday, 1994), 38–57.

31   E.g. G. Vermès and M. Goodman, *The Essenes According to the Classical Sources* (Sheffield: JSOT Press, 1989); Magness, *Archaeology*, 39–43; C. Hempel, *The Laws of the Damascus Document: Sources, Tradition and Redaction*, STDJ 29 (Leiden: Brill, 1998), 3–8; and VanderKam, *Dead Sea Scrolls Today*, 71–93.

32   A straightforward 'Qumran equals Essenes' identification seems far too simplistic for reasons Talmon outlines in 'Community of the Renewed', 128–29. F. García Martínez and A. van der Woude likewise view the Qumran community as resulting from a 'split' within the Essene movement ('A "Groningen" Hypothesis of Qumran Origins and Early History', *RevQ* 56 [1990], 537).

33   García Martínez and van der Woude, for their part, 'exclude the identification of the parent group with the Hasidim on the basis of the condemnation of Alcimus' ('Groningen', 540); but they unnecessarily and inaccurately narrow the profile of the 'Hasidim'.

of the community, were part of a 'rainbow' coalition of religious conservatives, then this would account for some of the diverse ideological
traits reflected in the Scrolls.[34] Even if this Essene–Hasidim move is not
taken, Qumran scholars have come to recognize that some of the beliefs
exhibited in the Scrolls represent a larger segment of Palestinian Second
Temple Judaism and not simply those of a small, sectarian community.[35]

David appears to be the referent for the metaphor in 4QWords of the
Luminaries (4Q504) and in Festival Prayers (1Q34; 4Q509).[36] Festival
Prayers and 4QWords of the Luminaries are Qumranic texts which seem
to represent more mainstream Jewish thought. Although scholars continue to debate whether the liturgical prayers of 1Q34 and 4Q509 are
Qumranic in origin or predate the community, the evidence seems to tilt
towards the latter position.[37] In the case of 4Q504, the second century
date of the copy, coupled with its general and not explicitly sectarian
language and ideas suggest that the original composition likely predated
the Qumran community and was part of the broader make-up of Second
Temple Judaism.[38]

A collection of prayers for the days of the week, 4Q504,[39] the prayer
in fragment 1-2 iv[40] begins with the petitioner reminding God of his

---

34   At some points the ideology of the community seems Essene-like (e.g. determin-
ism), at other points Sadducean (e.g. various halakhot) and at still others Pharisaic/proto-
rabbinic (e.g. the style of some of the biblical exegesis).

35   See C. Newsom, '"Sectually Explicit" Literature from Qumran', in *The Hebrew
Bible and Its Interpreters*, ed. W. Propp, B. Halpern and D. Freeman (Winona Lake:
Eisenbrauns, 1990), 167–87. In seeking to determine how to find 'sectually explicit' material in the Scrolls, the obvious assumption is that not all of the writings originated with
the Qumran community.

36   1Q34 (= 4Q509 97–98 i) is typically referred to as 1Q34–1Q34[bis] because the
document consists of five fragments: fragment one (1Q34), first published by J. T. Milik,
'Recueil de priers liturgiques (1Q34)', *DJD*, vol. 1 (Oxford: Clarendon Press, 1955), to which
J. Trever added four more (1Q34[bis]): 'Completion of the Publication of Some Fragments From
Qumran Cave I', *RevQ* 19 (1965): 323–36. For simplicity's sake, the full document will be
referred to as 1Q34. The copy of 1Q34 has been dated between 50–25 BCE.

37   See Newsom, 'Sectually Explicit' and D. Falk, *Daily, Sabbath, and Festival
Prayers in the Dead Sea Scrolls*, STDJ 27 (Leiden: Brill, 1998).

38   Cf. Falk, *Daily*, 63. The connection between these two texts has been noted:
Falk writes, '*Words of the Luminaries* and *Festival Prayers* exhibit a virtually identical
structure and form distinct from other prayer collections in the Dead Sea Scrolls, suggesting that they are of the same provenance' (*Daily*, 63).

39   According to palaeographical analysis, M. Baillet dates the oldest copy of
4Q504 to the middle of the second century BCE ('Paroles des Luminaires [Premier
Exemplaire: DibHam[a]]', *DJD* 7 [Oxford: Clarendon Press, 1982], 137).

40   Fragment 1-2 iv 3-9 reads: 'In Jerusa[lem the city which] you [cho]se from the
whole earth for [your Name] to be there for ever. For you loved Israel more than all the
peoples and you chose the tribe of Judah and your covenant you established for David
to be like a shepherd, a leader over your people; and he will sit upon the throne of Israel
before you for all days. And all nations saw your glory which you made holy in the midst
of your people Israel.'

sovereign election:[41] God chose Jerusalem as the place where his name would dwell forever (1-2 iv 2-4); and from out of the nation of Israel, he favoured the tribe of Judah and established his covenant with David so that David would be 'like a shepherd, a leader over your people, that he might sit on the throne of Israel before you' (1-2 iv 6-7).[42] This phrase (כרעי נגיד על עמכה [l. 7]), mentioned in close connection with YHWH establishing his covenant with David (l. 6), is almost certainly an allusion to 2 Sam. 5.2b (תרעה ... לנגיד על־ישראל). Thus, 'shepherd' refers to David's ruling as king over Israel. The eschatological-like language of the passage suggests that this specific petition expressed hopes for Jewish-national restoration.[43]

Similarly, in 1Q34, part of a larger corpus of prayers offered at various Jewish festivals, the shepherd metaphor appears within the context of covenant renewal:[44] '[. . . you raised up][45] for [th]em a faithful shepherd [. . .] poor and [. . .]' (ii l. 8). Although the Qumran community may have applied 'faithful shepherd' to the leader of their group, the

---

41   Each prayer represents a self-contained unit with a fixed superscription – appeal – summary structure; see E. Chazon, 'A Liturgical Document from Qumran and its Implications: 'Words of the Luminaries' (4QDibHam)' (PhD dissertation, Hebrew University, 1991).

42   There is some ambiguity in the beginning of this line. M. Baillet reads it as נגיד להיות כרעי ('to be like a shepherd, a leader [over your people] ('Paroles des Luminaires', 143, followed by K. Pomykala, *The Davidic Dynasty Tradition in Early Judaism: Its History and Significance for Messianism*, SBLEJL 7, ed. W. Adler [Atlanta: Scholars Press, 1995], 174, n. 14), et al. E. Qimron ('Improvements to the Editions of the Dead Sea Scrolls', *Eretz-Israel* 26 [1999], 142–43 [in Hebrew]), however, reads the line as כנגיד להיות מזרעו ('to be from his seed, a leader [over your people]', in which case 'shepherd' does not appear. If Qimron is correct, that would eliminate this text from consideration; its absence, however, would not affect the results of this survey since 4Q504 merely corroborates a pattern observed in other Second Temple Jewish texts.

43   The passage speaks of the shepherd as '[sitting] on the throne of Israel before [YHWH] for all days', of 'all nations [having seen YHWH's] glory' and consequently, 'to [YHWH's] great name they bring their offerings' to 'glorify [his] people and Zion, [the] holy city and [YHWH's] house'.

44   Fragment 3 ii 5b-8 reads: 'You chose for yourself a people in the time of your favour for you remembered your covenant. And you established them to be separated for yourself to be holy among all the peoples. And you renewed your covenant for them in the vision of glory and the words of your Holy [Spirit], by the works of your hand. And your right hand has written to make known to them the regulations of glory and the words of eternity. [. . . You raised up] for [th]em a faithful shepherd [. . .] poor and . . .'

45   While J. Charlesworth and D. Olson ('Prayers for Festivals' in *The Dead Sea Scrolls: Pseudepigraphic and Non-Masoretic Psalms and Prayers* 4a, ed. J. Charlesworth [Tübingen: Mohr Siebeck, 1997]) do not attempt to supply a verb to match רועה, F. García Martínez and E. Tigchelaar (*DSSSE*, vol. 2 [Leiden: Brill, 1998]) and Falk (*Daily*) seem correct in supplying 'you raised up' because God's actions are being described in the immediate context: God 'chose' a people ... God 'remembered' his covenant ... God 'established' his people ... God 'renewed' his covenant with them ... his right hand 'has written' glorious and eternal words. The idea that God 'raised up' for them a shepherd, then, would fit nicely with these other divine actions.

original referent would likely be King David for two reasons. On the one hand, 1Q34 represents one of those Qumran texts that predated the community and thus would have been used as a festival prayer for a much larger segment of Second Temple Judaism.[46] Hence, the 'faithful shepherd' whom God raised up would have been a figure widely recognized by Second Temple Jews as a faithful shepherd: David, with whom the shepherd metaphor is most frequently associated in the HB, would be one of the primary contenders. On the other hand, when the metaphor is used in connection with covenant language and divine election (as it is here), David would seem to be in view.[47] Thus, 'shepherd' here refers to David's ruling Israel as its king.[48] The mention of divine election, the renewal of the covenant, and the revelation of the Law also reveal concerns for Jewish-national restoration in this petition.

Quite a different use of the metaphor for rulers appears in the Dream Visions section of *1 Enoch*, one of the para-biblical manuscripts found at Qumran. While the earliest parts of the Enochic literature date to as early as 300 BCE,[49] most scholars date the Dream Visions (chs 83-90) to the second quarter of the second century BCE.[50] Scholars agree that, although *1 Enoch* shows traces of Hellenistic and Babylonian influences,[51] a community of Palestinian Jews stands behind the Enochic literature.[52] Given its use by NCB Jews and even Christ-believers,[53]

---

46   Cf. Falk, *Daily*, 156–57.

47   Cf. 4Q504, where David is explicitly identified in the text; in 4Q509, however, covenant language is absent and the referent for the metaphor is YHWH not David (cf. the discussion of this latter text in section 3.2.3 below).

48   Even if the referent for 'shepherd' here is YHWH or Moses or the like, the overall point of the chapter (that 'shepherd' refers to YHWH and to rulers) would not sustain any damage.

49   Cf. J. Charlesworth's comments in Charlesworth, 'A Rare Consensus among Enoch Specialists: The Date of the Earliest Enoch Books', in *Henoch: The Origins of Enochic Judaism, Proceedings of the First Enoch Seminar, University of Michigan, Sesto Fiorentino, Italy, June 19–23, 2001*, ed. G. Boccaccini (Torino: Silvio Zamorani editore, 2002), 234.

50   E.g. I. Fröhlich, 'The Symbolic Language of the Animal Apocalypse of Enoch: 1 Enoch 85-90', *RevQ* 14 (1989–90), 629; R. Beckwith, 'The Pre-History and Relationships of the Pharisees, Sadducees and Essenes: A Tentative Reconstruction', *RevQ* 11 (1982–84): 1–46; J. VanderKam, 'Exile in Jewish Apocalyptic Literature', in *Exile: Old Testament, Jewish, and Christian Conceptions*, ed. J. Scott, JSJSS 56 (Leiden: Brill, 1997), 96.

51   See G. Nickelsburg, *1 Enoch 1: A Commentary on the Book of Enoch Chapters 1–36; 81–108*, Hermeneia, ed. K. Baltzer (Minneapolis: Fortress Press, 2001), 62, for Hellenistic influences, and J. Collins, 'Apocalyptic Literature'. in *Early Judaism and Its Modern Interpreters*, ed. R. Kraft and G. Nickelsburg (Atlanta: Scholars Press, 1986), 357, for Babylonian.

52   For two recent discussions on the social origins of *1 Enoch*, see G. Boccaccini (ed.), *Enoch and Quman Origins: New Light on a Forgotten Connection* (Grand Rapids: Eerdmans, 2005), and Boccaccini, *Henoch*.

53   Besides manuscripts of *1 Enoch* appearing among the Dead Sea Scrolls,

1 Enoch would seem to represent a very influential movement. G. Boccaccini considers the highly cosmic orientation of *1 Enoch* to be representative of what he calls 'Enochic Judaism'.[54]

In the allegory of the history of Israel, the Gentile powers that previously ruled over Israel are depicted as angelic figures.[55] Although some scholars claim that these angelic beings are Gentiles rather than angels,[56] Nickelsburg makes a strong case for understanding these characters as angels not humans.[57] Despite being appointed by God, these angelic shepherds brutalize God's flock in ruling over them.[58] Ultimately, however, they are divinely condemned to the fiery abyss in the final judgement.[59]

Thus, when employing 'shepherd' for rulers, NCB Jewish writers such as Philo, Pseudo-Philo, Josephus, and the authors of 4Q504, 1Q34, and the Dream Visions, apply the metaphor for Israel's pre-monarchical rulers (like Moses), Israel's monarchy (most often David), and (in the case of *1 Enoch*) for the angelic beings that ruled Israel during its lengthy period of foreign oppression.

significant conceptual or literary parallels with *1 Enoch* appear in Daniel, *Jubilees*, Wisdom of Solomon, and, if it existed, the 'Book of Noah' (for a defence of the existence of this document and a core outline of its content, see W. Baxter, 'Noachic Traditions and the "Book of Noah"', *JSP* 15.3 [2006]: 179–94). The cosmic wisdom claimed by *1 Enoch* also seems to serve as a sparring partner for Ben Sira and possibly for *4 Ezra* and *2 Baruch* (see Nickelsburg, *1 Enoch*, 68–69). For a discussion of the influence of *1 Enoch* in the traditions of the Jesus movement and early Christianity, see Nickelsburg, *1 Enoch*, 83–87. Among its uses by Christ-believers, it is explicitly cited by the author of Jude.

54   While Boccaccini overemphasizes the importance of the aetiology of evil and theodicy as a means of distinguishing between different strands of Judaism, his core premise of a large (influential) Jewish group with cosmic-oriented expression of Judaism remains cogent.

55   In depicting Israel's suffering under foreign domination, for example, the author of Dream Visions writes: '[The Lord of the Sheep] summoned seventy shepherds and surrendered those sheep to them so that they might pasture them. He spoke to the shepherds and their colleagues, "From now on, let each and every one of you graze the sheep; and do everything which I command you. I shall hand them over to you duly counted and tell you which among them are to be destroyed; and you shall destroy them!" So he handed over those sheep to them' (*1 Enoch* 89.59-61a). These beings are referred to as 'shepherds' more than twenty times in the last two chapters of the Dream Visions.

56   E.g. Fröhlich, '1 Enoch 85–90', 631.

57   Nickelsburg, *1 Enoch*, 390–91. Perhaps his strongest point is that all identifiable people in the historical survey are symbolized as animals: the passage speaks of Jewish leaders who formerly led Israel as 'sheep': e.g. Moses (89.16-39), Joshua and the elders (89.37), the judges (89.41), Saul and David – who are sheep-turned rams (89.43-45), Solomon (89.48), and the prophets (89.51-54). Cf. the arguments of Tiller, *I Enoch*, 51–54, and Chae, *Davidic Shepherd*, 103–104.

58   Although they victimize the flock, the redactor speaks of them three times as 'pasturing' the flock (89.59, 72) – an otherwise pastoral description of their (angelic) shepherding activity.

59   Siebel suggests that 'the angelic shepherds play the same role of [the] bad shepherds' that are divinely judged in ancient oracles such as Ezekiel 34 and Zechariah 13 ('Shepherd & Sheep', 40–41).

3.2.3 YHWH as a shepherd

When likening YHWH to a shepherd, NCB Jews most commonly portray God as merciful or compassionate. Thus, in the very fragmented text of 4QFestival Prayers (4Q509)[60] IV, 10 ii-11 1-7,[61] YHWH[62] is implicitly referred to as a shepherd: 'you have shepherded' (l. 3).[63] The first two letters of the previous line, רח, probably represent the first part of רחם ('to have mercy/compassion'): hence, YHWH would be described here as a merciful shepherd to his people. Although it is hard to tell because of the lacuna, the appeal for YHWH to 'remember the distress and weeping' within a sombre acknowledgement of a community without its healer and comforter, suggests a concern, on the part of the petitioner, for Jewish-national restoration.

Mercy is explicitly associated with the image of YHWH as Israel's shepherd in Ben Sira. The usual date range for Ben Sira is 196 to 175 BCE.[64] While some have sought to locate Ben Sira within Sadduceeism (because of his priestly lineage and Hellenistic tendencies) or within Pharisaism (since he was a scribe and some of his theology aligns with what is known of Pharisees), these conflicting positions might suggest that Ben Sira represents a stream of Judaism wider than either one of these two sects.[65] Although his primary purpose for writing would be to encourage his fellow Jews against the pervasiveness of Hellenistic culture,[66] he does so, on the one hand, not by advocating a kind of cross-cultural abstinence, but rather, as one who embraced Hellenism insofar as it could be used to bolster Judaism.[67] He also seems to do so,

---

60   4QFestival Prayers would represent part of the same document as 1QFestival Prayers (discussed in section 3.2.2 above). These two manuscripts are different copies found in different caves.

61   The larger portion of 4Q509 reads as follows: 'And there is no one who heals [. . .] comforting those who stumbled in their transgressions [. . . Remem]ber the distress and weeping. You are the companion of prisoner[s . . .] ... [. . .] you have shepherded and ... in your ... [. . .] and your angels [. . .] and your inheritance [. . .] Lord [. . .]' (III 12 I-13 4-IV 10 ii-11 7).

62   YHWH is the obvious referent because the text also refers to 'your [i.e. YHWH's] angels' (l. 5) and 'your inheritance' (l. 6) as well as to אדוני ('Lord' [l. 7]).

63   García Martínez and Tigchelaar (*Scrolls*, 1025) correctly translate the last line from the previous column (III, 12 I-13 6), [. . . אסירי]ם תתרעה, as 'you are the companion of prisoner[s . . .]'. Because רעה/shepherd never occurs in the Hithpael form, רעה here is the alternative word, which means 'to associate with' (cf. BDB, 945).

64   For a brief summary of the dating issues, see R. Coggins, *Sirach*, GAP, ed. M. Knibb (Sheffield: Sheffield Academic Press, 1998), 18–20.

65   Coggins notes how both Sadducean and Pharisaic identifications are problematic (*Sirach*, 56–60).

66   Whether he does this as a leader in a religious movement or simply as a professional scribe, remains a matter of debate; see Tiller, 'Sociological Context', 17–22 and 23–26.

67   Two obvious signs of Hellenistic influence in Ben Sira include his use of a 'signature' (50.27) as well as his hymn to the fathers, which appears to be patterned after

on the other hand, by way of an implicit polemic against factions (like perhaps the group behind *1 Enoch*) who were opposed to the temple priesthood and who subordinated Torah to contemporary revelation.[68]

After extolling God for his all-surpassing mercy, Ben Sira writes:

> A person has mercy for his neighbour but the Lord has mercy upon all flesh, reproving and training and teaching and turning them around like a shepherd his flock; to those who receive his instruction he shows mercy, even to those who hasten to his judgments.

(18.13-14)

For Ben Sira, YHWH as a shepherd represents the embodiment of compassion,[69] extending his mercy to his entire creation, but especially to those who respond to his judgements. To his flock YHWH's mercy manifests itself as instruction to train them in the way they should live. This mention of YHWH teaching the flock resembles Eccl. 12.11, where the redactor describes YHWH as providing wisdom to the nation's wisdom teachers.[70]

The small, fifth fragment of the *Apocryphon of Ezekiel*, plainly citing Ezek. 34.14-16, fills out the picture of YHWH's mercy even further than

---

Hellenistic *encomia* (a eulogistic history in honour of a shrine or city). J. Sanders succinctly writes that '[Ben Sira] is entirely open to Hellenic thought *as long as it can be Judaized*. What he opposes is *the dismantling of Judaism*' (*Ben Sira and Demotic Wisdom*, SBLMS 28 [Chico: Scholars Press, 1983], 53, his emphasis).

68   Cf. B. Wright, 'Putting the Puzzle Together: Some Suggestions Concerning the Social Location of the Wisdom of Ben Sira', *SBLSP* 35 (Atlanta: Scholars Press, 1996): 133–49, and R. Argall, *1 Enoch and Sirach: A Comparative Literary and Conceptual Analysis of the Themes of Revelation, Creation and Judgment*, SBLEJL 8 (Atlanta: Scholars Press, 1995), 250.

69   Embedded in the shepherd imagery is the notion of divine compassion (v. 13a). In fact, the syntax of the Greek suggests that v. 13b is subordinate to and is governed by v. 13a (although the main verb [ἐστίν] in v. 13a must be supplied, that the four verbs of v. 13b are participles suggests that their actions depend on the main verb in the previous clause [v. 13a]: 'the Lord has mercy' [ἔλεος δὲ κυρίου]). Hence the four actions of 'reproving', 'training', 'teaching', and 'turning around' should be understood as expressions of God's mercy.

70   Being 'like a shepherd of his sheep' in Sir. 18.13 involves four overlapping activities. A shepherd rebukes (ἐλέγχω) his sheep so as to prevent the sheep from going astray. That this act of rebuking is more preventative than corrective is suggested by the use of ἐλέγχω in Sir. 19.13-17, where four of its other six occurrences appear. A shepherd trains those in his care the way a father does his child. A shepherd teaches his flock. Lastly, a shepherd turns his sheep, representing, bringing the lost to repentance. While the exact means by which YHWH rebukes, trains, teaches, and turns back his sheep is never specified, in light of Ben Sira's affiliation with other wisdom literature, specifically Ecclesiastes, YHWH would likely accomplish this through the agency of wisdom teachers; cf. M. Gilbert, 'God, Ben Sirach and Mercy: Sirach 15.11–18.14', in *Ben Sira's God: Proceedings of the International Ben Sira Conference, Durham – Ushaw College 2001*, ed. R. Egger-Wenzel, BZAW 321, ed. O. Kaiser [Berlin: Walter de Gruyter, 2002], 131).

Ben Sira. Because this text has not survived intact and four fragments survive only in secondary sources, determining its date and origin remains
difficult and highly speculative. Nevertheless, scholars tend to date
Apocryphon between 50 BCE and 50 CE.[71] Its noted Jewish character,[72]
the portion of fragment 1 preserved in Hebrew in b. Sanh. 91a-b, and
its fairly extensive use of Ezekiel 34 (a text commonly appropriated by
Second Temple Jews), would seem to suggest a Jewish Palestinian origin.
    The text of *Apocryphon* proclaims:

> Therefore he says by Ezekiel, 'And the lame I will bind up, and that which is
> troubled I will heal, and that which is led astray I will return, and I will feed
> them on my holy mountain ... and I will be', he says, 'their shepherd and I will
> be near to them as the garment to their skin'.

While closely following the sense of the original passage in Ezekiel 34,
the author supplements YHWH's pastoral shepherding activity of healing, leading, and feeding – all of which are expressions of divine mercy
– with the idea of being near his people. That is, according to the author
of this text, as Israel's shepherd, YHWH will be as close to them as the
very clothes they wear.[73] Further, the author of the text clearly takes up
Ezekiel's Jewish-national perspective, when he speaks of YHWH gathering
the strays, feeding them on his holy mountain, and being their shepherd.
    Both mercy and judgement are associated with the other use of the
metaphor by Pseudo-Philo. When Phinehas the priest recites to Kenaz
the judge, the prophets, and the elders a solemn message passed on to
him by his father Eleazar about the nation's future moral corruption,
Kenaz and the entire assembly lament, 'Will the Shepherd destroy his
flock for any reason except that it has sinned against him? And now he
is the one who will spare us according to the abundance of his mercy,
because he has toiled so much among us' (*LAB* 28.5). While possessing
great mercy as the nation's shepherd, God also has the sovereign authority to judge his people severely (i.e. 'destroy his flock') on account of
their sins. Pseudo-Philo describes God's 'toil' among his people in rather

---

71   Mueller and Robinson, 'Apocryphon', *OTP*, 1.488; K.-G. Eckart, 'Das
Apokryphon Ezechiel', *Jüdische Schriften aus hellenistisch-römischer Zeit* 5.1 (1974):
45–54. Its explicit use by 1 Clement and a (possible) allusion to it by Josephus would be
decisive factors in its *terminus a quo*.

72   Mueller and Robinson, 'Apocrypon', *OTP*, 1.489; Eckart, 'Apokryphon',
47–49; and A.-M. Denis, *Introduction aux pseudépigraphes grecs d'Ancien Testament*,
SVTP 1 (Leiden: Brill, 1970), 190.

73   This notion of God's presence or his glory with (or being absent from) his people
is a clear motif in the book of Ezekiel (cf. Ezek. 3.23; 8.4; 9.3; 10.18; 37.27-28; 43.4-5;
44.4; 48.35), although not explicitly a part of the shepherd imagery of Ezekiel 34. The
author of *Apocryphon* is likely making explicit what would be implicit in the metaphor; i.e.
YHWH's close presence with his people would be presupposed by his shepherding deeds
of searching, healing, leading, and pasturing done in their midst.

material terms, referring to his acts of creation and the formation, election, and care of his people Israel.[74] Furthermore, that this statement
appears within Kenaz's covenant with Israel, in which he warns the
nation about forsaking YHWH after his departure, reflects the text's
interest in Jewish nationalism.[75]

Mercy and judgement are also associated with the metaphor in the
Dream Visions. Although YHWH is never explicitly called a 'shepherd'
in the Dream Visions, this text deserves mention for several reasons. As
G. Manning suggests, the divine title 'Lord of the Sheep' (used some
twenty-eight times in the passage) would serve as a positive substitute
for 'Shepherd'.[76] Furthermore, the term 'Lord'[77] would elevate YHWH
as a shepherd above the other shepherding figures in the vision, viz. the
angelic shepherds and the sheep-shepherds (i.e. the Jewish leaders). In
other words, YHWH represents not simply the shepherd, but the owner
of the sheep. Moreover, YHWH as 'Lord of the sheep' explicitly functions in the role of a compassionate shepherd in the Dream Visions: he
hears and responds to his people's cries for help (*1 Enoch* 89.17), he protects them (89.25), tends or pastures them (89.28), gathers them from
the nations, brings them into this house (i.e. the temple) and restores
their sight (90.28-29).[78] But whereas YHWH can be a merciful shepherd
for his people, he can also sovereignly give them over to evil, angelic
shepherds who brutalize them for an extended period of time (89.59-65).
Ultimately, however, YHWH executes divine judgement upon these evil
shepherds on the Day of Judgment (89.71, 76; 90.15-26). Jewish nationalism is reflected in the eschatological tone near the end of the passage:
the Lord of the sheep builds 'a new house [i.e. the temple], greater and
loftier than the first one'; the nations fall down and worship the sheep
(i.e. the people of God); and YHWH gathers his flock from the nations
and brings them into this house.

---

74   According to the text, twice in Eleazar's final words to his son Phineas, God
speaks of toiling among his people (*LAB* 28.4, 5): this toil begins with the act of creation;
he continues: 'And I would plant a great vineyard, and from it I would choose a plant; and
I would care for it . . .' (v. 4).

75   *LAB* 28.2 reads: 'And now I will establish my covenant with you today so that
you do not abandon the LORD your God after my departure. ... Now therefore spare those
of your household and your children, and stay in the paths of the LORD your God lest the
Lord destroy his own inheritance.'

76   Manning states that the author avoids using 'shepherd' for YHWH (as well as
for Israel's heroes) because he has decided to give it a negative connotation (*Echoes of a
Prophet: The Use of Ezekiel in the Gospel of John and in Literature of the Second Temple
Period*, JSNTSS 270 [London: T&T Clark, 2004], 88–89).

77   The underlying word for 'Lord' would be מָרֵא (so Milik, *Enoch*, 204); cf. also
κύριος in *1 Enoch* 89.42 of the Chester Beatty Papyrus.

78   Nickelsburg remarks, '[T]hat the Lord was closely involved in the lives of those
sheep [was] evident, from a grammatical point of view, in the author's use of "the Lord
of the sheep" as the subject of a variety of verbs. The Lord was the immediate subject of
actions of which the sheep were the objects or beneficiaries' (*1 Enoch*, 389).

This idea of YHWH protecting his flock appears in the book of Judith. The modern consensus offers an early Hasmonaean date for this text, some time between 164–80 BCE.[79] The issue of provenance is a more difficult question. If S. Zeitlin et al. are correct about a Hebrew *Vorlage*, this would likely point to a Palestinian origin for Judith.[80] Although earlier scholars argued for Pharisaic authorship, nothing in the book would necessarily point in this direction.[81] T. Craven demonstrates how the piety reflected in Judith has points of resemblance with not only Pharisaic attitudes but also Sadducean, Zealot, and Essene.[82] Additional support for a non-sectarian perspective would come from the attitude of unity amongst Jews in general,[83] and the attitude towards Samaria in particular.[84] Rather than Pharisaic, these observations seem to suggest that Judith represents the broader Hasidim movement of the early Maccabaean era.

In seeking to deliver her people from their Assyrian invaders, Judith informs Holofernes that, although the Jews can never be conquered by another nation as long as they refrain from sin and walk according to the Law of their God, the Assyrian siege will force the people to eat food in violation of their Law. Consequently, the God who protects them will abandon them, leaving them defenceless. Holofernes will then be able to take Judaea and Jerusalem because the Jews will be 'like sheep for which there is no shepherd' (Jdt. 11.19).[85] While this phrase in the HB refers to Jewish monarchs, the referent for 'shepherd' here is not earthly rulers but YHWH. Thus YHWH as Israel's Shepherd refers here specifically to

---

79   For a list of scholars and dates, see B. Otzen, *Tobit and Judith*, Guides to Apocrypha and Pseudepigraph, ed. M. Knibb (Sheffield: Sheffield Academic Press, 2002), 132.

80   The Greek text of Judith represents, according to Zeitlin, 'from start to finish not only a translation but a very literal one, regularly following its Hebrew original in both idiom and *syntax*' (M. Enslin and S. Zeitlin, *The Book of Judith* [Leiden: E. J. Brill, 1972], 40; cf. C. Moore, *Judith: A New Translation with Introduction and Commentary*, AB (New York: Doubleday, 1985), 70.

81   H. Mantel, for example, argues that the religious perspective of Judith testifies to Sadducean authorship ('חסידות קדומה', *Studies in Judaism* [1976]: 60–80 [in Hebrew]).

82   T. Craven, *Artistry and Faith in the Book of Judith*, SBLDS 70 (Chico: Scholars Press, 1983), 118–22. Moore observes that the religious views of the book 'are not belligerently sectarian in character', i.e. even if they are Pharisaic (as he asserts) they are neither anti-Sadducee nor anti-Essene (*Judith*, 70).

83   Moore writes, 'The author [has an] irenic attitude toward all Jews, seeing them as being essentially one people and one religion' (*Judith*, 70).

84   According to the story, Judith is from Bethulia, in the region of Samaria; also, when all of the inhabitants of Samaria heard of Holofernes' impending invasion of Jerusalem and the temple, they blocked his path to Jerusalem (4.4-8).

85   If Craven is correct that the story of Judith draws upon the contest between Elijah and the prophets of Baal in 1 Kings 18 (*Artistry*, 47–48), then the phrase would likely represent an allusion to 1 Kgs 22.17.

his activity of protecting his people from military danger. In view of the story's setting of the crisis of Assyrian conquest, the specific meaning of the metaphor in 11.19 – YHWH as Israel's military protector – and the possible allusion to the Jewish-national text of 1 Kgs 22.17,[86] Jdt. 11.19 would also possess overtones of Jewish nationalism.

Much weaker Jewish-national sentiments can be found in Philo's appropriations of the metaphor for God. He notes that God is called a 'Shepherd' in Ps. 23.1,[87] and as such, his sovereign rule extends to the entire created order:

> For land and water and air and fire, and all plants and animals ... the sky, and the circuits of the sun and moon, and the revolutions and rhythmic move-ments of the other heavenly bodies, are like some flock under the hand of God its King and Shepherd (ὁ ποιμὴν καὶ βασιλεύς).[88] This hallowed flock he leads in accordance with right and law.
>
> *(Agric.* 51)

For Philo, then, because God is the universal, sovereign king and con-trols (rules over) every facet of creation, he therefore acts as its shepherd.

Thus, when YHWH is likened to a shepherd by these authors, his mercy is most often highlighted in the comparison, and overtones of Jewish-national restoration are frequently present.

3.2.4 *Messiah as a shepherd*

The metaphor is employed for the messiah in *Psalms of Solomon* 17. Like Judith, *Psalms of Solomon* may also suggest a broader Hasidim origin. Scholars generally maintain that the various psalms reflect the Pompeian era, ranging in date from 63 to 48 BCE,[89] with the final redaction of the document probably emerging some time before 70 CE – since Jerusalem (according to *Psalms*) has been desecrated but not destroyed. M. Winninge lists the three central views on the socio-political and religious provenance

---

86   The military tone of the passage would support the idea of an allusion to 1 Kgs 22.17. While Huntzinger correctly notes that this expression 'signifies the vulnerability of the people and their need for proper leadership' ('End of Exile', 165), he incorrectly links this passage to Ezek. 34.5, leading him to conclude that the metaphor here is a subtle attack on Israel's leaders.

87   Philo refers to God as the 'all-good Shepherd' (πάντα ἀγαθοῦ ποιμένος [*Agric.* 49]).

88   When an article precedes two substantives connected by καί, this often indicates apposition: hence, 'the shepherd and king' should be understood as 'the shepherd-king' (cf. BDF, 144–45). Thus Philo, like the exilic prophets before him, connects royal rule to pastoral care.

89   Pompei's invasion of Jerusalem in 63 BCE seems to be described in *Psalms* 2, 8, and 17, while his assassination in Egypt in 48 BCE appears to be alluded to in the latter part of *Psalm* 2; this would suggest that the community predated the *Psalms* by a genera-tion or so.

of *Psalms*: Hasidic, Pharisaic, or non-Qumran-Essene.[90] Many scholars advocate the Pharisaic composition of *Psalms*.[91] Because of their affinities with the Dead Sea Scrolls, however, a growing number of scholars assert that *Psalms* are not Pharisaic but have a broader socio-religious origin.[92] The origin of the *Psalms* can likely be traced to the Hasidim and perhaps narrowed from this rather inclusive movement to the broader form of the 'Essenes' – i.e. the parent group that would have spawned the Qumran community.[93]

The author of *Psalms of Solomon* 17 paints a bleak picture of the moral state of his nation (viz. the defiling of Jerusalem and the temple by the Hasmonaeans and the Romans), prompting him to cry out to YHWH for a messianic deliverer to save his people. The nature and works of this messiah, described as one who 'shepherds the Lord's flock' (v. 40b), comprise the second part of the psalm.[94] There are four primary traits of the Davidic shepherd. The Son of David is a royal figure: he is the true heir to David's throne and will reign over the nation as the 'King of Israel' (vv. 21, 32, 42) in fulfilment of ancient expectation. The Son of David is a warrior-like judge,[95] and as such, the psalmist expects him to destroy the Gentile rulers for trampling Jerusalem (v. 22), to punish arrogant Jewish 'sinners' who have turned their backs on the covenant (vv. 23-25),[96] and to 'judge peoples and nations' (and so put

90   M. Winninge, *Sinners and Righteous: A Comparative Study of the Psalms of Solomon and Paul's Letters*, CB/NTS 26 (Stockholm: Almqvist & Wiksell International, 1995), 12–14.

91   See L. DiTommaso, *A Bibliography of Pseudepigrapha Research 1859–1999*, JSPSS 39 (Sheffield: Sheffield Academic Press, 2001), 873–93.

92   E.g. G. Stemberger (*Jewish Contemporaries of Jesus: Pharisees, Sadducees, Essenes* [Minneapolis: Fortress Press, 1995]) believes that they are the work of some unidentified segment of pluralistic, early Judaism; cf. R. Wright, 'The Psalms of Solomon, the Pharisees and the Essenes', in *1972 Proceedings for the International Organization for Septuagint and Cognate Studies*, SCSS 2, ed. R. Kraft (Los Angeles: 1972): 136–47, and R. Hann, 'The Pious', 189. For Hann the similarities between the *Psalms* and the Scrolls would be explained by their common parent group, 'proto-Essenism'.

93   That is, if the Qumran community was a subgroup of Essenes, who were, in turn, part of a larger, broad-based coalition of Palestinian Jewish religious conservatives, the Hasidim; cf. the analysis of Winninge, *Sinners*, 141–80. In any scholarly reconstruction, however, *Psalms of Solomon* would represent a Palestinian Jewish setting.

94   Although the shepherd metaphor comes near the end of this section of the psalm, Willitts cogently argues (*Shepherd-King*, 80–85) that 'the motif encapsulates the whole description [of the Davidic Messiah] and, thus, functions as a unifying framework for the vision of the future Davidic King' (*Shepherd-King*, 83).

95   The author achieves this warrior-like imagery by alluding to Isaiah 11: Isa. 11.4c in vv. 24 and 35, Isa. 11.12 in v. 26, and Isa. 11.2 in v. 37.

96   These 'sinners' would be the 'children of the covenant' who adopted Gentile practices (v. 15). The use of shepherd imagery (i.e. the 'iron rod' by which he executes punishment) would seem to suggest that Jews are being taken to task here, not Gentiles. Jerusalem will be purged of its defilement – when the messiah judges Gentile invaders and lapsed Jews – and become holy once more (v. 30).

other Gentiles under his yoke [vv. 29-30]). The prayer's interest in the security and purity of Jerusalem as well as in the righteous state of the Jewish nation reflects clear nationalistic concerns of the psalm's author.

Third, the Davidic messiah will take care of his people. In pastoral fashion, he will gather them together, lead them in faithfulness and righteousness, and settle them in their land (vv. 26-28), 'not allowing any among them to become weak in their pasture' [v. 40b]). His flock will ultimately consist of the righteous Jewish remnant and reverential Gentiles, who obey the messiah and receive mercy from him (17.35, 40). The final trait of the Davidic shepherd is his close relationship with YHWH: on the one hand, God represents the source of the messiah's power, enabling him to accomplish the deeds expected of him (v. 22)[97] – deeds which YHWH executes through the messiah's word.[98] On the other hand, YHWH has made the Son of David 'pure from sin' (v. 36), so that he can rule over the nations. This intimate affiliation between YHWH and the Son of David is reflected in the author's co-extensive view of Israel's kingship: the Son of David is 'Israel's King' (cf. vv. 21, 32, 42) but so, too, is YHWH.[99] In other words, YHWH rules through the agency of the Davidic shepherd.

As will be observed in chapter 4 below, the strong overtones of Jewish nationalism present in this depiction of a coming son of David, possessing a unique relationship with God, who shall reign as King of Israel, shepherding and caring for God's people, while judging the nations, correlates quite closely with Matthew's view of Jesus as the Son of David.

3.2.5 Other usages of 'shepherd'

The notion of judgement that factors so significantly in the portrayal of the Davidic shepherd in *Psalms of Solomon* 17 is also the focus of the metaphor in one of its uses in the Damascus Document (CD).[100] The scholarly consensus maintains that CD is a product of Qumran

---

97   The allusion to Isa. 11.1-2 in 17.37 suggests that the Davidic ruler has been appointed specifically by YHWH to accomplish these deeds.

98   As Willitts notes, the normally distinctive roles of gatherer (YHWH) and governor (messiah) coalesce in *Psalms of Solomon* 17.

99   The opening and closing of the psalm represents an inclusio that projects YHWH's kingship: 'Lord, you are our king forevermore' (v. 1a) and 'The Lord himself is our king forevermore' (v. 46).

100   The literary relationship between the Old Cairo A and B manuscripts of CD has been debated for some time; cf. Hempel, *Laws*, 77–79, and S. White, 'A Comparison of the "A" and "B" Manuscripts of the Damascus Document', *RevQ* 48/12 (1987): 537–53. The general timeframe for the final redaction of each would be the latter part of the second century BCE. Of principal importance for this present study is the subtle thematic difference between the parallels of B and A: in manuscript A, the stress lies on the act of apostasy, i.e. on the act of turning away from the covenant (which results in divine judgement).

ideology,[101] i.e. of a highly apocalyptic, isolationist group that separated not just from mainstream Palestinian Judaism, but from their parent body, a subgroup of Essenes.

Towards the end of the text appears a discussion of members about the sect who reside in the camps scattered throughout Palestine (XIX, 4b-6a). Members who refuse to live according to the Law will receive judgement when God visits the earth:

> When the word comes which is written by the hand of Zechariah the prophet, 'O sword, awake against my shepherd and against the man close to me', declares God. 'Strike the shepherd and the flock will be scattered and I will put my hand against the little ones'. Those that watch him – they are 'the afflicted one of flock' – these ones will escape in the time of the visitation. But those who remain will be delivered up to the sword when the messiah of Aaron and Israel comes.
>
> (XIX, 7-11a)

According to this text, those Jews who reject the teachings of the Qumran community will be harshly judged when the messiah comes: they will be divinely struck down – in similar fashion to the shepherd of Zech. 13.7.[102] Thus it is not the 'shepherd' per se that is the focus of the metaphor but rather what happens to the shepherd in Zech. 13.7 that occupies the redactor's sights: he is struck down.[103] This point is germane to the author's message: although the shepherd was close to YHWH he became an object of his wrath and was struck down by him in judgement; similarly, those Jews who are unfaithful to the covenant will experience divine judgement in the day of the messiah.[104] A Jewish-national outlook is present within the text, i.e. a concern for the moral purification (through divine judgement) of God's people: the covenant God made with ancient Israel has since been renewed with the predecessors of the Qumran community (cf. CD I); consequently, the author of the text emphasizes the centrality of obedience to the Mosaic Law and

---

101   Cf. Baumgarten and Schwartz, *Dead Sea Scrolls*, 7. Hempel persuasively argues otherwise (*Laws*, 20) but her thesis would only affect the legal section of CD and not cols XIII or XIX, where the shepherd metaphor appears.

102   The emphasis in the B manuscript (unlike the A) is on the judgement itself.

103   The contrast in the text is between the 'afflicted of the flock' (an implicit citation of Zech. 11.11) and 'those that remain': the former group is rescued from judgement while the latter is not; instead, this latter group will be delivered up to the sword in judgement. The delivering up of the disobedient to the sword in judgement is reiterated in l. 13, where the sword is described as 'executing the vengeance of the covenant' upon those 'who do not remain strong in these precepts' (l. 14). Similar to the position advocated here, P. Davies (*The Damascus Document: An Interpretation of the 'Damascus Document'*, JSOTSS 25 [Sheffield: JSOT Press, 1982]) also espouses a corporate identification.

104   Cf. the discussion of CD XIX in Huntzinger, 'End of Exile', 166–69. The parallel in CD VII, 10-21 would confirm this interpretation.

to the communal regulations (cf. VII, 4-8; XIX, 2-5, 13-14) so that the community will avoid incurring 'the curses of his covenant' – as opposed to ancient Israel – as prophesied by Zech. 13.7 (and Isa. 7.17 in VII, 9-12).

Another innovative use of the metaphor in CD occurs in the second part of the document.[105] The passage discusses three offices of leadership for the Essene camps: the priest, the Levite, and the 'Examiner' (מבקר).[106] The role of the Examiner receives its fullest explanation in XIII, 7-12, where he is described as '[having] compassion on them as a father does for his sons, and he will watch over (וישקוד)[107] all the afflicted among them as a shepherd over his flock' (XIII, 9).[108] According to the whole passage, the Examiner represents a religious ruler in the community who exercises a high level of authority over it in the areas of recruiting, commerce, marital affairs, and instruction.[109] The Examiner must perform these duties with a fatherly compassion: he is to keep diligent watch over those who are particularly distressed – the way a shepherd would his flock – by 'loosening the chains that bind' the flock in order to ensure that no one under his care will be 'oppressed or crushed' (XIII, 10). Although the description of the Examiner's duties is not overtly pastoral (i.e. using language pertaining to literal shepherding), there is, nevertheless, a pastoral or earthy element to them: he watches over the afflicted, loosens their chains, and has particular regard for the 'oppressed and crushed'.[110]

Like CD XIII, *4 Ezra* employs the metaphor for a religious leader. A first-century CE date is typically assumed for *4 Ezra*. Some scholars consider the date of composition to be around 100 CE.[111] The likelihood of a Hebrew original,[112] the highly theodicy-oriented nature of the book concerning Zion's desolation by the 'Babylonians' (i.e. the Romans), and parallels with the (probably) Palestinian texts of *2 Baruch* and

---

105   The second part of CD treats biblical halakhah and organizational rules for the community (cols IX–XVI); רעה appears within a subunit dealing with 'the rule for those dwelling in the camps' (XII, 22b).

106   Scholars render מבקר variously: 'Overseer' (Milik), 'Inspector' (García Martínez and Tigchelaar), and 'Examiner' (Baumgarten and Schwartz).

107   While other options exist, the reading of Baumgarten and Schwartz (*Dead Sea Scrolls*) as וישקוד ('and he will watch over') seems most probable. For a fuller analysis of this translation issue, see Baxter, 'Shepherd', 119.

108   The parallel for CD XIII, 7-12 appears in 4Q267 9 iv 3-9.

109   See XIII, 11-16, ll. 12b-13, and ll. 14-16b.

110   The particular regard for the 'oppressed and crushed' echoes the sentiments of Ezek. 34.16 and Zech. 11.7, where the weak (in Ezek. 34.16) and the oppressed (in Zech. 11.7) are especially singled out for shepherding.

111   For a survey of approaches to dating *4 Ezra*, see M. Stone, *Features of the Eschatology of IV Ezra*, HSS 35, ed. F. M. Cross (Atlanta: Scholars Press, 1989), 2–4; B. Longenecker, *2 Esdras* (Sheffield: Sheffield Academic Press, 1995), 13–16; and B. Metzger, 'The Fourth Book of Ezra', OTP, 1.520.

112   See Stone, *IV Ezra*, 35–38 and Metzger, 'Ezra', 1.519–20.

1 Enoch, along with possibly *Psalms of Solomon*, Pseudo-Philo, and *Apocalypse of Abraham*, would point in the direction of a Palestinian provenance for *4 Ezra*.[113]

The story of *4 Ezra* opens with Ezra grieving over Zion's destruction at the hands of the Babylonians. He begins to ponder the origin and pervasiveness of sin, and the current predicament of his people, when an angel appears to him in a vision to encourage and warn him. At the end of the vision, Phaltiel ('a chief of the people') comes to Ezra, asking:

> Where have you been? And why is your face sad? Or do you now know that Israel has been entrusted to you in the land of exile? Rise therefore and eat some bread, so that you may not forsake us, like a shepherd who leaves his flock in the power of savage wolves.
>
> (5.16b-18)

A number of things stand out in the passage. Ezra occupies a high seat of authority within the community such that other leaders look to his leadership.[114] He has been (divinely) 'entrusted' with the leadership of exilic Israel. Without his leadership Israel will fall prey to their enemies; and 'savage wolves' in this passage probably refers to Israel's Gentile oppressors, the 'Babylonians'. The wider narrative does give definition to the kind of leadership Ezra exercised, but it is probably enough to say that 'shepherd' here refers to the religious leadership of Israel, without which the people are virtually helpless to know and observe the Law and to find hope in God amid their disastrous circumstances. While the metaphor is not used so pastorally here, there remains a measure of earthiness to it: Ezra the shepherd must eat to have strength to defend his flock against the savage wolves threatening his sheep.[115] Moreover, in view of the story's Babylonian exilic setting and Jerusalem's destruction (3.1-2), Ezra's anxiety over Israel's subjugation to Gentiles (4.22-25), his complaints about divine inequity (5.22-34), and the apocalyptic visions comprising most of the book, when Phaltiel frets over exilic Israel being like abandoned sheep left in the power of savage wolves, clear Jewish-national concerns are in view.

---

113   Cf. Stone, *4 Ezra*, 10; Longenecker, *2 Esdras*, 14; Metzger, 'Ezra', 1.522–23.

114   A 'chief of the people' considers Israel as having been 'entrusted' to 'you' – viz. to Ezra – not to 'us', i.e. Ezra and the other chiefs.

115   For further comment on and comparison of this verse, see section 3.5 below.

The use of the metaphor in *2 Baruch* resembles its use in *4 Ezra*. The accepted date range for *2 Baruch* is after 70 CE but some time before the Bar Kochba revolt of 132 CE.[116] A Palestinian provenance seems to be suggested by Baruch's stand in the story with the inhabitants of Palestine over and against the Diaspora Jews, to whom the people of the story earnestly petition Baruch to write.[117] Additionally, the questions the author raises throughout the book concerning the loss of land and leadership, as well as the likelihood of a Hebrew *Vorlage*,[118] may suggest a Palestinian origin.[119]

Unlike in *4 Ezra*, the appropriation of the metaphor for a religious leader in *2 Baruch* has a narrower focus for the activity of the leader. Baruch warns his people that, in view of how God dealt with his people in the past, unless they live uprightly they, too, will join the rest of the nation in exile (77.1-10). Baruch's impending death, however, leads to uncertainty in the minds of the people and they request that he write a letter to the Jews in Babylon before his departure to encourage the Diaspora Jews in their exilic plight. Their reason for their request is that 'the shepherds of Israel have perished, and the lamps which gave light are extinguished, and the fountains from which we used to drink have withheld their streams' (v. 13). The author appropriates the shepherd metaphor for Law teachers, i.e. authoritative teachers of the Law – like the author.[120] By their teaching these religious teachers provide light and refreshment to the people.[121]

Because the community considers Baruch to be the sole surviving leader in the wake of Jerusalem's destruction, they believe his impending death will leave a huge void in religious leadership.[122] But Baruch reassures his followers:

> Shepherds and lamps and fountains came from the Law and when we go away, the Law will abide. If you, therefore, look upon the Law and are intent

---

116   For an examination of the date range, see G. Sayler, *Have the Promises Failed? A Literary Analysis of 2 Baruch*, SBLDS 72 (Chico: Scholars Press, 1984), 103–110.

117   The letter comprises the final section of the document; cf. Klijn, '2 Baruch', 1.617.

118   See M. Desjardins, 'Law in 2 Baruch and 4 Ezra', *Studies in Religion* 14 (1985), 25 (and n. 3), also Klijn, '2 Baruch', 1.616.

119   For a discussion of the internal evidence of the author's world, see Sayler, *2 Baruch*, 110–18.

120   According to R. Wright ('The Social Setting of the Syriac Apocalypse of Baruch', *JSP* 16 [1997]: 81–96), the author of *2 Baruch* considered himself to be 'a recognized/authorized "Baruch" intermediary'.

121   The parallelism between 'extinguished lamps', 'dry fountains', and 'perished shepherds' implies that Israel's shepherds were supposed to offer light to the people, lest they walk about in darkness, and drink, lest they thirst; consequently, the people speak of being 'left in the darkness and in the thick forest and in the aridness of the desert' (77.14).

122   Cf. *2 Baruch* 44–46.

upon wisdom, then the lamp will not be wanting and the shepherd will not give way and the fountain will not dry up.

(77.15b-16)

As in v. 13, 'shepherds', 'lamps', and 'fountains' represent teachers of the Mosaic Law. The larger point here, however, is that these recognized teachers ultimately derive their authority from the Law (and not merely from some communal appointment). Moreover, the Jewish-national concern of the text is obvious: Baruch has just warned the people that in order to avoid exile they must remain faithful to God's Law (77.1-10); in view of Baruch's imminent departure, however, the people express anxiety over how to do this without his help. Baruch therefore encourages them that as long as they remain faithful God will provide them with other religious teachers, i.e. other shepherds to guide them.[123]

Although Philo employs the shepherd metaphor for kings and for God, he most frequently deploys the metaphor innovatively for the human mind (twenty-six times, mostly in *De Agricultura*).[124] To shepherd bodily passions means to exercise perfect self-control over them. Philo appeals to Moses to underscore the importance of being a good shepherd: just as Moses prayed that the flock would be given a good shepherd to lead them out of wickedness and into virtue, so also a person should pray for a mind that can rule like a shepherd over unlawful bodily dispositions (*Agric.* 44–48).

In another use of 'shepherd', Philo expresses an awareness of a critical attitude towards the shepherding vocation. When speaking of Joseph's brothers' admission to Pharaoh about being shepherds (according to Genesis), Philo writes:

[I]f the care of literal goats or sheep was what was meant, they would perhaps, in their shrinking from disgrace, have been actually ashamed to own what they were; for such pursuits are held mean and inglorious in the eyes of those who have compassed that importance, wholly devoid of wisdom, that comes with prosperity, and most of all in the eyes of monarchs.

(*Agric.* 61)

123   Hunziker-Rodewald asserts, 'Dass in der syrischen Baruch-Apokalypse nicht eindeutig zwischen der lichtspendenden Funktion des Gesetzes und derer, die das Gesetz dem Volk vermitteln, zu unterscheiden ist, liegt daran, dass die Vermittler aus dem Gesetz stammen (77.15), d.h. nur entfalten, was jenes bereits enthält' (*Hirt*, 211). The teachers of the Law do derive both their teaching and authority from the Law; nevertheless, the author of 2 *Baruch* views the teachers as the shepherds not the Law itself (cf. 77.13). Moreover, 2 *Baruch* made this same point previously in 46.4b-6.

124   Other less substantial occurrences of the metaphor being applied to the mind are *Abr.* 221; *Det.* 3, 9, 25; *Ios.* 2; *Migr.* 213; *Mut.* 110; *Post.* 67, 98; *Prob.* 31; *Sacr.* 45, 48–49, 51; *Sobr.* 14; *Somn.* 2.151–54.

Philo does not merely adopt the perspective of Gen. 46.34bβ (viz. 'all shepherds are detestable to the Egyptians'). On the one hand, his explanation of their vocation substantially amplifies the critical attitude inherent in the biblical text. On the other hand, he seeks to justify Joseph's brothers' claim of being shepherds, contrary to Gen. 46.34β. In Genesis, it is precisely because Egyptians detest shepherds that Joseph instructs his brothers to inform Pharaoh of their occupation: so that they can live in Goshen. The Egyptians' low view of shepherds is not a problem for the redactor of Genesis; it is, however, for Philo (or perhaps for his readers): hence he attempts to rationalize the vocation of Israel's Patriarchs.

Similarly, in one of his literal uses of 'shepherd', Josephus reveals a negative attitude towards shepherds. In *AJ* 17.278, Josephus describes Athronges, one of the challengers to Herod's throne as aspiring to the kingship despite not being distinguished by his ancestry, character, or wealth – but on the contrary, he was only a shepherd and unknown to the general populace. Here, Josephus implies that there is a definite lowliness to the social status of a shepherd.[125]

3.2.6 Summary of the shepherd metaphor in the writings of NCB Jews

The range of uses for the shepherd metaphor can be mapped as illustrated in Table 3.1. Similar to the HB, Second Temple Jews most commonly appropriate the metaphor for rulers and for YHWH.

Table 3.1 General referents for the shepherd metaphor

Rulers	YHWH	Messiah	Act of Judgment	Teachers of the Law
1 Enoch	1 Enoch	Pss. Sol. 17	CD XIX	2 Baruch
4Q504	4Q509			
1Q34	Ben Sira			
CD XIII	Judith			
Philo	Apoc. Ezek.			
LAB	Philo			
Josephus	LAB			
4 Ezra				

---

125   This contrast between being of noble ancestry and being a shepherd is lacking in the parallel account of *BJ* 2.60 and is maybe due to a difference in the respective audiences Josephus addresses; cf. the discussion of the social setting of *AJ* in section 3.2.2 above.

Within the category of 'Rulers as Shepherds', there are further correspondences with the HB but also some differences: see Table 3.2. While 4Q504 and 1Q34 are too fragmentary to offer further insight here, *1 Enoch*, CD XIII, Philo, and *4 Ezra* depict shepherd-rulers, similar to the HB, in fairly pastoral terms,[126] i.e. in language that corresponds to literal shepherding: the redactor of *1 Enoch* refers three times to the evil shepherds governing Israel as 'pasturing' the flock; the Examiner of CD XIII is responsible for watching over the afflicted, loosening their chains, and paying particular regard to the 'oppressed and crushed'; Philo speaks of shepherd-rulers as guarding, protecting, leading, and guiding the flock; and in *4 Ezra*, the shepherd must eat to have strength to defend the flock against savage wolves.

Table 3.2 Specific referents of the 'rulers as shepherds' metaphor

Referent	1 Enoch	4Q504	1Q34	CD XIII	Philo	LAB	4 Ezra	Jos.
Monarchs					X			X
King David		X	X					X
Intercessor					X	X		
Angels	X							
Religious leader				X			X	
Virtuous mind					X			

NCB Jewish authors can also use the metaphor innovatively. Pseudo-Philo uses 'shepherd' for pre-monarchical rulers of Israel: Moses and the Judges. But the particular aspect of their leadership that Pseudo-Philo highlights is their role of intercessor for the nation's iniquity. In *1 Enoch* Israel's rulers during their period of foreign domination are described as angelic beings: the demonic forces whose activity, according to the author, resulted in the nation's captivity and oppression. The author of CD XIII describes the Examiner as a 'shepherd' who exercises authority over the community in the areas of admittance, commerce, marital affairs, and religious instruction.[127] Philo, for his part, uses the metaphor for the virtuous mind that successfully rules over bodily passions. Thus, compared to the HB, Second Temple Jewish authors appropriate the shepherd metaphor for non-political figures (e.g. religious leaders/ teachers, human mind) and for non-political functions (e.g. interceding, controlling bodily passions, teaching) with greater frequency.

---

126   Josephus does not use the metaphor in this way, but this may be because he is merely following the specific contours of the biblical text: he quotes 1 Kgs 22.17 in *AJ* 8.404 and 2 Sam. 24.17 in *AJ* 3.328.

127   Cf. the more general depiction of a religious leader in *4 Ezra* 5.

Table 3.3 Implicit or explicit traits of YHWH as a shepherd

Shepherd-trait	Ben Sira	1 Enoch	Jdt	4Q509	Apoc. Ezek.	Philo	LAB
Merciful	X	X		X	X		X
Judge		X					X
Protector			X				
Sovereign Ruler						X	

When applied to YHWH, the shepherd metaphor parallels what is observed in the HB: see Table 3.3. YHWH is most commonly portrayed as merciful or compassionate. Similarly to the HB, YHWH's shepherding is described in pastoral terms: according to the *Apocryphon of Ezekiel*, YHWH binds up and heals the troubled and the lame, and feeds them; the redactor of *1 Enoch* speaks of the 'Lord of the sheep' as protecting his people, pasturing them, gathering them in his house, and restoring their sight; and according to Judith, YHWH as Israel's Shepherd protects his people from physical dangers.[128]

The metaphor is deployed uniquely in three passages: see Table 3.4. In CD XIX the focus is not so much on the shepherd of Zech. 13.7 per se, but on his being struck down by God. This striking down of the shepherd represents the execution of God's wrath, in the day of the messiah, upon those Jews who were once faithful but who turned away from the Covenant. In *Psalms of Solomon* 17, the messianic Son of David is depicted as a warrior who will sternly judge the Gentiles and apostate Jews, but gather together the people of God and extend YHWH's rule over the nation, shepherding them in righteousness. The author of *2 Baruch* describes the teachers of the Law as Israel's shepherds, who, by their teaching, provide light, guidance, and refreshment for Israel.

Table 3.4 Specific referents for other uses of 'shepherd'

Text	Referent	Characteristics
CD XIX	Act of Judgment	Apostates receive divine condemnation when messiah comes
Pss. Sol. 17	Davidic Messiah	Eschatological Davidic warrior-ruler and judge
2 Baruch	Law teachers	Provide light/guidance/spiritual refreshment

---

128   While Pseudo-Philo's use of the metaphor is not as pastoral as the others, it is still 'earthy': he describes God's toiling amongst his people in terms of creation and the formation, election, and care of his people Israel.

As observed above, Second Temple Jewish authors often idealize the activities of the model shepherd (e.g. YHWH) in pastoral terms – in language commonly used to describe the shepherding vocation: see Table 3.5.

Table 3.5 Degree of pastoral imagery used in the texts of NCB Jews when idealizing a shepherd

Pronounced imagery	Modest imagery	Little or no imagery
1 Enoch	Judith	Ben Sira
CD	LAB	Philo
Pss. Sol. 17		
Apoc. Ezek.		

One of the defining characteristics of the appropriation of the shepherd metaphor by NCB Jews is the overtones of Jewish-national restoration: see Table 3.6. As in the HB, there is a clear tendency for NCB Jewish writers to associate Jewish-national concerns with the metaphor.

Table 3.6 Jewish-national overtones in the metaphor's use by NCB Jews

Strong overtones	Modest overtones	Little or no overtones
1 Enoch	1Q34	Ben Sira
4Q504	4Q509	Philo
CD XIII; XIX	Judith	
Pss. Sol. 17	Josephus	
Apoc. Ezek.		
LAB		
4 Ezra		
2 Baruch		

It is obvious that the shepherd metaphor appears most frequently in Jewish Palestinian literature and is deployed by Jewish authors for Jewish communities. The only Diaspora Jewish writers who appear to use the metaphor are Philo and Josephus. The metaphor is altogether absent in, for example, the Diaspora Jewish writings of Artapanus, Aristobulus, *Letter of Aristeas*, *Joseph and Aseneth*, Ezekiel the Tragedian, Pseudo-Phocylides, and Wisdom of Solomon, which (with the exceptions of Aristobulus and Pseudo-Phocylides) present material which would have, at least potentially, provided a suitable context for the shepherd metaphor's appropriation: for example, although fragmented, Artapanus deals with Joseph and Moses in the context of kings and rulers; two of the questions posed in *Letter of Aristeas* concern the chief characteristic and the definition of kingship; *Joseph and Aseneth* has descriptions of Joseph, the ruler of Egypt, and YHWH; there are also fairly lengthy depictions of Moses and YHWH in Ezekiel the Tragedian; and the sixth chapter (especially) of Wisdom of Solomon deals with the rule of kings.

Philo and Josephus are Diaspora Jews writing for other Diaspora Jews, as well as for Gentiles in the case of Josephus, and possibly Philo.[129] Only in their texts does 'shepherd' receive negative connotations. By way of contrast, among the numerous uses of 'shepherd' by Palestinian Jewish authors, only CD XIX employs the metaphor with negative connotations. Thus, the general tendency of Palestinian authors is to deploy the metaphor positively.[130] The reason for this difference might be their respective Diaspora contexts and the intended recipients of their texts: Philo writes for Egyptian Jews (and possibly Gentiles), while Josephus writes from Rome primarily for Gentile authorities – the vocation was held in low regard by Egyptians and Romans.[131] While this observation cannot be pressed too far, it may be that, based on the available albeit limited data, the shepherd metaphor possessed a greater interest for Palestinian Jews than it did for their Diaspora counterparts. Part II of this study will discuss how Matthew's appropriation of the metaphor fits with these basic patterns of thought observed in the metaphor's use by NCB Jews.

3.3 The Use of 'Shepherd' in the Writings of NCB Romans

3.3.1 Introduction

Among non-Jewish, NCB groups, Roman texts possess the most impact for any study of Matthew because of the strong political and social influence the Roman Empire would have wielded over its Jewish and CB inhabitants. Generally, people's beliefs and behaviours are shaped by

---

129　Their respective destinations would likely include Gentiles because of their more religio-cultural and apologetic concerns. That is, both Philo and Josephus sought to defend and extol Judaism against its Gentile detractors. This type of orientation is lacking in the other texts discussed in this section of the study.

130　While *4 Ezra* 5.16b-18 could be deemed negative, it actually is not. The text does not in any way make a general characterization about shepherds, viz. that they are prone to abandoning their flock in times of danger – according to the Fourth Gospel such a person would be regarded only as a hired hand and not a 'good' shepherd. All that should be taken from *4 Ezra* 5.18 is that some shepherds do (forsake the flock), some do not, and Ezra is being admonished not to be like the former – 'like a shepherd who leaves his flock in the power of savage wolves'; the inference is that he should rise up and look after his flock of exiles like a responsible shepherd.

131　Cf. the discussion of 'shepherd' in Roman texts in section 3.3 below.

their social-historical context.[132] First-century residents of the Roman Empire unambiguously felt the impact of Roman rule in terms of taxation and military force. J. Kautsky notes that 'to rule in aristocratic empires is, above all, to tax'.[133] Scholarship is clear that in the hierarchical society of the Roman Empire the poor were exceptionally taxed to sustain the wealth and lifestyle of the ruling elite.[134] Roman taxes, tribute, or other expenses were experienced in nearly every sphere of daily life, e.g. in land value and production, rent, goods, and services, and in the use of various public facilities.[135] Indeed, because as much as 70 per cent of their production was claimed through taxes, most peasants in the empire lived at or close to the subsistence level.[136]

Besides excessive taxation Roman rule was keenly felt in the empire's displays of military might. The presence of Roman soldiers in the cities of the empire served as a constant visual reminder of Rome's ever-present power on the one hand,[137] and the defeated state of non-Roman inhabitants, on the other.[138] The Gospels make it clear that Roman soldiers could be gratuitously cruel to whomever they incarcerated,[139] and they also suggest that Roman soldiers freely flexed their military muscle with civilians. For example, commentators recognize that the thought behind the logion in Mt. 5.41 ('And whoever shall force you to go one mile, go two') is that soldiers could, for the sake of personal convenience, force someone – on the spot – to carry their cumbersome belongings for a distance of one mile.[140]

The empire also made a definite impact in terms of some of the religious practices of its residents. In order to generate and maintain the relationship between the emperor and his people, emperor-centric liturgical practices entailing prayers, vows, sacrifices, and festivals were instituted.[141] Involvement

132   See the discussion in section 1.4.1 above.

133   J. Kautsky, *The Politics of Aristocratic Empires* (Chapel Hill: University of North Carolina Press, 1982), 150.

134   See, for example, Kautsky, *Politics*, G. Lenski, *Power and Privilege: A Theory of Social Stratification* (New York: McGraw Hill, 1966), and D. Oakman, *Jesus and the Economic Questions of His Day* (Lewiston: Edwin Mellen, 1986).

135   Carter, *Empire*, 13–14, 134–35.

136   Carter, *Empire*, 18.

137   T. R. Hobbs notes that the military had become the 'face of the empire' that most residents saw and experienced ('The Political Jesus: Discipleship and Disengagement', in *The Social Setting of Jesus and the Gospels*, ed. W. Stegemann, B. Malina and G. Theissen [Minneapolis: Fortress Press, 2002], 251–52).

138   While its military presence would have been much stronger in urban centres, the Gospels suggest that Roman soldiers lived in more rural areas as well (e.g. Mt. 5.40-41; 8.5).

139   E.g. Mk 15.16-20 and parallels.

140   Cf. Mt. 20.25; 27.32. As Carter and others note, Roman soldiers often forced people into service to build bridges and roads – for the express purpose of raising Rome's income through extra tolls.

141   See S. Price, *Rituals and Power: The Roman Imperial Cult in Asia Minor* (Cambridge: Cambridge University Press, 1984).

in these rites could at times be fairly extensive. Some first-century Jews, for example, held public posts that would have required significant participation in the Roman cult.[142] Philo, however, describes an instance that suggests participation could be much more minimalistic: when Emperor Gaius is informed that everyone but the Jews have been offering sacrifices of thanksgiving for his preservation, Philo and his delegation protest that the Jewish priests have as well; but Gaius complains that they offer sacrifices only for the emperor but not to him.[143]

Of course, Roman imperial persuasion was also manifested in less antagonistic ways. Non-Romans often embraced various aspects of Roman culture in order to make their lot more secure with Rome or to improve social status.[144] For example, the city of Sepphoris adopted a pro-Roman stance early on in the first Jewish revolt, which led to its moniker, 'City of Peace';[145] and Barclay notes that although Agrippa I was a staunch defender of his fellow Jews, 'the ease with which [he] moved in both Gentile and Jewish worlds [served as an example] of the social integration desired by many Jews of high social status'.[146]

Furthermore, some residents of the empire would have accepted elements of Roman culture rather unintentionally with no reasoned deliberation. That is to say, they picked up a Roman practice of some kind not to become more Roman or to gain specific favour from Roman authorities, but merely for the sake of personal preference. Berlin, for example, observes that Roman-style cooking pans were easily and widely adopted throughout the region of Galilee;[147] and in view of the explicitly Roman adornment of Jewish tombs, Barclay remarks that 'the fact remains that it must have been perfectly normal for a Jew to walk into a non-Jewish workshop to order a sarcophagus'.[148]

Roman culture could also be expressed negatively, whereby aspects of Roman rule were purposefully rejected or subverted – leading to a kind of counter-practice – as a way of making a specific anti-Rome statement.[149]

---

142   See Barclay, *Jews*, 321–23.

143   Philo, *Legat.* 355–57.

144   For some examples of Jewish cultural assimilation in the Roman Empire, see M. Williams, 'Jews and Jewish Communities in the Roman Empire', in *Experiencing Rome: Culture, Identity and Power in the Roman Empire*, ed. J. Huskinson (London: Routledge, 2000), 316–23.

145   See E. Meyers, 'Sepphoris: City of Peace', in *The First Jewish Revolt: Archaeology, History, and Ideology*, ed. A. Berlin and J. A. Overman (London: Routledge, 2002), 110–20.

146   Barclay, *Jews*, 254. Barclay categorizes these Jews as 'social climbers' and, besides Agrippa I, he thus characterizes the Herodians, whose transference from their native Jewish customs to Roman ones led to careers in imperial administration or as client kings in eastern nations (cf. *AJ* 18.141).

147   Berlin, 'Romanization', 68–69.

148   Barclay, *Jews*, 329–30.

149   For a list of some of these ways, see Hobbs, 'Political', 270.

Josephus mentions that when Gaius planned to construct a statue of himself in the Jewish Temple the peasants en masse abandoned their regular work in the fields for a prolonged period, causing Rome to see the 'economic handwriting on the wall', and dispense with installing the statue;[150] and although its exact meaning is disputed, subversion may be the order of the Temple tax logion in Mt. 17.24-27, where the Matthean Jesus instructs his followers to pay the tax for the Temple of Jupiter Capitolinus – formerly the pre-70 Temple tax – as a way of publicly proclaiming God's sovereignty and power over the Roman Empire.[151]

Carter has probably drawn the most attention to the relationship between Matthew's Gospel and the Roman Empire, asserting that 'the Gospel comes from and addresses a world dominated by the Roman Empire'.[152] Matthew would thus represent a response – at least in part – to this context of Roman political, economic, ideological, and social domination in which the Jesus movement seeks to carve out a place for itself. How close or how far off Matthew's deployment of the shepherd metaphor is with the use of 'shepherd' in Roman texts will have direct bearing on determining the socio-religious orientation of Matthew (perhaps even more so, his audience).

Because Roman authors overwhelmingly tend to appropriate the shepherd metaphor infrequently – which itself suggests something – several other dimensions of 'shepherd' usage will be taken into account in this present section of the study. Besides analysing occurrences of the metaphor,[153] the general attitudes of Roman authors towards vocational shepherds will be examined: sometimes the manner in which they discuss shepherds as a vocation or as a social class produces additional insight into the attitude that NCB Romans had towards shepherds in Matthew's day; and as will be immediately evident, this attitude stands in very sharp relief to that of NCB Jews and Christ-believers.

Also of special importance for understanding 'shepherd' usage here are the titles of honour bestowed upon Roman emperors. Carter correctly points out that Matthew's presentation of Jesus closely echoes and challenges the claims of Roman imperial theology.[154] In view of these parallel claims, some

---

150   Josephus, *AJ* 18.270-84; cf. R. Horsley, *Jesus and the Spiral of Violence: Popular Jewish Resistance in Roman Palestine* (Minneapolis: Fortress Press, 1993), 114–16.

151   See Carter, *Empire*, 130–44; Barclay, *Jews*, 310–13.

152   Carter, *Empire*, 1.

153   One occurrence that shall not be analysed is *Inst.* 8.6.18.1, where Quintilian (c. 40–118 CE) explicitly quotes Homer's metaphor, 'shepherd of the people'. Philo also cites this phrase three times for kings, similar to Homer, who uses the expression for Agamemnon (*Il.* 2.253). But in the case of Quintilian, he cites Homer's phrase only to demonstrate the need to employ metaphors appropriately and not simply for the sake of using a well-known figurative expression.

154   Carter (*Empire*, 57–74) focuses on the claims of divine sovereignty, presence, agency, and societal well-being. Imperial claims, for example, assert that the emperor of Rome has been anointed by the gods as their agent through whom their presence in and

measure of overlap in the titles and terms applied to the emperor and to Matthew's Jesus would be expected.[155] Hence, section 3.3.4 will survey the titles given to Roman emperors to determine if 'shepherd' – an important descriptor Matthew employs for Jesus – was among these honorific Roman titles. Finally, characteristics and tendencies of 'shepherd' usage shall be synthesized and conclusions drawn.

3.3.2 *The shepherd metaphor in Roman texts*

Although Roman authors typically do not appropriate 'shepherd' as a metaphor, some do. Dio Chrysostom (c. 40–120 CE), a Roman orator of Greek heritage, uses the metaphor a number of times in *De regno*, specifically in his first four discourses that deal with kingship. Chrysostom uses a citation from Homer[156] to tease out some of the qualities of the ideal king. He asserts that only the good king derives his office from Zeus (rather than from some other god), and that he receives his appointment precisely because he is wholly concerned with the welfare of his flock (*1 Regn.* 12). Chrysostom contrasts the king's devotion to his subjects with a list of vices to avoid: '[The king] shall plan and study the welfare of his subjects; he is not to become licentious or profligate, stuffing and gorging with folly, insolence, arrogance ... [but] he is to devote his attention to himself and his subjects, becoming indeed a guide and shepherd of his people' (*1 Regn.* 13). He then describes what it means to be a 'shepherd of his people' by stating what it does not entail: '[becoming a] shepherd of his people, not, as someone has said,[157] a caterer and banqueter at this expense'. Chrysostom thus employs the shepherd metaphor for the ideal king,[158] who avoids self-indulgence and distinguishes himself by his selfless devotion to care for and to protect his subjects, never exploiting them for selfish gain.[159]

---

power over the Roman Empire are manifest: e.g. Domitian is called 'present god' (*deus praesens*) – the god's presence and favour reside in him (*Sil.* 5.2.170). Matthew makes similar claims for Jesus: in Jesus and in his mission, God's presence and his sovereign rule (i.e. the kingdom of God) are revealed.

155   This overlap would especially be anticipated if, as Carter correctly asserts, Matthew, on the one hand, seeks implicitly to challenge the Romans' view of divine sovereignty, divine presence, agency, and societal well-being, since these concepts relate both to the emperor and to Jesus. It would also be expected if, on the other hand, Matthew wrote as someone steeped in Roman culture – whether by virtue of ethnic identity or a high degree of Roman acculturation.

156   *Iliad* 2.205–206: '[T]o whom the son of Saturn gives the sceptre, making him the lawgiver that he may rule the rest'.

157   Viz. Plato: *Resp.* 4.421b.

158   Cf. Chrysostom's use of the metaphor in *2 Regn.* 6, where he cites Homer's phrase, 'shepherd of the people', to describe how the poet referred to earthly rulers.

159   This use of the metaphor is echoed in *1 Regn.* 17, 28; *3 Regn.* 40–41; and *4 Regn.* 43–44.

Another Graeco-Roman author, the biographer Plutarch (c. 45–125 CE), twice employs 'shepherd' metaphorically in *Moralia*. In the first, Plutarch uses 'shepherd' to describe the actions of a royal servant named Philopoemen, who 'tends' (ποιμαίνω) King Attalus by fattening his master with food and drink, thereby contributing to the king's inactivity. Consequently, rather than Attalus's eminence increasing – as typically occurs through kings' military campaigns – leisure and inactivity lead to his diminished status (*An seni* 792A–B). 'Shepherding' here refers to filling up a monarch with luxuries resulting in tarnishing the king's status and thus it possesses negative overtones: it results in a monarch's diminished rank. Plutarch remarks how the glutted Attalus is mocked by the Romans: 'does the king have any influence with Philopoemen?' In other words, it seems as if Philopoemen the servant can do more for the people than the king can. While the act of 'tending' in itself would not necessarily imply an unfavourable connotation, the name of the servant responsible for sullying the king's reputation would: 'Philopoemen' (Φιλοποίμην), which means 'shepherd-associate'. A shepherd, then, is the one responsible for soiling the king's reputation.

In the second occurrence of the metaphor, Plutarch uses it in relation to Epicurean philosophers. He describes them as 'tending' (ποιμαίνω) their philosophies (*Def. orac.* 420B). Here, 'shepherding' would essentially refer to practising and peddling philosophical teachings. Tending/shepherding philosophies would not by itself elicit negative overtones; however, it is the Epicureans who do the shepherding and no one else. Plutarch's character Cleombrotus is quite critical of Epicureans and, although Cleombrotus also opposes some of the teachings of the Stoics,[160] he does not attack them in the virulent way that he does the Epicureans. Hence, 'shepherd' receives a critical connotation by association.

The Roman historian Suetonius (c. 69–121 CE) appropriates the metaphor for Tiberius in his *De Vita Caesarum*. In recounting the reign of Tiberius he describes a time when his governors recommended that he increase the already burdensome taxes for his provinces. In response to their counsel he wrote to them that 'it was the part of a good shepherd to shear his flock not skin it' (*Tib.* 32.2). Suetonius then follows this account with some ways by which Tiberius, more often than not, 'showed himself kindly and devoted to the public weal' (*Tib.* 33.1), for example by introducing regulations to curb senatorial abuses, and by reducing the cost of the games (33.1 and 34.1, respectively). Hence, Suetonius employs the metaphor to depict the responsible care rulers are to offer their subjects.

Thus, Roman authors appropriate the shepherd metaphor infrequently: on the one hand, Dio Chrysostom and Suetonius employ the metaphor for kings and their responsibility to provide proper care for their subjects. On the other hand, Plutarch uses it with quite negative connotations.

160   See *Def. orac.* 420 A.

3.3.3 The portrayal of shepherds in Roman texts

Roman authors writing near the time of Matthew normally refer to shepherds in very minor ways. In a few instances they use 'shepherd' (Latin, *pastor*) as a proper name.[161] Without question, however, they most commonly refer to shepherds simply in passing, and consequently, shepherds have no significance in their works.[162] But there are some significant cases that reveal the author's attitude towards shepherds.

Livy[163] uses 'shepherd' some twenty-one times in *Ab Urbe Condita Libri*, which describes the rise of the Roman Empire. Livy portrays shepherds – even within their very minor role in his literary history – as semi-violent, unprincipled rabble-rousers (*Ab Urbe*. 1.4.9, 5.7; 5.53.8–9), and unscrupulous assassins (1.40.5–7; cf. 39.29.9). In a similar vein, Seneca the Younger[164] draws a negative comparison between the high social rank of a senator and the low rank of a shepherd (*Ep.* 47.10.7).[165]

The bellicose conduct of and low regard for shepherds observed in Livy appear in the Roman history, *Historiae Romanae* by Velleius Paterculus.[166] In an account of the war between Athens and Lacedaemonia, King Codrus, to secure victory for Athens as foretold by a Pythian oracle, disguises himself as a shepherd, provokes a quarrel, and is slain in the ensuing skirmish (*Hist.* I, 2.1–2).[167] Paterculus writes that Codrus '[laid] aside his kingly robes and [donned] the garb of a shepherd'. The first part of this phrase seems somewhat superfluous unless the author intended to contrast implicitly the social classes of a shepherd and a king. The contrast between these two social

---

161   Pliny the Younger (c. 61–113 CE) uses it as a proper name, 'Junius Pastor' (*Ep.* 1.18.3), as does Seneca the Younger, who uses it as the name of a Roman knight (*Ira* 2.33.3–4).

162   For 'shepherd' as a vocation, see Ovid (c. 43 BCE–17 CE), *Fast.* 1.379; 2.369; 3.879; 4.487, 735, 776, 795, 810; *Trist.* 4.1.12; *Metam.* 1.573, 676, 681; 3.408; 4.276; passim; Seneca the Younger (c. 4 BCE–65 CE), *Ep.* 34.1; 122.12.2; *Herc. fur.* 139, 232, 451; *Med.* 101; *Phaed.* 422; *Oed.* 146, 808, 816; *Herc. Ot.* 128; *Oct.* 774; *Nat.* 2.22.1.8; Pliny the Elder (23–79 CE), *Nat.* 8.54.3, 100.5, 106.2, 114.3; 10.40.6, 115.3; 12.22.5; 16.75.5, 179.4, 208.1; 18.330.3; 19.27.3; 22.56.2; 25.14.8; Martial (c. 40–104 CE), *Epi.* 5.65.11; 8.53.3; 11.41.1; 13.38.1; 14.156.1; Petronius (first century CE), *Fr.* 27.10; Statius (c. 45–96 CE), *Achill.* 1.20; 2.51; *Theb.* 1.367; 2.378; 4.301, 368, 715; 6.188; 7.393, 437; 8.692; 9.191; 10.574; 11.310; 12.268; *Sil.* 1.2.43, 214; 1.4.105.

163   Titus Livius (c. 59 BCE–17 CE) spent most of his life in Rome and was a member of the elite literary circle patronized by Augustus.

164   Lucius Annaeus Seneca (c. 4 BCE–65 CE) was born in Spain but raised and educated in Rome in rhetoric and philosophy.

165   Elsewhere for the sake of contrast he tries to establish, Seneca juxtaposes 'shepherd' and 'goddesses' (*Ag.* 731): in other words, shepherds represent the antithesis of gods and goddesses.

166   Gaius Velleius Paterculus (c. 19 BCE–30 CE) served in the military in Germany under the future Emperor Tiberius, and was appointed quaestor (in 6 CE) and later praetor (15 CE).

167   This idea of a shepherd provoking a quarrel resembles the scene in Livy, *Ab Urbe*. 1.40.5-7, discussed above.

classes, when combined with the shepherd's murder – which happens during a simple domestic dispute – suggests that the social status of a shepherd was so low that even the murder of one would not raise as much as an eyebrow.[168]

Alongside these instances where shepherds are portrayed rather unfavourably, two references seem to move in the opposite direction. In his twelve-volume treatise *Des Rustica*, Columella[169] speaks of shepherds in a more positive manner, describing them as possessing a keen mind (*Rust.* 1.9.1–5; cf. 7.3.13–15), while Tacitus[170] presents a sympathetic depiction of shepherds in the *Annales*.[171] Before offering a synthesis of these texts, it will be necessary to examine one further piece of information.

3.3.4 Honorific titles for Roman emperors

Of the honorific titles ascribed to Roman emperors, the most common of these given to Julius Caesar (49–44 BCE) and to Octavius Caesar (27 BCE–14 CE) are 'Saviour' (Σωτήρ), 'Benefactor' (Εὐεργέτης), 'God' (Θεός), and 'Founder' (Κτίστης).[172] According to Suetonius, while Augustus always rejected being called 'Lord' (*Aug.* 53.1), he eventually accepted the title 'Father of his Country' (*Aug.* 58.2). Suetonius also notes that Gaius Caligula (37–41 CE) assumed the titles 'Pious', 'Child of the Camp', 'Father of the Armies', and 'Greatest and Best of Caesars' (*Cal.* 22.1). In addition to these titles, F. Sauter notes that Martial[173] and Statius[174] ascribe to Domitian (81–96 CE) the names 'Peacemaker', 'Favourite of God [and Humans]', and 'Lord/Master of the World',[175] as well as the names of popular Roman gods such as 'Jupiter' and 'Hercules'.[176] Other

---

168   Cf. Pliny's subtle yet critical attitude towards shepherds in *Nat. His.* 35.25.1–4.

169   Lucius Junius Moderatus Columella (c. 4 BCE–65 CE) was a native of Spain but lived most of his life in the environs of Rome. He served for a time in the military and also owned several farms at various points in his life.

170   Cornelius Tacitus (c. 55–116 CE) was a Roman historian, who also served as praetor (in 88), *consul suffectus* (97), and later as proconsul in 112–13 CE.

171   Shepherds find the body of King Radamistus's pregnant wife Zenobia floating in a river, and because she still shows signs of life, they care for her (*Ann.* XII, 51).

172   Other honorific names include: *parens patriae, pontifex maximus,* and *Divus Iulius* for Julius Caesar, and *divi filius* and *Augustus* for Octavius Caesar. For a list of inscriptions that accord divine honours to Caesar, Antony, Augustus, and his house, see L. Taylor, *The Divinity of the Roman Emperor* (Philadelphia: Porcupine Press, 1975), 267–83.

173   Marcus Valerius Martialis (c. 40–104 CE) was a Spanish-born poet who lived two-thirds of his life in Rome.

174   Publius Papinius Statius (c. 45–96 CE) was the son of a prominent schoolteacher and became prize-winning poet.

175   Suetonius also asserts that Domitian sought to be called 'our Lord and God' (*dominus et deus noster*).

176   F. Sauter, *Der Römische Kaiserkult Bei Martial und Statius* (Stuttgart-Berlin: Verlag Von W. Kohlhammer, 1934).

titles for Domitian include 'Lord of the Earth' (Statius, *Sil.* 3.4.20), 'Ruler of the Nations' (*Sil.* 4.2.14–15), 'Master of the Sea and Land' (Philostratus, *Vit. Apoll.* 7.3), and 'Ruler of Lands and Seas and Nations' (Juvenal, *Sat.* 4.83–84). Despite the variety of titles of honour bestowed upon living and dead emperors of the Roman Empire, the ascription of 'shepherd' never appears among them as it plainly does for monarchs in ANE, Classical Greek, and Hellenistic sources. How, then, is this absence best synthesized with the other uses of 'shepherd' in Roman writings?

3.3.5 *Characteristics and tendencies in the use of 'shepherd' in Roman writings*

Because Roman authors frequently employ shepherds only incidentally in their writings, it is quite clear that they viewed shepherds as a social class and as a vocation as unimportant at best. But numerous uses push this attitude of indifference even further: shepherds are bellicose, outcasts given to varying degrees of violence. Still, there are some texts that seem to contradict this general conclusion, and that would seem to argue for a mixed view, i.e. Romans viewed shepherds both positively and negatively. How best can the data be put together? While a mixed view is possible, it should be rejected because the balance of evidence does not support it. The vast majority of texts indicate that shepherds were peripheral at best;[177] and of those texts which offer a further glimpse into how shepherds were viewed, the perception is quite negative. Hence, the few texts should be explained in light of the majority and not vice versa.

In terms of the literal usages of 'shepherd', two texts stand apart from the others and thus need explanation. In Columella, the strength of his more positive statements would largely be muted in view of the purpose of his treatise, which is to defend the agricultural enterprise against its highly vocal Epicurean detractors (*Rust.* 1.1–12); he thus extols the merits of every aspect of his enterprise – including shepherding.

In the *Annales*, the sensitive depiction of shepherds is probably better explained by Tacitus' tendency to use 'type-characters', specifically the 'Noble Savage' character.[178] Of the Noble Savage character type, B. Walker observes, '[T]heir virtues are placed in the strongest contrast with Roman vices ... Above all they have not been tainted by greed.'[179] Thus, this seemingly positive portrayal of shepherds serves less as an implicit editorial about them and more as a narrative device to convict Tacitus' Roman

---

177   See the beginning of section 3.3.3 above.

178   See B. Walker, *The Annals of Tacitus: A Study in the Writing of History* (Manchester: Manchester University Press, 1960), 204–34.

179   Walker, *Annals*, 225.

readers with its 'shock value'.[180] This reading of Columella and Tacitus fits seamlessly with the other literal uses of 'shepherd'.

In terms of 'shepherd' as a metaphor Dio Chrysostom and Suetonius use it favourably, while Plutarch does not. Plutarch's usage would thus fit with the general tendency observed above. But how can the former two authors' appropriations be accounted for? Chrysostom employs the metaphor several times for the ideal king, but his own social-historical context must be kept in mind. While Chrysostom was a Roman citizen, he was also of Greek heritage – like Plutarch – and the significance of this cannot be understated, for his cultural loyalties would have been divided between Roman and Greek. Consequently, D. Russell asserts that 'Dio is typical of Greek men of letters who practised in the world of the Roman Empire ... They addressed themselves both to Greek and to Roman audiences.'[181] Chrysostom thus would have had both Greek and Roman sensibilities since he sought to speak to Greeks and Romans.

While Classical Greek writers such as Xenophon, Plato, and Demosthenes were studied in Rome from at least the days of Augustus, it was the Greek authors who sought to emulate the style of their literary forbearers. Russell recognizes that 'Dio is one of the closer followers of classical models ... and he clearly had a marvellous ear for the cadences and idioms of fourth-century prose. ... Dio also quotes the poets – we shall hear him on Homer and Euripides – but not more recent ones.'[182] In the Greek literary tradition which Chrysostom inherited and sought to preserve, classical Greek authors regularly employed the shepherd metaphor.[183] Hence, because Dio Chrysostom the Roman also belonged to this rich, Greek literary tradition in which authors regularly employed the shepherd metaphor for rulers or for the activity of ruling, his use of the metaphor in *De regno 1–4* fits seamlessly with his Greek heritage, but stands out conspicuously among his contemporary Roman writers.

---

180   There would be similar shock value, for example, in Luke's parable of the Good Samaritan: Jesus is not concerned with demonstrating the virtues of Samaritans, but rather, with exposing and shaming the religious elite.

181   D. Russell, *Dio Chrysostom: Orations VII, XII, XXXVI*, CGLCIL, gen. ed. E. Kenney and P. Easterling (Cambridge: Cambridge University Press, 1992), 1. Cf. J. Cohoon, *Dio Chrysostom*, vol. 1, LCL, ed. E. Warmington (Cambridge, MA: Harvard University Press, 1971), xi. F. Millar (*A Study of Cassius Dio* [Oxford: Clarendon Press, 1964], 7) recognizes the significance of this dual allegiance in the third-century history of Cassius Dio (c. 164–231 CE), who uses the shepherd metaphor once in a manner parallel to Chrysostom (56.16.3). For a discussion of how Greek and Roman cultures interacted during the Roman Empire, see J. Huskinson, 'Élite Culture and the Identity of Empire', in *Experiencing Rome: Culture, Identity and Power in the Roman Empire*, ed. J. Huskinson (London: Routlege, 2000), 98–101.

182   Russell, *Orations*, 2.

183   E.g. Homer, Aeschylus (*Ag.* 657), Euripes (*Supp.* 191), Plato (*Resp.* 1.342, 343, passim); cf. Vancil's in depth assessment of the metaphor in ANE and Classical Greek texts in Vancil, 'Shepherd', 14–127.

As for Suetonius, the literary context suggests that Suetonius uses the metaphor in *Tib.* 32.2 for dramatic effect. In recounting the history of Tiberius, Suetonius highlights how different Tiberius was (early in his reign) from other emperors – especially Augustus – in terms of his humility (26.1–2), dislike of flattery (27.1), and his seemingly over-the-top tolerance for criticism (28.1). It is Tiberius' smaller-than-life personality that serves as the lead-up to the use of the shepherd metaphor. It is also extremely significant that, consonant with Suetonius' portrayal of Tiberius in this section of his text, the shepherd metaphor does not come through narration but rather appears on the lips of the king: '[Tiberius] wrote in answer that it was the part of a good shepherd to shear his flock not skin it' (32.2). In other words, it is not so much Suetonius likening Tiberius to a shepherd but rather Tiberius likening himself to one; and herein lies the dramatic effect. Roman authors generally view shepherds negatively. While Gaius exclaims with reference to himself, 'Let there be one Lord, one King' (*Cal.* 22.1), Tiberius, who has previously eschewed titles of honour, now compares himself to a lowly shepherd. This self-deprecating reference, then, would serve to punctuate Suetonius' depiction of Tiberius as one who 'played a most unassuming part, almost humbler than that of a private citizen' (*Tib.* 26.1).

Thus, understanding these passages in the light of their respective social-historical settings and paying attention to the wider literary contexts leads to the readings offered above, which allow for a more accurate explanation of the data pertaining to 'shepherd' usage in Roman texts. Roman authors held shepherds in low regard; and this critical attitude towards shepherds would likely explain why they never use 'shepherd' for Roman emperors: it would have been offensive.[184]

This non-use of 'shepherd' for monarchs by Roman authors clearly diverges with the term's employment for kings by ANE, Classical Greek, and Hellenistic sources. The absence of this particular usage of 'shepherd' in the writings of Roman authors (approximately) contemporary with Matthew is particularly intriguing because most of the Roman titles observed in section 3.3.4 above are applied to Jesus by his early followers. Jesus is called 'Saviour' (σωτήρ [Lk. 2.11; Jn 4.42; Phil. 3.20]), 'God' (θεός [Jn 20.28; Rom. 9.5]), 'Holy One' (Mk 1.24), 'Source of Creation' (ἡ ἀρχὴ τῆς κτίσεως [Rev. 3.14; cf. Jn 1.3; Col. 1.16]), 'Ruler' (1 Tim. 6.15; Rev. 1.5), and 'Lord' (or 'Master'); further, John's expression for Jesus, ὁ μονογενής (Jn 3.16; cf. μου ὁ ἀγαπητός in Mk 1.11), would approximate 'Favourite of God'. The reasons why Roman authors avoided using 'shepherd' likely have to do with what seems to be the prevailing attitude of Romans towards shepherds, as evidenced by how they are often depicted in their writings.

184 Not surprisingly, then, when Dio Chrysostom offers a lengthy list of titles for Zeus (*1 Regn.* 37–41), 'shepherd' never finds its way onto his list – as it could, however, if a such a list was compiled by an ANE, a Hellenistic, or a Jewish author.

3.3.6 *Summary of 'shepherd' in Roman writings*

That Roman authors most frequently employ 'shepherd' incidentally suggests that they viewed shepherds as unimportant at best.
R. MacMullen comments, 'No one's social relations were so limited and
tenuous, so close to no relations at all, as the shepherd's in the hills. His
work kept him away from people. *In those he did meet he had reason
to fear an enemy.*'[185] Moreover, numerous texts suggest that Roman
writers had a disparaging attitude towards them, and this would likely
account for the absence of 'shepherd' among the numerous honorific
ascriptions given to Roman emperors. The unfavourable portrayal of
shepherds and the absence of the term as a title for Roman emperors
demonstrate the insignificance these authors placed on the shepherd as
a metaphor for leadership. Although only the texts of Roman authors
whose dates intersect with the early first to early second century CE
range of Matthew have been considered here, interestingly, the results
of this analysis receive support from K. Chew's study dealing with the
use of 'shepherd' by Virgil in the *Aeneid*.[186] He demonstrates that 'shepherds' – particularly as the vocation relates to Aeneas, Virgil's central
character – become a locus for violence in the story.

This negative view of shepherds contrasts with the use of the shepherd as
a metaphor in the writings of NCB Jews and Christ-believers. This characteristic attitude of Roman writers towards shepherds will help further situate
Matthew's appropriation of the shepherd metaphor in Part II of the study.
Since there is otherwise clear overlap between early titles for Jesus and
Roman titles for emperors, this distinction – at least in the case of Matthew
– may, on the one hand, imply something about the cultural setting in which
Matthew wrote and expected his Gospel to be read. The distinction, on the
other hand, may allow the author, against the backdrop of first-century
Roman imperialism, to present Jesus in an overtly political manner – insofar
as Jews of the empire would be concerned, that is. The study shall return to
the interplay between Matthew and his Roman imperial context in chapter 5.

3.4 *The Use of the Shepherd Metaphor in the Writings of Christ-believers*

3.4.1 *Introduction*

To ascertain Matthew's socio-religious orientation, his shepherd motif
must also be compared with the shepherd metaphor's use by other
Christ-believers. This section will examine the shepherd metaphor in

---

185   R. MacMullen, *Roman Social Relations: 50 BC to AD 284* (New Haven: Yale
University Press, 1974), 1 (emphasis added).
186   K. Chew, '*Inscius pastor*: Ignorance and Aeneas' Identity in the *Aeneid*',
Latomus 61/3 (2002): 616–27.

the following texts: the Gospels of Mark, Luke, and John, the book of
Acts, the Letters of Hebrews, 1 Peter, Jude, and Ephesians, the book of
Revelation, and the *Shepherd of Hermas*. The analysis will seek to identify tendencies or patterns of usage which characterize the metaphor's
appropriation by Christ-believers approximately contemporaneous with
Matthew. These patterns of thought will then provide another point
of comparison for locating Matthew on a spectrum describing socio-
religious orientation.

3.4.2 Jesus as the messianic shepherd

Christ-believers commonly apply the shepherd metaphor to Jesus. The
author of the Gospel of Mark uses 'shepherd' twice. In the first part
of the Gospel, when Jesus sees the crowds his compassion for them
is aroused because 'they were like sheep not having a shepherd' (Mk
6.34a).[187] Consequently, Jesus' response is that 'he began to teach them
at length' (v. 34b). Since the lesson lasts well into the day, it becomes
difficult for the people to tend to their need for physical nourishment
(vv. 35-36). Jesus, however, supplies this need by multiplying the disciples' supply of five loaves and two fish to feed and satisfy the over
five-thousand-member crowd (vv. 36-44).

While there are a number of HB texts to which 'like sheep not having a
shepherd' here may possibly allude, the most probable contender would be
Num. 27.17 for a few reasons. First, scholars recognize that the wilderness
is an important motif in Mark's Gospel.[188] In fact, within this section of
the narrative, its importance is suggested by the triple usage of 'wilderness'
(ἔρημος) in 6.31, 32, and 35, a term which occurs in almost stereotypical
fashion in the book of Numbers,[189] even appearing within the broader
context of Num. 27.17.[190] Second, Jesus' immediate response to seeing the
crowd 'like sheep not having a shepherd' is that he begins to teach them
(v. 34c). Moses is recognized not simply as the Lawgiver but as Israel's
teacher.[191] Lastly, the feeding miracle that immediately follows in Mark's

187   Here the reference to Jesus would be indirect: the masses are helpless – like
a flock without its shepherd – so Jesus steps in and does for them what their (absentee)
shepherds should be doing, viz. he tends to their needs.

188   E.g. U. Mauser (*Christ in the Wilderness: The Wilderness Theme in the Second
Gospel and Its Basis in the Biblical Tradition* [London: SCM Press, 1963]) maintains that
the wilderness in Mark must be interpreted against the background of the wilderness of
the exodus; cf. W. Lane, *The Gospel of Mark*, NICNT (Grand Rapids: Eerdmans, 1974),
39–62. Bracewell also recognizes the importance of this setting in Mark's appropriation
of the shepherd metaphor ('Shepherd Imagery', 92–108).

189   ἔρημος occurs fifty-five times in Numbers [LXX], followed in frequency by
Isaiah (thirty-six times), Exodus, and Jeremiah (twenty-seven times each).

190   I.e. in Num. 27.3 and 14. F. Moloney notes that the exodus theme – associated
with Moses – is alluded to throughout Mk 6.31-44 (*The Gospel of Mark: A Commentary*
[Peabody: Hendrickson, 2002], 130–31).

191   E.g. Deut. 4.14; 5.31; 6.1; 31.19; cf. Mt. 23.2, and Jn 9.28.

narrative – necessitated by the length of Jesus' teaching session – would certainly evoke thoughts of Moses and the miracle of manna in the wilderness.[192]

Given the connection between 6.34a and 34b, i.e. Jesus observes the shepherd-less state of the crowds so he begins to teach them, as well as the likely allusion to Num. 27.17, Jesus' primary (but not exclusive) role as Israel's shepherd would be that of teacher.[193] The shepherds that the people lack would likely refer to the various religious leaders previously mentioned in Mark's narrative: the scribes (1.22), the priests (1.44), the Pharisees (2.16, 18, passim), and the Herodians (3.6). The negative responses of these leaders to 'Jesus Christ, the Son of God' (1.1b) at this point of the narrative would seem to exemplify why the Evangelist can characterize the Jewish people as being without a shepherd: the leaders care more about strict legal observance than about the sick and the outcast among the flock.[194]

The identity of the crowd for whom Jesus feels compassion and whom he teaches and feeds in 6.34-44 is disputed. Cranfield notes that the leftovers of the first meal were collected in 'baskets' (κόφινοι),[195] a term the satirist Juvenal considered especially characteristic of Jews. Hence, it would seem that the crowd in 6.34-44 would be Jewish. Jesus' flock, then, at least at this juncture of Mark's narrative, would be comprised of Galilean Jews: these are the people for whom Jesus serves as the messianic, Moses-like shepherd who teaches the people of Israel and who compassionately satisfies the nation's needs while they are in the wilderness.[196] Chapter 4 below will show that Matthew transposes Mark's shepherd-teacher tradition to one of shepherd-healer.

The second half of Mark reaches its climax in the passion and resurrection narratives of 14.1–16.8. At the conclusion of the last supper, Jesus and his disciples go out to the Mount of Olives, where Jesus predicts their impending failure and denial, declaring, 'You will all fall away, because it has been written, "I will strike down the shepherd and the sheep will be scattered"' (14.27b). In Mark's appropriation of Zech. 13.7 ('I will strike

---

192   This is evidenced in John's Gospel where, after the sign of the feeding of the five thousand, John writes, 'When the people saw the sign that he had done, they began to say, "This is indeed the prophet who is to come into world"' (Jn 6.14). This connection between Jesus' miraculous provision and Moses' manna provision (and hence, the connection between Jesus and Moses) is made even more explicit in the 'bread of life' discourse (Jn 6.41-58).

193   Within the broader context of the feeding miracle (vv. 35-44), a second role as Israel's Shepherd would be that of provider/feeder.

194   The scribes accuse Jesus of blasphemy when he absolves the paralytic of his sins (2.7); the scribes of the Pharisees accuse Jesus of improper table fellowship because he eats with notorious sinners (2.16); the Pharisees and Herodians plot Jesus' murder after he healed on the Sabbath (3.6).

195   Mark 6.43; the same term is used again in 8.19 with reference to this first feeding.

196   Cf. the assessment of this verse by Broadhead, *Naming Jesus*, 94, and Bracewell, 'Shepherd Imagery', 132–35.

down the shepherd and the sheep will be scattered'), it seems clear that his purpose in citing this text is to demonstrate God's sovereignty over the events of the passion:[197] the falling away of the disciples does not contravene God's design but rather, it aligns with God's purpose for Jesus in his passion. Mark maintains the broad sense of 'striking down', 'shepherd', and 'scattered' found in Deutero-Zechariah.[198] But while preserving the general sense of these terms, he does, nevertheless, modify and extend them. Whereas the striking down of the shepherd refers to the violent end of the Davidic line in Deutero-Zechariah, here it refers to the crucifixion of Christ. It is also clear from the syntactical parallel between 'fall away' and 'scattered' that the scattering, while involving physical dispersion, is self-imposed and caused by taking offence at Jesus' suffering at the hands of the authorities.[199] Furthermore, Mark extends the shepherd imagery of Zech. 13.7 in the next verse: 'But after I have been raised, I will go ahead (προάγω) of you to Galilee' (v. 28). While προάγω/ἄγω ('go ahead'/'lead') does not necessarily bear shepherding imagery, it can;[200] and in view of its close connection with the shepherd citation in the previous verse,[201] προάγω would doubtless bear that imagery here. Mark, then, extends the shepherd metaphor beyond the striking down of the crucifixion to the resurrection of Jesus and the reconstitution of his dispersed disciples in Galilee.

Thus, Mark adds to his earlier depiction of Jesus as Israel's messianic shepherd-teacher and provider in the wilderness. He portrays Jesus as Israel's prophesied shepherd, who was struck down and his followers dispersed – according to the sovereign plan of God revealed in the scriptures – only to be raised again to gather together his dispersed flock of disciples in Galilee.

A similar portrait of Jesus as the messianic shepherd appears in John's Gospel, where the shepherd metaphor appears in the so-called Good Shepherd Discourse. This discourse consists of two parts: the figure of speech or parable (10.1-6) and the expansion of this figure (10.7-18).[202]

---

197   The ὅτι here would be causative: 'because it is written'.

198   That is, for both Deutero-Zechariah and Mark 'strike down' means to be killed, 'shepherd' refers to God's appointed leader of his people, and 'scattered' includes physical dispersion.

199   Cf. Mk 14.29-31.

200   E.g. in the LXX: Gen. 46.32; Exod. 3.1; Ps. 77.52; Isa. 63.12-14; Jdt. 11.19; cf. 2 Sam. 5.2; Isa. 40.11, and Ezek. 34.13, for cognates bearing this same type of association.

201   There is a definite A-B/A-B parallelism between v. 27b, 'I will strike down the shepherd and the sheep will be scattered', and v. 28, 'But after I have been raised, I will go ahead of you to Galilee':

Πατάξω τὸν ποιμένα,
        καὶ τὰ πρόβατα διασκορπισθήσονται
ἀλλὰ μετὰ τὸ ἐγερθῆναί με
        προάξω ὑμᾶς εἰς τὴν Γαλιλαίαν

202   The switch in metaphors (from 'sheep' to 'gate') and the change in Jesus' role in the metaphor (i.e. from opening the door to being the door) would suggest that the second part of the discourse represents an expansion in thought rather than an explanation.

The parable involves a comparison between Jesus, on the one hand, who, as the true shepherd, has access to the sheep through the door of the sheepfold, and strangers, on the other, who access the sheep through some other means. Since there is but one means of legitimately accessing the sheep in the sheepfold (i.e. through the door of the pen), everyone who seeks to enter through any other means must be considered a 'thief' or a 'robber'; the mark of the true shepherd is that he enters through the gate of the pen (v. 2). If Manning is correct that the first section of the discourse alludes to the sanctioning of Joshua as Moses' successor in Num. 27.16-23,[203] then according to John, Jesus' legitimacy as the true 'shepherd of the sheep' comes via divine appointment.

John expands this point because according to the story Jesus' audience fails to understand the teaching (v. 6). There are three chief elements of comparison in vv. 7-18 between Jesus and false shepherds. While Manning asserts that the gatekeeper symbolizes the religious leaders (i.e. the Pharisees and the priesthood),[204] it seems more likely that the text alludes to messianic pretenders.[205] The first comparison between Jesus and these pretenders concerns the exclusive relationship between the shepherd and the sheep (vv. 7-9). As the true shepherd of the sheep, Jesus represents the only gate to the sheepfold – sheep cannot enter or leave the fold except through Jesus. As for those who came before Jesus, i.e. the 'thieves and robbers', who sought unauthorized access to the sheepfold, the sheep did not listen to them (v. 8). This contrast between Jesus and his illegitimate predecessors, as well as the reference to a united flock under 'one shepherd' (in v. 16), suggest an allusion to Ezekiel 34:[206] John views Jesus as the fulfilment of Ezekiel's prophecy of a coming Davidic shepherd.

Another element in the contrast is the quality of the care offered by the shepherds. Jesus offers his flock the pasture of salvation: 'by me [the door of the sheepfold] if anyone should enter, he will be saved ... I myself have come so that they might have life (ζωὴν)' (vv. 9a, 10b). Illegitimate shepherds, however, only steal, kill, and destroy the flock (v. 10a).

The final element in the comparison between Jesus and the false shepherds concerns their commitment to the sheep (vv. 11-18). According to the text, the false shepherd or 'hired hand' flees from the flock during times of distress (causing the sheep to scatter) because he is neither the shepherd nor

---

203   Manning, *Echoes*, 103–108; cf. J. Turner, 'The History of Religions Background of John 10', in *The Shepherd Discourse of John 10 and Its Contexts*, ed. J. Beutler and R. Fortna, SNTSMS 67 (Cambridge: Cambridge University Press, 1991), 38.

204   Manning, *Echoes*, 107–108.

205   Cf. C. Barrett, *The Gospel According to St. John: An Introduction with Commentary and Notes on the Greek Text*, 2nd edn (Philadelphia: Westminster Press, 1978), 371. For detailed arguments supporting this view, see Baxter, 'Shepherd', 148.

206   For a detailed discussion of John's use of Ezekiel 34, see Manning, *Echoes*, 111–24.

the owner of the sheep (v. 13). The 'good shepherd',[207] however, does not flee at the first sign of trouble; rather, he will lay down his life for the sheep (v. 11). Moreover, this sacrificial act, far from being unintentional (one of the hazards of the job, so to speak), is by divine design: 'no one takes [my life] from me but rather, I lay it down by myself; I have authority to lay it down and I have authority to take it up again; this commandment I received from my Father' (v. 18). The intentionality of Jesus' sacrifice is grounded in Jesus' close relationship with his sheep ('I am the good shepherd and I know my own [sheep] and my own [sheep] know me' [v. 14]), expressed in the intimate knowledge he shares with them,[208] and also grounded in the intimacy Jesus shares with his heavenly Father: 'just as the Father knows me and I know the Father' (v. 15a).[209]

Of some importance for the discussion of the shepherd metaphor in John is the composition of Jesus' flock. In view of John's allusion to Ezekiel 34, it would be tempting to understand 'one flock with one shepherd' (v. 16) as referring to Diaspora Jews – as it does in Ezekiel 34. If, however, the 'sheepfold' in the parable of vv. 1-5 stands for Judaism – as most scholars maintain – the position of Diaspora Jews would be unlikely.[210] The consensus view is likely correct: the flock consists of Jews and Gentiles.[211] Hence, the Johannine Shepherd's flock consists (ultimately) of CB Jews and Gentiles. Moreover, if the sheepfold that Jesus enters represents Judaism, out of which he 'calls his own sheep' who follow him out of the pen – in contradistinction to the 'Jews' – and for whom he dies sacrificially, then Jewish-national sentiments here would be minimal.

207   J. Neyrey makes a strong case for translating 'Good Shepherd' as 'Noble Shepherd' ('The 'Noble Shepherd' in John 10', *JBL* 120/2 [2001], 267–68), but his thesis does not affect the point of this section.

208   This point seems presupposed in vv. 1-6; cf. 10.27; 14.21, 26; 15.26-27; 16.12-15; 17.6-7, 26.

209   This reciprocal knowledge between the Father and Son highlights for John the uniqueness of Jesus: Jesus stands alone as God's special agent for bringing about redemption.

210   J. Painter suggests that John has 'other Jewish Christians in mind, or perhaps the re-gathering of his own [scattered] community' ('Tradition, History and Interpretation in John 10', in *Shepherd Discourse of John 10*, 65–66). But here again, this kind of 'Jewish' position seems unlikely if the 'sheepfold' that Jesus enters to lead out his sheep is Judaism.

211   Barrett typifies this position: 'John was written in the context of the Gentile mission' (*St. John*, 376). According to story, Jesus has already preached to and gained adherents among the Samaritans (Jn 4.4-30, 39-42). Later in the narrative, several things occur: the Pharisees mention that 'the world' follows Jesus (12.19); John immediately follows this statement with an account of Greeks seeking to meet Jesus (12.20-22), which prompts Jesus to announce the nearness of his passion (12.23-24) by which he will draw 'all people' to himself (12.32). In Jn 10.16 Jesus speaks of having 'other sheep' (in addition to his Jewish followers), who 'will hear' (ἀκούσουσιν) his voice and 'will become' (γενήσονται) one flock under his leadership. The future tenses of these verbs suggest that 10.16 should be viewed within the story as predictive/prophetic, and hence, would point to the inclusion of Gentiles.

Thus, Jn 10.1-18 depicts Jesus as the messianic fulfilment of Ezekiel 34: unlike his illegitimate, mal-intending predecessors, Jesus is the true shepherd. As such, he not only possesses a unique and intimate relationship with YHWH, but intimately knows his flock, which ultimately consists of Jewish and non-Jewish Christ-believers, whom he offers abundant pasture and, finally, his own life to ensure their redemption.

The Johannine notion of a shepherd who sacrifices himself for his sheep appears in the closing section of the letter to the Hebrews (13.20-21). The first part of this prayer represents the basis for which the petitioner can expectantly make an appeal to God: 'And the God of peace, the one who brought back from the dead the great Shepherd of the sheep by the blood of the eternal covenant, our Lord Jesus' (v. 20). The author of Hebrews makes an implicit comparison between Moses, the shepherd of Israel under the old covenant, and Jesus, the shepherd of God's people under the new covenant, by alluding to Isa. 63.11. In keeping with the earlier part of his letter, the author continues to elevate Jesus over Moses by inserting into his biblical allusion, 'the great [one]', to describe Jesus.[212] Not only is Jesus intrinsically greater than Moses, but so is the scope of God's intervention in his life: whereas God merely brought Moses up from Egyptian oppression (Isa. 63.11), he raised Jesus up from the realm of the dead.[213] According to the author's appropriation of Zech. 9.11 in v. 20,[214] God brought Jesus up from the realm of the dead 'because' when Jesus shed his blood, he offered a unique and perfect sacrifice for his people (cf. Heb. 7.26-28) to accomplish their eternal salvation in a way that the old covenant never could (cf. Heb. 9.11-15).[215] His sacrifice, then, was ratified by his resurrection.

Hebrews 13.20 thus depicts Jesus as the messianic shepherd whose greatness surpasses Moses', a superiority reflected in God bringing Jesus up from the realm of the dead. Additionally, the author of Hebrews attaches a priestly element to the shepherd metaphor insofar as he asserts that the 'great' Shepherd was raised from the dead precisely because of Christ's

---

212   The author used μέγας ('great') previously in his letter with reference to Christ's priesthood (in 4.14 and 10.21, with the latter verse echoing the discussion of 3.1-6, where Christ and Moses are compared). The use of 'great', then, may serve to link the concept of 'shepherd' with 'priest', which becomes the focus of the final strophe of 13.20.

213   The term, ἀνάγειν ('bring up'), its cognate ἄγειν ('lead'), as well as the corresponding Hebrew term, אֵלָה, are frequently associated with the shepherd metaphor in the Jewish scriptures (e.g. Exod. 3.1; Num. 27.17; 1 Sam. 17.34; 2 Sam. 5.2; Ps. 78.52-54, 71; Isa. 49.10-12).

214   Hebrews 13.20bα reads ἐν αἵματι διαθήκης αἰωνίου, while Zech. 9.11a [LXX] has ἐν αἵματι διαθήκης.

215   The implicit citation of Zech. 9.11 suggests that ἐν should be understood instrumentally, i.e. 'by means of the blood of the eternal covenant', rather than as introducing an attendant circumstance ('with the blood of the eternal covenant'). According to N. Turner, the causal sense would be in view here (*Syntax*, vol. 3 in J. Moulton, *GNTG* [Edinburgh: T&T Clark, 1993], 252–53).

sacrificial work on the cross as the 'great' high priest for believers.[216] While this shepherd-sacrifice connection is seen elsewhere,[217] its explicit association with the covenant would represent a new dimension to the metaphor: the shepherd is the mediator of the New Covenant.

Christ's sacrifice is also associated with the metaphor in 1 Peter. In discussing Christ's substitutionary suffering (2.21-25), the author states that believers have been healed of their penchant for sin – an inclination he likens to straying sheep – by Christ's sacrifice on the cross.[218] Thus, believers are no longer considered lost strays, 'but rather', they have 'now returned to the Shepherd and Overseer of [their] souls' (v. 25b). Scholars correctly note that 'shepherd' here refers specifically to the activity of watching over and guarding the flock.[219] This could perhaps be nuanced further: not only are the straying sheep healed of their proclivity to sin by Christ's sacrifice,[220] they are restored to being the people of God under Christ's care and leadership. Added to this would be Peter's reference to Christ as the coming Chief Shepherd (5.4):[221] Christ as the Chief Shepherd will return to reward those leaders who faithfully shepherded their flock.

A somewhat different portrait of the messianic shepherd emerges from the book of Revelation. The metaphor initially appears in the letter to the church at Thyatira. To everyone who overcomes in the struggle against evil teaching, heeding Christ's criticism and keeping to his works until his return, a promise is given: 'I will give him authority over the nations and he will rule (ποιμανεῖ) them with a rod of iron, as clay vessels are shattered' (Rev. 2.26b-27a). While the New Testament alludes to Psalm 2 elsewhere, only here (as well as in Rev. 12.5 and 19.15, discussed below) is shepherding imagery employed. Psalm 2.8-9 recites the privilege accompanying the divine sonship of the king: ruling authority over the nations. The author of Revelation applies this privilege – originally given to the Davidic king – to the faithful saints of Thyatira: Christ extends this privilege of worldwide dominion to those in Thyatira who overcome evil. The inclusion of the iron rod–clay pot imagery[222] suggests that Jezebel, her followers, and those like them will be

---

216   See H. Attridge, *The Epistle to the Hebrews: A Commentary on the Epistle to the Hebrews*, Hermeneia, ed. H. Koester (Philadelphia: Fortress Press, 1989), 406.

217   E.g. the citation of Zech. 13.7 in Mark and Matthew, and John 10.

218   Cf. the γάρ ('for') clause of v. 25a, which clarifies the nature of their healing in the previous verse.

219   That ἐπίσκοπος qualifies the meaning of ποιμήν is suggested by the grammatical structure: the use of one article for two nouns of similar case connected by καί means that the two nouns should be taken together, as 'the shepherd-overseer' rather than as 'the shepherd and overseer' (cf. BDF, 144–45).

220   The γάρ of v. 25a would connect it to v. 24: the sheep had strayed (from the shepherd) because of their penchant for sin (v. 25a); once healed of this proclivity (v. 24) they rather naturally return to their shepherd-leader (v. 25b).

221   This text relates more specifically to 'Assembly Leaders as Shepherds'; consequently, it is discussed more fully in section 3.4.3 below.

222   The author could have (presumably) omitted this reference – as he did with 'the

subject to appropriately severe rule which they will be unable to withstand (in a vein similar to Psalm 2). Thus, the shepherd metaphor refers here to Jesus ruling over the nations jointly with the faithful members of his flock.

This notion of messianic rule appears in two other passages in Revelation. It occurs in a vision of a pregnant woman of royal status with a fierce dragon who seeks to devour her child (12.1-6): the woman gives birth to a son, 'who is about to rule (ποιμαίνειν) all the nations with a rod of iron' (v. 5aβ). As with Rev. 2.27, this verse alludes to Ps. 2.9a and the focus of this allusion is on the son's deeds, viz. he will rule the nations with a rod of iron. But unlike 2.27, which extends the scope of the son's shepherding/ruling activity to include those who overcome (in Thyatira), messianic rule here is limited only to the son. The use of μέλλω ('about') gives the phrase a sense of futurity, i.e. this worldwide rule of the son will take place in the imminent future (at the Parousia). The other passage is the vision of the Parousia (19.11-16). Perhaps the trait most underscored in this vision is that of supreme Judge: Christ is the 'faithful and true' Judge who judges righteously (19.11b). He also judges with strict severity: 'And from out of his mouth comes a sharp sword, so that with it he may strike the nations and he himself will rule (ποιμανεῖ) them with a rod of iron; and he treads the winepress of the intense wrath of God Almighty' (v. 15). Here, ποιμαίνω connotes 'rule' in the sense of meting out punishment.

Quite a different use of the metaphor occurs in the interlude of Rev. 7.1-17, which answers the question, 'who is able to stand' in the great day of the wrath of God and the Lamb (6.17)? John is shown a vision of a great multitude dressed in white, standing before the throne of God, who find their shelter and their needs provided for by the Lamb, who resides 'in the middle of the throne [and who] shepherds them and will lead them to the springs of living water' (v. 17a). That a lamb serves as a shepherd would seem unprec-edented – although not an entirely unexpected use of the shepherd metaphor in Revelation.[223] The figure of a lamb as a shepherd highlights the centrality of Christ's sacrifice in redeeming and leading his people.[224]

Thus, the book of Revelation depicts Jesus as the messiah who will shepherd all the nations of the earth. Jesus' shepherding is equated with ruling over the nations at the Parousia: he will gently shepherd his followers, sheltering them and providing for their needs forever, even sharing his ruling authority over the nations with those who overcome their difficult circum-stances; but as far as the rebellious nations are concerned, he will rule them with harsh severity.

---

ends of the earth as your possession' (Ps. 2.8b) – had it not served to advance his thought.

223   In the vision of the God's throne, the sole figure found worthy to open and read the book of judgements is 'the Lion from the tribe of Judah, the Root of David' (5.5), who is depicted as a 'lamb standing [in the middle of the throne] like one having been slaughtered' (5.6).

224   Seibel notes that 'lamb' and not 'shepherd' is the usual term New Testament authors use to discuss Christ's sacrifice. For a discussion of the 'lamb' metaphor as it relates to Christ's sacrifice, see Seibel, 'Shepherd and Sheep', 233–62.

In sum, Christ-believers highlight a variety of Jesus' attributes when appropriating the shepherd metaphor for him. He is a Moses-like teacher; he is the object of scriptural prophecy; he sacrifices his life for his flock, with whom he relates intimately, to redeem them but is raised from the dead; he is his flock's caregiver and judge, as well as the ultimate ruler of the nations.

3.4.3 Assembly leaders as shepherds

The shepherd metaphor appears in the second part of the epilogue of the Fourth Gospel, concerning Jesus' reinstatement of Peter (Jn 21.15-25). Jesus asks Peter three times if he loves him, to which Peter responds each time in the affirmative. After each of Peter's declarations of love, Jesus gives him the charge: 'Tend my lambs' (βόσκε τὰ ἀρνία μου), 'Shepherd my sheep' (ποίμαινε τὰ πρόβατά μου), and 'Tend my sheep' (βόσκε τα πρόβατά μου).[225] His charge to Peter centres on leadership: Peter is restored to his Christ-determined position of leadership within the CB community. Although Peter is commissioned to shepherd the flock, he serves merely as an 'under-shepherd' to Christ, who has already been uniquely identified in the Gospel as the 'good shepherd' (10.1-18). Thus, in the epilogue to the Fourth Gospel, 'shepherd' refers to the office of leadership in CB assemblies. Peter, likely serving as a paradigm for leaders, is called by Jesus to shepherd and care for Jesus' flock, motivated ultimately by a shepherd's love for Jesus the good shepherd.

The idea of an assembly leader as an under-shepherd also appears in 1 Peter. In his parting instructions to the elders in 1 Peter 5, the author essentially gives one command: 'shepherd the flock of God among you' (v. 2a). The author clarifies the meaning of his command in the latter part of v. 2: the imperative form of 'shepherd' is modified by the participle that follows it, 'overseeing' (ἐπισκοποῦντες).[226] The activity of shepherding, then, refers to watching over the people in the sense of caring for and protecting them. The motivation for this imperative to shepherd the flock is that when God ultimately judges his people (4.17-18), he will especially judge those given charge over the flock.[227] Should the elders faithfully shepherd those allotted to their care, they will receive a reward when Christ the 'Chief Shepherd' (ἀρχιποίμενος) appears (5.4). The author thus draws a distinction between the elders as shepherds and Christ as the Chief Shepherd: despite the importance of their position and duties, elders remain under-shepherds. That is,

225   Unlike in John 10, these verses in the epilogue probably do not allude to any HB passages; cf. Manning, *Echoes*, 131–32.

226   Cf. Achtemeier, *1 Peter*, 325. Although ἐπισκοποῦντες is absent in the early witnesses ℵ and B, it is present in ρ[72] and A. Additionally, as Michaels points out, the author often places an imperative immediately before a participle, which would support the witness of ρ[72] and A.

227   The οὖν ('therefore') in v. 1a connects this exhortation to the preceding pericope, 4.12-19, specifically the last part dealing with God judging his household. The sense of this pericope, then, would be: 'Therefore in view of God's future judgment . . .'.

their authority over their sheep is derived from their calling as assembly leaders in Christ, for whom they shepherd the flock and to whom they will ultimately give an account of their shepherding at the Parousia.

The accountability of the shepherds for the sheep is made even more explicit in the *Shepherd of Hermas*.[228] The metaphor appears toward the end of the ninth Similitude, where the Shepherd exhorts the CB community to forgive one another and to be united in spirit so as to bring joy to the 'lord of the sheep' (i.e. Christ). But should they fail to heed this admonition, the shepherds – not the sheep – will be held accountable:

> [I]f some of [the flock] are found missing,[229] woe be to the shepherds. But if the shepherds themselves are found missing, what will they say to the owner of the flock? That they are missing because of the sheep? They will not be believed, for it is incredible that a shepherd could suffer at the hands of the sheep. Instead, they will be punished for their lie. I, too, am a shepherd, and it is exceedingly necessary for me to give an account for you.
>
> (Herm. *Sim.* 108.5b–6)

While the topic of leadership has been discussed earlier in *Hermas*, only here are the leaders explicitly identified as 'shepherds'.[230] According to this passage, shepherds are judged (more harshly than the sheep) for the manner in which they contribute to congregational unity, for this would seem to be their chief aim as shepherds: to help establish unity in the congregation. The shepherds clearly exercise ruling authority over the sheep, but they themselves are under the authority of another, viz. the 'owner of the flock' ('lord of the sheep'): Christ, to whom they will ultimately give an account of their shepherding.

This pronouncement of woe upon evil shepherds in *Hermas* is echoed in the letter of Jude. The author of Jude pronounces a curse on the false teachers troubling his readers. He describes them as following in the path of Cain's wickedness, falling into Balaam's error of prophesying for illicit gain; like Korah, they will perish because of their rejection of divine and divinely sanctioned authority (v. 11). Jude's scathing rebuke of these self-proclaimed leaders moves from biblical comparisons to nature metaphors in vv. 12-13, highlighting the emptiness of their teaching: 'They are the dangerous threats at your love feasts, eating together without fear, shepherding themselves' (v. 12a). Commentators sometimes construe 'shepherding themselves' (ἑαυτοὺς ποιμαίνοντες) with the mention of irreverent love feasting in the

---

228   The chapter-verse configurations for *Hermas* in this study follow G. Snyder, *The Shepherd of Hermas*, AFNTC 6, ed. R. Grant (Camden: Thomas Nelson and Sons, 1968).

229   While Snyder translates διαπίπτω as 'missing', the word has a wide range of meanings and probably connotes here something like 'lost'.

230   Some of the terms in *Hermas* used earlier for leaders include προηγούμενοι (6.6), πρεσβύτεροι (8.3), and ἐπίσκοποί (104.2).

immediately preceding phrase. The author, however, seems to allude to Ezek. 34.2, where Ezekiel accuses the rulers of Israel of feeding themselves at the expense of their flock: Ezek. 34.2 reads היו רעים אותם ('they are those who shepherd themselves'), while Jude 12 reads οὗτοί εἰσιν οἱ ... ἑαυτοὺς ποιμαίνοντες ('they are those ... who shepherd themselves').[231] In view of this probable allusion to Ezekiel 34, as well as the comparison to Cain, Balaam, and Korah in v. 11, 'shepherding themselves' should include the idea that these false believers claimed to be religious leaders or shepherds of the assembly; but in contrast to true shepherds, they only looked after their own needs rather than the flock's.[232]

A much less critical but still sombre warning is sounded by Paul to the Ephesian elders, in the book of Acts. According to the narrative, Paul, in view of his (possibly) impending death in Jerusalem, leaves the leaders of this local assembly with the final charge: 'Watch out for yourselves and for all the flock, among whom the Holy Spirit has made you overseers to shepherd the church of God, which he purchased with his own blood' (20.28). According to this text, shepherding duties belong to the overseers (ἐπίσκοποι) – those occupying formal leadership roles in the assembly.[233] The type of leadership implied by the meaning of ἐπίσκοπος is oversight and caring for diverse needs.[234] The Ephesian elders have been placed in this position of leadership in the assembly by the Holy Spirit for the expressed purpose of caring for their congregation.[235] In caring for their flock, the elders are to protect them from enemies,[236] and to follow Paul's example of selfless giving.[237] The opponents here are probably false teachers, in which case the elders would protect their flock through diligent instruction. Teaching would then be implicit in the use of the metaphor here. Thus, according to Acts 20.28, shepherds refer to those exercising leadership in the oversight of the local assembly, caring for the needs of the members and protecting them from being exploited by false teachers.

While the activity of teaching seems implicit in Acts 20.28, it becomes explicit in the metaphor's use in the letter to the Ephesians. In a call for

---

231   R. Bauckham demonstrates that the author's preference in his allusions to the Jewish scriptures is for the Hebrew text rather than the LXX (*Jude, 2 Peter*, WBC 50 [Dallas: Word Books, 1983], 7). Here, for example, Ezek. 34.2 in the LXX reads, μὴ βόσκουσι ποιμένες ἑαυτούς ('do they not tend, [that is], the shepherds, themselves?').

232   According to the respective accounts in the scripture, each figure to which Jude refers (Cain, Balaam, and Korah) illicitly sought some form of personal gain.

233   The closely related term, ἐπισκοπή, appears in Acts 1.20, referring to the office of leadership among the Twelve which had been vacated by Judas.

234   Cf. BAGD, 298–99, and E. Selwyn, *The First Epistle of St. Peter*, 2nd edn (Grand Rapids: Baker Book House, 1981), 230.

235   Since the verse would make sense without the infinitival phrase ποιμαίνειν τὴν ἐκκλησίαν τοῦ θεοῦ ('to shepherd the church of God'), ποιμαίνειν is best taken here as an infinitive of purpose (cf. BDF, 197).

236   Acts 20.29-30.

237   Paul offers himself as an example of how to shepherd in vv. 33-35.

church unity, the author of Ephesians insists that Christ ascended to pour out gifts of the Holy Spirit: 'And he gave some apostles and some prophets and some evangelists and some shepherd-teachers' (τοὺς δὲ ποιμένας καὶ διδασκάλους) (4.11). The grammatical construction of an article governing two nouns with the same number and case connected by καί suggests that the last two nouns of the verse are to be viewed as one role, i.e. shepherd-teacher, rather than two.[238] Consequently, while 'shepherd' typically connotes protection, care, and oversight, here it is explicitly connected to teaching. Thus, according to this text, an integral component of a shepherd's task involves instructing the members of the assembly. In this way, shepherd-teachers help to build up the local body of Christ to attain a thoroughgoing unity and maturity, as well as to help keep believers from false doctrine.

Thus, while they are likened to shepherds, assembly leaders function more as under-shepherds to Jesus: they are accountable to him for how they manage the flock – which includes teaching. Consequently, they are to shepherd his people knowing that they will be judged by him when he returns.

3.4.4 Rulers as shepherds

The author of *Hermas* employs the shepherd metaphor in a manner quite different from its other uses in a parable about indulging in luxuries (chs 61-65). A shepherd of luxury leads a flock that lives lavishly, while a second shepherd receives members of the former shepherd's flock and drives them harshly. While Snyder suggests that this parable may reflect rival leaders, in view of the explicit identification of these shepherds with angels, i.e. with the angel of luxury and deception, and the angel of punishment, and in view of 'angel' being used synonymously throughout *Hermas* for 'spirit', it would seem more likely that these shepherds refer not to rival leaders, but to an inner disposition that ultimately leads to suffering for the Christ-believer. In other words, the use of 'shepherd' here would somewhat parallel Philo's deployment of the metaphor for the mind in that the metaphor refers to an internal ruling disposition or attitude – one that, here, inclines a person to live a life of reckless indulgence.

3.4.5 Other uses of 'shepherd'

The bulk of the material in *Hermas* (chs 25-110) is mediated by a 'shepherd'.[239] That the shepherd is 'glorious to the sight' and possesses

---

238   See BDF, 144–45. This structure prompts M. Barth, for example, to translate this particular ministry as 'teaching shepherds' (*Ephesians*, 2 vols, AB [New York: Doubleday 1974], 2.425, 438–39).

239   The other material in *Hermas* comes through the mediation of an 'elderly lady' and 'the great angel'. The tone and thrust of the Shepherd's revelation stands apart from the messages of the elderly lady and the great angel in that, whereas the message of the

the ability to change his form (25.4; cf. 47.1) suggests that he is an angelic being, explicitly identified at the end of this vision and elsewhere (47.7; 49.1; 91.3; 101.4; 108.3; 110.1) as 'the angel of repentance': the one who oversees the act of repentance (a primary motif throughout *Hermas*),[240] giving aid and understanding to those who repent of their sins. Into this angel's care, Hermas has been entrusted (25.3–4) to keep the commandments of God. In addition to this role, the Shepherd's primary task is to give to Hermas mandates to keep and parables to learn in order to strengthen him in his faith, and to record these commands and parables in order to strengthen Hermas' community (25.5–7). Thus, according to this reading of *Hermas*, the shepherd represents an angelic mediator, sent by Christ to abide with the repentant, helping them and instructing them in the faith.

Whereas the author of *Hermas* uses 'shepherd' metaphorically, the author of Luke's Gospel does not.[241] Something, however, can be said of how his literal use of 'shepherds' contributes to his birth narrative. Luke's birth narrative emphasizes the humble beginnings of Jesus: he is born in a manger 'because there was no place for [his parents] in the inn' (Lk. 2.7b); and the news of Jesus' birth is first announced by the angel of the Lord to shepherds. That the shepherds were 'in the same region' (ἐν τῇ χώρᾳ τῇ αὐτῇ) watching over their flock would connect the shepherds in 2.8 with the birth of Jesus in the lowly manger in v. 7. The marginalized circumstances of Jesus' birth – circumstances that will foreshadow the direction of Jesus' mission to the marginalized in Luke – are amplified, on the one hand, by the birth announcement being made to mere shepherds first, and by these shepherds, on the other hand, being the first visitors to pay homage to the infant Christ. In this way, then, Luke uses shepherds to convey the humble origins of Jesus and his messianic mission.

3.4.6 *Summary of the shepherd metaphor in the writings of Christ-believers*

The range of uses for the shepherd metaphor in the writings of early Christ-believers is summarized in Table 3.7. Typically, the metaphor is used either for Jesus as the messianic Shepherd or for assembly leaders. The categories of 'assembly leader' and 'ruler' would most closely mirror the 'rulers as shepherd' category in the HB and in the texts of NCB Jews; in contrast, Christ-believers never employ the metaphor for kings

elderly lady focuses on sin and the church, and that of the great angel on Hermas' commission (to instruct the church), the message of the angel-shepherd consists primarily of instruction.

240   See C. Osiek, *Shepherd of Hermas*, Hermeneia, ed. H. Koester (Minneapolis: Fortress Press, 1999), 28, n. 218.

241   Although neither ποιμήν nor ποιμαίνω are used metaphorically in Luke's Gospel, broader shepherding imagery does appear. For a detailed discussion of this imagery, see Baxter, 'Shepherd', 166–67.

or for other political leaders; and 'ruler' in *Hermas* refers to inner passions that can cause a person to live over-indulgently.

Table 3.7 Referents for the shepherd metaphor

Jesus the Messiah	Assembly leaders	Angelic mediator	'Ruler'
Mark			
John	John		
	Acts		
	Ephesians		
Hebrews			
1 Peter	1 Peter		
	Jude		
Revelation			
	Hermas	*Hermas*	*Hermas*

Table 3.8 summarizes the individual emphases within the 'assembly leaders as shepherds' category. A 'shepherd' is viewed quintessentially as a ruler of the flock: assembly leaders would exercise ruling authority over their communities, insofar as they would be responsible for looking after the various needs of their flock.[242] The authors of *Hermas* and Ephesians, however, explicitly associate teaching with the metaphor (Acts does so implicitly). The connection between teaching with shepherding would exemplify the tendency towards a non-pastoral depiction of the activity of shepherds by Christ-believers, unlike NCB Jews, who portray the activity of shepherd-rulers using language that corresponds to literal shepherding.

Table 3.8 Emphases within 'assembly leaders as shepherds'

Assembly leader/ruler	Assembly leader/teacher
John	
Acts	(Acts)
	Ephesians
1 Peter	
Jude	
Hermas	*Hermas*

242   The book of Acts offers a partial window into this type of governance by assembly leaders: the apostles seemed to be in charge – at least initially – of collecting and distributing monetary funds (4.34-35; 5.2), as well as food distribution (6.1-2).

When authors apply the metaphor to Jesus, they usually accent some particular feature(s): see Table 3.9. When compared to the specific traits of 'YHWH as a Shepherd' in the HB (cf. Table 2.2 above), Jesus parallels YHWH insofar as he offers abundant care. An important distinction, however, would be the nature of that care. In the HB, YHWH is portrayed as providing for his people's physical and material needs, protecting and delivering them from their enemies, and reconstituting them in the land of Israel. With the exceptions of Mark and Revelation (discussed in section 3.5 below), the care Jesus offers as a shepherd is not so pastoral;[243] and it is anchored in self-sacrifice – an act completely foreign to the metaphor in the HB, as well as in the writings of NCB Jews, since shepherds typically save their flock through physical rescue (Table 3.10 thus summarizes the use of pastoral imagery).

Table 3.9 Implicit and explicit traits of Jesus as the messianic shepherd

Jesus-Shepherd trait	Mark	John	Hebrews	1 Peter	Rev
Offers sacrifice for the sheep	X	X	X		X
Offers abundant care	X	X		X	X
Raised from the dead	X	X	X		
Moses-like	X	X	X		
Compassionate	X	X			
Object of scriptural prophecy	X	X			
Davidic ancestry		X			X
Gatherer of disciples	X	X			
Teacher	X				
Universal ruler					X
Universal judge				X	X
Relates intimately to flock		X			

243   The authors of Mark (in 6.35-44) and Revelation (in 7.16-17) depict Jesus using pastoral imagery. The emphasis of the metaphor in John 10 is on the exclusive relationship between the sheep and the shepherd; additionally, the pasture that the Good Shepherd offers is eternal life – which he obtains by sacrificing his life for his sheep. In Hebrews, the Shepherd is described in terms of his resurrection and his relationship to the 'eternal covenant'. In 1 Peter the messianic shepherd cares for the soul and offers a crown of glory to the faithful. By way of contrast, of the NCB Jewish texts which appropriate the metaphor for YHWH (*1 Enoch*, 1Q509, Ben Sira, Judith, Philo, *Apocryphon of Ezekiel*, and *LAB*), only Philo and Ben Sira do not associate pastoral imagery with the metaphor; although elsewhere, as observed in section 3.2.2 above, Philo actually does employ pastoral imagery when describing Moses as Israel's shepherd.

Table 3.10 Degree of pastoral imagery in texts idealizing a shepherd

Pronounced imagery	Modest imagery	Little or no imagery
Mark 6.34	Mark 14.27	Acts
John		Ephesians
Revelation 7.17		Hebrews
		1 Peter
		Jude
		Revelation 2; 12; 19
		Hermas

In addition to not using the shepherd metaphor for monarchs or for other political rulers, Christ-believers' appropriations of the metaphor typically lack the overtones of Jewish-national restoration that so often characterize its use by NCB Jews: see Table 3.11.

Table 3.11 Overtones of Jewish-national restoration

Jewish-national overtones	No Jewish-national overtones
Mark	John
	Acts
	Ephesians
	Hebrews
	1 Peter
	Jude
	Revelation
	Hermas

3.5 Summary and Conclusions

A survey of the shepherd metaphor in the writings of NCB Jews, NCB Romans, and Christ-believers reveals some distinctive patterns. 'Shepherd' remains a very peripheral term in the texts of NCB Romans and is rarely employed metaphorically. Moreover, these authors often reflect a disparaging attitude towards shepherds and consequently, they do not typically appropriate the metaphor for emperors, unlike ANE, Classical Greek, and Hellenistic authors. Non-Christ-believing Roman authors' use of 'shepherd' stands far apart from its deployment by NCB Jews and Christ-believers.

Similarly to the HB, there would seem to be three basic patterns of usage concerning the metaphor's employment by Second Temple NCB Jews. The first concerns the metaphor's referent: see Table 3.12. NCB Jews commonly appropriate the metaphor, on the one hand, for earthly rulers or for the activity of ruling. A few innovations within this category appear, however. Shepherd-rulers can refer to intercessors who act on behalf of Israel for the nation's iniquity (*LAB*); they can represent the destructive governing of Israel by angelic beings (*1 Enoch*); the metaphor can be associated with local religious leaders who exercise ruling authority over a group in different areas of communal life (CD XIII); it can also symbolize the virtuous mind that controls bodily passions (Philo). On the other hand, NCB Jews regularly use the metaphor for YHWH, especially to underline his mercy and compassion.[244]

Table 3.12 Comparison of shepherd metaphor referents in the texts of NCB Jews[245]

Ruler	*YHWH*
Num. 27.17	Gen. 48.15
Deuteronomistic History	Gen. 49.24
Chronicles	Psalm 23
Psalm 78	Psalm 28
Deutero-Isaiah	Psalm 80
Trito-Isaiah	Ecclesiastes
Jeremiah	Deutero-Isaiah
Ezekiel	Jeremiah
Micah	Ezekiel
Nahum	Hosea
Deutero-Zechariah	Micah
1 Enoch	Deutero-Zechariah
4Q504	**1 Enoch**
1Q34	**4Q509**
CD	**Ben Sira**
Philo	**Judith**
L.AB.	***Apoc. Ezek.***
Josephus	**Philo**
4 Ezra	**LAB**

244   For the more innovative referents of the metaphor in the texts of NCB Jews, see Table 3.15 below.

245   The texts of later, NCB Jews are in bold (so also in Tables 3.13 and 3.14 below) to help distinguish them visually from HB texts.

The second pattern concerns pastoral imagery: see Table 3.13. NCB Jews' appropriations of the shepherd metaphor frequently bear pastoral imagery. When idealizing the activities of a model shepherd these authors commonly speak of shepherd-rulers in terms appropriate for the shepherding vocation: they pasture or graze the flock; they guard, protect, and lead it; they watch over the afflicted, and so on. Similarly, YHWH, as a shepherd, is described as gathering his sheep together and pasturing them, as binding up, healing, and feeding his flock, and as protecting them from physical dangers.

Table 3.13   Comparison of pastoral imagery in texts idealizing a shepherd

Pronounced imagery	Modest imagery	Little or no imagery
Psalm 23.1	Gen. 48.15	Ecclesiastes
Psalm 28.9	Gen. 49.24	Ben Sira
Psalm 80.1	Judith	Philo
Isaiah 40.11	*LAB*	
Jeremiah 31.10		
Ezekiel 34		
Hosea 4.16		
Micah 7.14		
Zechariah 11.13		
1 Enoch		
CD XIII		
Pss. Sol. 17		
Apoc. Ezek.		

The third pattern of usage concerns the sentiments of political-national and/or moral restoration of the nation of Israel associated with the metaphor: see Table 3.14. Usually it is YHWH who accomplishes this work of restoration, but in a few instances this hope is associated with Israel's leaders: at times royal, at other times messianic or religious.

Table 3.14 Comparison of Jewish-national/non-Jewish-national over-tones in the shepherd metaphor

Jewish-national overtones	No Jewish-national overtones
Gen. 48.15	Ecclesiastes
Gen. 49.24	**Ben Sira**
Num. 27.17	**Philo**
Deuteronomistic history	
Chronicles	
Psalm 23	
Psalm 28	
Psalm 78	
Psalm 80	
Deutero-Isaiah	
Trito-Isaiah	
Jeremiah	
Ezekiel	
Hosea	
Micah	
Nahum	
Deutero-Zechariah	
1 Enoch	
4Q504	
4Q509	
1Q34	
CD	
Judith	
Pss. Sol. 17	
Apoc. Ezek.	
LAB	
4 Ezra	
2 Baruch	
Josephus	

Christ-believers tend to appropriate the shepherd metaphor differently from NCB Jews in terms of referent: see Table 3.15. Christ-believers tend to refrain from using the metaphor for political rulers or for the activity of ruling,[246] and for YHWH, employing it instead for Jesus (as the messiah) and for assembly leaders. Although Christ-believers apply the shepherd metaphor to Jesus, they do not actually connect the metaphor to the title 'messiah' – a designation that bears definite political

---

246 Only Revelation offers an exception to this tendency: 'shepherding' designates the 'ruling' of Jesus in Rev. 2.27; 12.5; and 19.15.

overtones;[247] only Matthew makes this 'shepherd'–'messiah' connection (cf. Mt. 2.4-6).

Table 3.15 Overall comparison of shepherd metaphor referents[248]

Ruler	YHWH	Messiah	Assembly leader	Unique usages
Jeremiah	Gen. 48.15	*Pss. Sol.* 17	**John 21**	Philo
Num. 27.17	Gen. 49.24	**John 10**	**Acts**	*2 Baruch*
Ezekiel	Psalm 23	**Mark**	**Ephesians**	*Hermas*
Deutero-Zech.	Psalm 28	**Hebrews**	**1 Peter 5**	CD
DtH	Psalm 80	**1 Peter 2, 5**	**Jude**	
Chronicles	Ecclesiastes	**Revelation**	*Hermas*	
Psalm 78	Deutero-Isaiah			
Deutero-Isaiah	Jeremiah			
Trito-Isaiah	Ezekiel			
Micah	Hosea			
Nahum	Micah			
1 Enoch	Deutero-Zech.			
4Q504	*1 Enoch*			
1Q34	4Q509			
CD	Ben Sira			
Philo	Judith			
LAB	*Apoc. Ezek.*			
Josephus	Philo			
4 Ezra	*LAB*			
Revelation				

In using the metaphor for assembly leaders, Christ-believers do something that sharply distinguishes them from NCB Jews and Romans: Christ-believers refer to their assembly leaders as 'shepherds',[249] but

247   'Messiah' represents a political figure, for example, in Isa. 45.1, where it designates the Persian king, Cyrus. While occasionally Christ-believers can use 'messiah' with political overtones (e.g. Mk 12.35; 14.61; 15.32, and their respective parallels; also Lk. 23.2; Acts 2.36; Rev. 1.5), in the vast majority of instances where 'messiah' occurs in the New Testament (almost 500 times), it lacks any such political connotations.

248   The texts of Christ-believers are in bold font (so also in Tables 3.16 and 3.17 below) to help distinguish them visually from the other texts.

249   This assembly leaders-as-shepherds usage also appears in the writings of later Christ-believers not included here, e.g. 1 Clement and Ignatius.

Jews refrain from using this title for the leaders of their synagogues.[250] Romans also avoid the term for *collegium* leaders.[251]

Christ-believers tend to use the shepherd metaphor differently than NCB Jews in terms of pastoral imagery: see Table 3.16. Christ-believers' appropriations of the metaphor tend not to depict the activity of the shepherd in earthy, pastoral terms. Although they commonly depict Jesus as a shepherd who, like YHWH, offers his flock abundant care, their description of the messianic shepherd typically lacks the pastoral imagery found in the portraits of YHWH as a shepherd in the HB and in Second Temple Jewish texts, as well as in the profile of the Davidic messiah in *Psalms of Solomon* 17. Additionally, Christ-believers link the metaphor to Jesus' death on the cross: the shepherd dies to secure his sheep's salvation – quite unlike the deliverance YHWH as a shepherd works on behalf of his flock, which involves some physical display of power,[252] according to the HB and Second Temple Jewish texts.

---

250   'Shepherd' never appears as a title for synagogue leaders in any of the extant primary sources (literary texts, papyri, and inscriptions); cf. the comprehensive study of A. Runesson, D. Binder, and B. Olsson, *The Ancient Synagogue from Its Origins to 200 CE: A Source Book*, AJEC 72, ed. M. Hengel et al. (Leiden: Brill, 2008).

251   Cf. Harland, *Associations*. Harland does note that the worshipers of Dionysos at Pergamum are sometimes referred to as βουκόλοι ('cowherds'), and their leaders, who offered prayers, sang hymns, and danced in honour of Dionysos, as οἱ χορεύσαντες βουκόλοι ('dancing cowherds').

252   Although Deutero-Zechariah speaks of the purification of a remnant in relation to the striking down of his shepherd (13.7-9), the text is actually silent as to how the death of a Jewish ruler accomplishes this cleansing (see the discussion of Zech. 13.7 in section 2.2.2 above). In fact, 13.7-9 does not make this connection and the relationship between the two events could be chronological rather than causative. In other words, rather than the passage meaning that the death of this ruler will bring about the purification of a Jewish remnant (causative), it could simply mean that after the death of this ruler – and not before – a Jewish remnant will be purified (chronological). While the Gospel writers, in applying this text to Jesus, take these two events as causative (the striking down of Jesus brings about cleansing from sin), the author of CD XIX does not: in the day of the messiah, the striking down of the shepherd represents the outpouring of divine wrath upon apostates, while the faithful escape judgement – they are not 'purified' by the former event.

Table 3.16 Overall comparison of pastoral imagery in texts idealizing a shepherd

Pronounced imagery	Modest imagery	Little or no imagery
Ps. 23.1	Gen. 48.15	Ecclesiastes
Ps. 28.9	Gen. 49.24	Ben Sira
Ps. 80.1	Judith	Philo
Isa. 40.11	Pseudo-Philo	Acts[4]
Jer. 31.10	**Mk 14.27**	**Ephesians**
Ezek. 34		**Hebrews**
Hos. 4.16		**1 Peter**
Mic. 7.14		**Jude**
Zech. 11.13		**Revelation 2; 12; 19**
1 Enoch		*Hermas*
CD XIII		
Pss. Sol. 17		
Apoc. Ezek.		
Mk 6.34		
John		
Rev. 7.17		

This more non-pastoral use of the shepherd metaphor (for Jesus) finds corroboration in the other major category of usage for Christ-believers: assembly leaders. While assembly leaders exercise ruling authority over their communities, Christ-believers (either explicitly or implicitly) associate teaching with shepherding. This connection between teaching and shepherding exemplifies how Christ-believers usually employ the metaphor for assembly leaders: without the pastoral imagery that so often marks the metaphor's usage by NCB Jews.

Finally, Christ-believers typically lack a concern for the political-national restoration and/or moral renewal of the nation Israel: see Table 3.17. The nation of Israel's moral or geo-political well-being is not typically the focus of Christ-believers; their concern, rather, is much more universal: 'the church of God' (Acts 20.28), 'the body of Christ' (Eph. 4.11-12), or the overcoming church (Revelation).

Table 3.17 Overall comparison of Jewish-national overtones in the shepherd metaphor

Jewish-national overtones	No Jewish-national overtones
Gen. 48.15; 49.24; Num. 27.17	Ben Sira
Deuteronomistic History	Philo
Chronicles	**John**
Psalms 23; 28; 78; 80	**Acts**
Deutero-Isaiah; Trito-Isaiah	**Ephesians**
Jeremiah	**Hebrews**
Ezekiel	**1 Peter**
Hosea	**Jude**
Micah	**Revelation**
Nahum	***Hermas***
Deutero-Zechariah	
1 Enoch	
4Q504; 4Q509; 1Q34; CD	
Judith	
Pss. Sol. 17	
Apoc. Ezek.	
LAB	
4 Ezra	
2 Baruch	
Josephus	
Mark	

While there are no exceptions to the pattern of referents, there seem to be some exceptions to the latter two patterns regarding pastoral imagery and Jewish nationalism. On the one hand, Jn 21.15-17 is the lone instance where assembly leaders are depicted in pastoral terms ('Feed my lambs. ... Tend my sheep. ... Feed my sheep'). But while John 21 cuts against the grain of the pattern of thought for Christ-believers employing the metaphor for assembly leaders, it nevertheless cannot overthrow the clear tendency: Christ-believers typically do not deploy the shepherd metaphor for assembly leaders in the terms commonly used for describing the duties of literal shepherds.

On the other hand, when applying the metaphor to Jesus, Mk 6.34 (and to a lesser degree 14.27) and Rev. 7.17 employ pastoral imagery, and the first text also bears some overtones of Jewish nationalism. Two things can be said here. First, the counter-evidence of these three passages from two authors provides insufficient grounds to deny the general pattern generated by the other fourteen passages from eight different authors. 'Patterns' of usage/thought do not represent unalterable laws void of exceptions, but only general tendencies among authors. Second, it could be argued that Mark and Revelation (7.17) merely give evidence of why the socio-religious orientation of NCB Jews and Christ-believers should be described spectrally rather than in terms of an either/or configuration: the thought patterns of some CB groups can resemble types of Second Temple Jewish thought.[253]

There are two interesting parallels that perhaps best highlight the ruler/non-ruler, pastoral/non-pastoral, and Jewish-national/no Jewish-national sentiments differences in usage between NCB Jews and Christ-believers. *Fourth Ezra* 5.18 and Acts 20.29-30 offer a parallel for the first difference. Both texts speak of a 'flock' being threatened by 'savage wolves'. In the latter text, the 'savage wolves', who come in after Paul's departure and do 'not spare the flock' are identified as men who 'arise from among [their midst], speaking distorted things to draw away disciples after them' (20.30). In other words, the 'savage wolves' represent false teachers not rulers: hence, Paul admonishes the 'overseers' to beware of these men and to follow his example as a leader. By contrast, the wider context of *4 Ezra* 5.18, makes it plain that the 'savage wolves' in whose 'power' exilic Israel would have remained without Ezra's leadership, are not false teachers but Babylonian rulers: hence, Chief Phaltiel's concern for Ezra's whereabouts. In addition, the central concern in Acts 20 is doctrinal purity or apostasy, whereas in *4 Ezra* 5 it is the national well-being of exilic Israel.

Fourth Ezra 5.18 and the much later Christian addition of *4 Ezra* 2.34 offer a parallel for the differences in pastoral and Jewish-national usage.[254] As observed (section 3.2.5 above), the NCB Jewish author of 5.18 employs the shepherd metaphor in a (somewhat) pastoral manner with definite overtones of Jewish-national restoration. The CB author of 2.34 applies the metaphor for Jesus but in a very different manner. On the one hand, he uses it without pastoral language: the shepherd brings 'everlasting rest' (i.e. salvation) and the 'rewards of the kingdom', which features 'joy of glory', 'glorious garments', and white clothing (2.34-39). On the other hand, the author takes a decidedly anti-Jewish-national stance: God sent Ezra to the people of Israel but they rejected his message: hence the author exhorts the 'nations' to hear and understand (2.33-34). These parallels, then, more clearly illustrate the differences in thought between NCB Jews and most Christ-believers concerning the shepherd metaphor.

In order to situate Matthew on a socio-religious spectrum, this study will compare the patterns of thought reflected by his shepherd motif with the observable patterns of thought concerning the shepherd metaphor in the writings of other Christ-believers, NCB Jews, and NCB Romans.

253 For further discussion of this point, see section 5.2.3 below.
254 *Fourth Ezra* 2.34 reads, 'Await your shepherd; he will give you everlasting rest, because he who will come at the end of the age is close at hand.' As mentioned previously, Bergren argues for a date range of mid-second century CE to mid-third century CE for this addition (*Fifth Ezra*, 24–26); cf. Metzger, '4 Ezra', *OTP*, 1.520.

Does Matthew's deployment of the metaphor resemble the tendencies of his contemporary Christ-believers? Does it align more closely with the patterns of usage evident in the texts of NCB Jews or NCB Romans? These questions will be addressed in Part II of this inquiry.

Part II

Matthew's Shepherd Motif
and Its Socio-religious Implications

Chapter 4

A LITERARY ANALYSIS OF MATTHEW'S SHEPHERD MOTIF

4.1 Introduction

Virtually all scholars agree that the Gospel of Matthew is a first-century text written by a follower of Jesus of Nazareth.[1] From there agreement drops off sharply.[2] This chapter will examine Matthew's shepherd motif, concentrating on his explicit uses of 'shepherd' (ποιμήν/ποιμαίνω).[3] The study will pause at points where Matthew appropriates 'shepherd' texts from the HB to analyse how his appropriation compares with them as another means of discerning the Evangelist's literary and theological emphases. The chapter will end by summarizing Matthew's appropriation of the shepherd metaphor and discussing how the motif contributes to the Gospel's Christology and soteriology.

4.2 Matthew's Depiction of Jesus as the Shepherd

4.2.1 The shepherd's identity: the Davidic messiah

Matthew introduces the shepherd motif in the birth and infancy narratives.[4] Although ποιμαίνω does not occur until 2.6, ch. 2 is closely con-

---

1   For a helpful spectrum of opinions on the dating of Matthew, see Davies and Allison, *Matthew*, 1.127–28. An overwhelming majority of commentators date the Gospel between 70 and 100 CE. Few scholars argue for a pre-70 composition and fewer still for a post-100 date.

2   The guiding assumption for this study of Matthew is the Two-Source Hypothesis. For a recent defence of this position, see Davies and Allison, *Matthew*, 1.97–127.

3   Because explicit occurrences of ποιμήν/ποιμαίνω remain the focus of this study, passages like Mt. 10.6; 15.24; and 18.12-14, where the shepherd motif occurs without the use of 'shepherd', will not be analysed. This does not mean that these instances of shepherding imagery without the use of 'shepherd' have been overlooked. These texts have indeed been analysed, but in the end, they do not add appreciably to the use of the ποιμήν/ποιμαίνω metaphor. As will be observed in this chapter, they merely follow the pattern of usage established by the ποιμήν/ποιμαίνω motif. One 'shepherd'-less passage bearing shepherd imagery that will be treated because of the unique point it contributes is Mt. 27.9-10 (see section 4.2.5 below).

4   Unlike some of the other Christological motifs in the Gospel, 'shepherd' is distributed fairly evenly throughout the narrative. The structure of the Gospel is unset-

nected syntactically, lexically, thematically, and narratively to the first chapter.[5] The first chapter essentially answers the question of who Jesus is: the Davidic messiah.[6] The first line of the Gospel ascribes to Jesus the titles of Messiah, Son of David, and Son of Abraham (1.1).[7] The purpose of the ensuing genealogy (1.2-17) is largely to substantiate Jesus' Davidic lineage and thereby legitimize his claim to Israel's throne:[8] Jesus is not merely 'a son of David' (like his father Joseph [1.20b]); he is *the* Son of David (1.1), the rightful successor to 'David the king' (1.6), and the one who will ascend the Davidic throne.

After describing Jesus' Davidic ancestry, the Evangelist offers an account of Jesus' birth in 1.18-25, whereby he establishes three further points. First, Jesus is conceived by the Holy Spirit (1.18b, 20b) and thus, relates to God in a unique way. Second, Jesus the Son of David has come for a salvific mission: 'and you shall call his name Jesus for he will save his people from their sins' (1.21b, cf. v. 23b). And third, Jesus' birth and mission to Israel were foreseen by and fulfil the scriptures (1.22-23; cf. Isa. 7.14).

tled: see Luz, *Matthäus*, 1.18–19 for a discussion of some of the difficulties of assessing the structure, and Davies and Allison, *Matthew*, 1.58–72 for a survey of structural breakdowns. The lowest common denominator for the Gospel's structure would at least recognize a beginning, a middle, and an end. 'Shepherd' appears in each of these sections – something that cannot be said for 'Son of Man' or 'Lord' (which do not appear in the beginning section) or 'Son of Abraham' (which disappears after 1.1).

5   Syntactically, the genitive absolute of Mt. 2.1aα, Τοῦ δὲ Ἰησοῦ γεννηθέντος ('Now when Jesus was born') serves to connect the story of 2.1-12 with the preceding paragraph of 1.18-25, which describes the circumstances of Jesus' birth: 1.18-25 begins with Τοῦ δὲ Ἰησοῦ Χριστοῦ ἡ γένεσις ('Now the birth of Jesus Christ') and ends with Ἰησοῦς. Matthew frequently deploys the genitive absolute as a means of interlocking pericopes within his narrative (e.g. 1.18; 2.13, 19; 8.1, 5, 28); cf. Soares Prabhu, *Formula*, 180–83. Lexically, chs 1 and 2 share a number of significant vocabulary terms: Χριστός (1.1, 16, 17, 18; cf. 2.4), Ἰούδας (1.2-3; cf. 2.5-6), γεννάω (1.2, 3, 4, passim; cf. 2.1), ὁ βασιλεύς (1.6; cf. 2.1), κατ' ὄναρ (1.20; cf. 2.12), τίκτω (1.21; cf. 2.2), καλέω (1.21, 23, 25; cf. 2.7), λαός (1.21; cf. 2.6), and διὰ τοῦ προφήτου (1.22; cf. 2.5). Thematically, the genealogy presents Jesus as the true heir to David's throne, while 2.1-12 develops this kingship theme further. Narratively, 2.1-12 chronologically follows the events of 1.18-25: Jesus the true heir is born (1.18-25), and 2.1-12 presents how some groups of people respond to news of his birth.

6   Cf. K. Stendahl, 'Quis et Unde? An Analysis of Matthew 1–2', in *The Interpretation of Matthew*, ed. G. Stanton (Philadelphia: Fortress Press, 1983), and Kingsbury, *Matthew*.

7   While P. Bonnard (*L'Évangile selon saint Matthieu*, CNT [Neuchâtel: Delachaux & Niestlé, 1963], 15–16) is probably correct that the superscription is intentionally ambiguous and introduces both the genealogy and the entire Gospel. Hence, 1.1 would not only introduce who Jesus is in terms of his ancestral origin, but would also foreshadow the direction and focus of the Gospel: how these titles are realized in Jesus.

8   That this is the main point of the genealogy is demonstrated by the frequent use of the name 'David' (four times), the appellation of 'the king' at the first mention of David (1.6), the three 'fourteens' that make up the genealogy's structure, the threefold repetition of 'fourteen' – according to gematria the three consonants of David's name in Hebrew (דוד) numerically add up to fourteen – as well as David's position within the structure of the genealogy: 'David' serves as a kind of bridge between Abraham and the exile.

The central theme of the story in chs 1 and 2 is kingship, specifically who Israel's true king really is. If the first chapter is concerned with Jesus' identity (who Jesus is), the second answers the question of his geographical origin (where Jesus is from).[9] The second chapter consists of two sections: vv. 1-12, which introduce the shepherd motif, deal with the events in Bethlehem; and vv. 13-23, which deal with the geographical movement of the infant Jesus after he is forced to flee because of Herod's death plot. Matthew unfolds this kingship theme largely through two implicit, interrelated contrasts between the Jewish leaders and the eastern Magi, and between Jesus and Herod.[10]

While Matthew's Magi remain anonymous in the narrative, widespread agreement among scholars exists about a few things concerning them. They are clearly Gentiles: they come from 'another land' (2.12b) from the east (2.1).[11] While the notion of 'kingship' is a much later Christian association with the Magi,[12] they would nonetheless represent a social class of some standing, possibly priests.[13] Additionally, although magical powers and superior understanding were often associated with Magi,[14] their knowledge about the coming king remained inferior to that of the Jewish leaders: their wisdom helped bring them to Jerusalem but it took the biblical knowledge of the chief priests and scribes of Israel to lead them directly to the Christ-child (2.1-2a, 4-5). Lastly, through their arts, the Magi recognized (without the aid of the scriptures) the greatness of the 'king of the Jews' and consequently desired to pay him homage,[15] offering him precious gifts (vv. 2b, 10-11).[16] The leaders

9   This query is tightly connected to the first Christological question: in the Gospel of John, questions of the messiah's place of origin flow rather naturally from questions concerning his identity (Jn 1.44-46; 7.40-42, 52).

10   Nolan combines these two contrasts into one: between 'unbelieving, semi-Jewish, but non-Davidic (Herodian) Jerusalem, and believing, non-Jewish (Magian), but Davidic Bethlehem' (*Royal Son*, 205).

11   Early scholarship posits their origin to be Arabia, Babylon, or Persia; cf. Davies and Allison, *Matthew*, 1.228, and R. Brown, *The Birth of the Messiah: A Commentary on the Infancy Narratives in the Gospels of Matthew and Luke*, ABRL, new edn (New York: Doubleday, 1993), 168–70.

12   Davies and Allison, *Matthew*, 1.231.

13   While the gifts of the Magi probably signify something like tribute given to a king, frankincense and myrrh have cultic functions in the HB (see Exod. 30.34-38; Leviticus 2, passim; 24.7, 15 for frankincense, and Exod. 30.23 for myrrh), and as such, would colour their gifts with a priestly tinge. Luz notes that μάγος, in the first instance, refers to someone belonging to the Persian caste of priests. Soares Prabhu remarks that although magi as 'magicians' would have represented the popular thinking of the times, according to their deployment by Matthew in his narrative, the Evangelist seems to restore 'their ancient exalted role' (*Formula*, 281).

14   E.g. Dan. [LXX] 1.20; 2.2; 4.4; 5.7; Acts 8.9-11; *AJ* 10.195, 216.

15   R. Horsley asserts that the homage of the Magi is 'an act of the highest respect for, homage to, and submission to a king, a political ruler, not an act of worship of divinity, further expressing the worldwide political import of what is happening here' (*Sociology and the Jesus Movement* [New York: Crossroads, 1989], 58).

16   In their 'pilgrimage' to the Christ-child, many scholars see an allusion to Isa. 60.6. First Kings 10.1-10/2 Chron. 9.1-12 presents an interesting parallel: a member of

of the Jewish people (represented in the narrative by Herod, the chief priests, and the scribes), however, when informed of the Magi's request, are deeply troubled by it (v. 3). Despite knowing through the scriptures where the coming king would be born, as well as identifying this king with the coming messiah (vv. 2a, 4-5), despite residing only five miles from the birthplace, and despite being named among the specific recipients of the messiah's rule (2.6b), the Jewish leaders refrain from visiting the Christ-child.[17] Rather, they – as epitomized by Herod – seek to destroy him because of the threat he poses to their rule.[18]

Thus, when the news of Jesus' birth becomes public, according to Matthew's story the Magi – Gentiles possessing only a veiled knowledge of the royal messiah, and who must travel a great distance to see the Christ-child – respond to him with joy, homage, and offerings. The Jewish leaders, however, despite enjoying the guidance of the scriptures and living in close proximity to the Christ-child, show only a feigned interest in the child, and ultimately seek the demise of the one divinely appointed to shepherd them.[19]

The more important contrast in the infancy narrative is between Herod, who for Matthew typifies the Jerusalem leadership, and Jesus. Matthew's genealogy presents Jesus, the Son of David, as the rightful heir to the throne of 'David the king'. In ch. 2, the reader is introduced to Israel's monarch at the time of Jesus' birth, 'Herod the king' (2.1a). The Magi ask Herod, 'Where is the one born king of the Jews?' The question is ironic for Herod *is* the king of the Jews (v. 3a).[20] Consequently, Herod finds their question disturbing (v. 3),[21] thus revealing his insecurity, which ultimately leads to his plot against the child (vv. 13, 16). Although Herod ruled over the Jews,

Gentile royalty pays homage (bringing gifts that include spices) to King Solomon, the son of David, because she recognizes his greatness (cf. the reference to this story in Mt. 12.42).

17   Although the 'crowds' visit Jesus early into the story (4.25), and the Jerusalem leaders travel to the wilderness to meet John the Baptist early in the narrative (3.5), it is not until 15.1 that Jewish leaders (viz. Pharisees and scribes) come to Jesus from Jerusalem; and not long after their visit Jesus informs his disciples of his impending passion in Jerusalem (16.21).

18   Although this treacherous plot is not explicitly revealed until 2.13, it is anticipated by the admonishing dream given to the Magi in 2.12a.

19   Luz, in his Matthew commentary, slightly misses the mark here: the story does not have an 'Akzent antijüdisch' but, more specifically, an anti-Jewish-leaders point.

20   By the time of Jesus' birth, Herod the Great (as he had become known) had been in power for over thirty years. Moreover, based on the inscription, *Regi Herodi Iudaic(o)* ('king of the Jews') on some pottery found at Masada (see H. Cotton and J. Geiger, 'Wine for Herod', *Cathedra* 53 [1989]: 3–12 [in Hebrew]), Mendels asserts that Herod desired not merely to be 'King of Judea' but 'King of the Jews' (*Jewish Nationalism*, 284, 322, n. 22).

21   Josephus records an interesting legend about Herod: when Herod was still a boy, he was met by an Essene prophet who greeted him as 'king of the Jews', predicting that one day he would rule the nation (*AJ* 15.373–74). If this legend became well known during the time of Jesus, then it would have added to the irony of the story – something not lost on Matthew's first audience.

controversy existed over the legitimacy of his throne because of his Idumaean ancestry,[22] his friendship with Rome and attraction to its culture,[23] and his excessive cruelty.[24]

Thus, while Herod's kingship was seen by some as illegitimate from the start, Matthew presents Jesus as the legitimate heir to the throne of Israel. Verseput comments, '[Matthew] even juxtaposes the legitimate child-heir with the house of Herod, so that comparisons with an earlier protest against the Hasmonaean dynasty in *Ps. Sol. 17* are difficult to avoid.'[25] Unlike Herod, Jesus belongs to the royal line of King David; and far from ascending to the throne through wealth or political guile, Jesus' appointment as king of the Jews comes via divine sanction as prophesied by the scriptures. Hence, the ultimate reason why Herod's throne is illegitimate is because he is not the one God has appointed to rule his people; rather, it is Jesus.

While Matthew appropriates scripture earlier in the narrative to delineate Jesus' identity, his next citation in 2.6 confirms Jesus' legitimacy as the true heir to the throne, as well as tersely summarizes and foreshadows his mission to Israel. Jesus' claim to the throne is legitimized in two ways. The inquiry described in the verses leading up to the citation (vv. 4-5), reveals that the scripture about to be quoted refers to the birthplace not of the king but of the 'messiah' (v. 4b). In other words, in the response to the Magi's query of where the 'king of the Jews' would be born, the religious leaders seek the birthplace of the 'messiah'. Hence, part of Jesus' legitimacy as Israel's true king derives not simply from being of royal lineage (for even Joseph is called a 'son of David' [1.20]), but from being Israel's 'messiah' – the first Christological title appearing in the superscription of the Gospel (1.1; cf. 1.16, 17). Also, his birthplace has already been announced in the scriptures: the messiah will be born 'in Bethlehem of Judea, for so it is written by the prophet' (2.5b). For Matthew, the scriptures are divinely revealed and therefore authoritative and binding. Consequently, that Jesus' birth is foreseen by the scriptures would be an implicit affirmation both of his special character and also of the validity of his claim to the throne.

But just as the geographical origin of the messiah is anchored in the biblical citation, so too is the nature of his mission: 'And you Bethlehem, land of Judah, by no means are you least among the rulers of Judah, for out

---

22   Herod's father was an Idumaean, making Herod unfit to rule in the eyes of some Jews; cf. H. Hoehner, 'Herodian Dynasty', *DJG* (Downers Grove: IVP, 1992), 319.

23   P. Richardson notes that in his architecture, 'Herod balanced two competing needs: his commitment to Judaism caused him to give little offense in his building, especially the Temple in Jerusalem; but his attachment to Rome caused him to include, in as politically astute a way as possible, a symbol of Roman authority' (*Herod: King of the Jews and Friend of the Romans* [Columbia: University of South Carolina Press, 1996], 18).

24   In the latter part of his reign (near the time of Jesus' birth), his cruelty manifested itself in (among other things) the execution of his wife Marianne (along with their three sons) because, being of Hasmonaean descent, she possessed a greater claim to Israel's throne; cf. Hoehner, 'Herodian Dynasty', 320–21, and Richardson, *Herod*, 33–38.

25   Verseput, 'Davidic Messiah', 102.

of you will come a ruler who will shepherd my people Israel' (v. 6). This citation represents a conflation of Mic. 5.1 (v. 6a) and 2 Sam. 5.2bβ (v. 6b), and is without parallel in the other Gospels.[26] Davies and Allison note that the citation conforms neither to the LXX nor to the MT,[27] and subsequently should be viewed as an interpretation rather than a quotation of scripture.[28] That is, implicit within this citation itself would be Matthew's understanding of how these texts relate to Jesus. A few points can be made here.

First, in his appropriation of Mic. 5.1a, two elements are changed: 'Ephrathah' becomes 'Judah', and 'you are least' becomes 'you are by no means least'. Matthew eliminates a point of reference that would have meant little to his readers,[29] in favour of a term with much greater relevance, 'Judah'.[30] This would especially be so within the infancy narrative, where the patriarch Judah has already been mentioned in the genealogy (1.2-3), and according to Jacob's testament in the book of Genesis, a messianic figure would come through the line of his son Judah (Gen. 49.10-12).[31]

At one point, Matthew also seems to reverse the meaning of the Micah text: according to the MT, Bethlehem is the least but Matthew seems to deny this.[32] This reversal should probably be understood in this way: although Bethlehem is the least among the rulers of Judah, because Jesus the messiah is born there, the city can no longer be considered insignificant but rather, great.[33] Matthew's use of Mic. 5.1, however, actually mirrors the larger context within Micah: Bethlehem Ephrathah is small but in the future it will produce a great leader who will rule over Israel in the majesty of the name of YHWH (Mic. 5.1b, 3). The difference would seem to be one of emphasis, whereby Matthew accentuates the greatness of Bethlehem after this prominent leader emerges. This may be one of the reasons why the Evangelist neglects to quote the last part of the verse in Micah, which speaks of the ancient origin of David's descendant (which would seem to fit with

---

26   A small number of scholars (e.g. Chae, *Davidic Shepherd*, 174–84) have argued for an additional text within this conflation: Gen. 49.10.

27   Cf. Stendahl, *School*, 99; Soares Prabhu, *Formula*, 37; Brown, *Messiah*, 184–86.

28   Davies and Allison, *Matthew*, 1.242; cf. D. A. Carson, *Matthew*, EBC 8 (Grand Rapids: Zondervan, 1984), 87.

29   Ephrathah appears only six times in the HB and all but one refers explicitly to Bethlehem.

30   Soares Prabhu suggests that Matthew's aim is not geographical precision but theological, insofar as he may be alluding to 1 Sam. 17.12, which refers to David as a son of an Ephrathite of Bethlehem in Judah, thus reinforcing the Davidic lineage of Jesus (*Formula*, 262–63).

31   That Gen. 49.10-12 is understood messianically by early Jews can be seen, for example, in 4Q252 (4QGenesis Pesherᵃ) and b. Sanh 98b.

32   The LXX, for example, maintains the sense of the MT: 'least you are among the clans of Judah' (ὀλιγοστὸς εἶ τοῦ εἶναι ἐν χιλιάσιν Ἰούδα).

33   If Micah could refer to Bethlehem as 'least' – despite it being the birthplace of King David – then clearly Matthew's reversal of this text means that Jesus' greatness far outstrips David's.

Matthew's genealogy): the Evangelist is most concerned here with justifying Jesus' Bethlehem origin.

In addition to these changes, Matthew also takes the somewhat ambiguous term אֶלֶף, which literally means 'thousand' but can connote either a 'tribe' or a 'tribal chief',[34] and opts for the latter connotation by using ἡγεμών ('rulers'),[35] which acts as a link to ἡγέομαι in the 2 Sam. 5.2 citation in the second part of the verse. Moreover, the use of ἡγεμών (rather than, say, χιλιάς) may serve to underscore, within this brief citation, the reason for the messiah's emergence from Bethlehem: to replace those who currently lead (ἡγέομαι) Israel.[36] Certainly, Jesus' replacement of the Jewish leaders is one of the ways that Matthew echoes the wider literary context of Mic. 5.1.[37]

Second, if Matthew's sole purpose in citing scripture here was to justify the geographical origin of Jesus, then 2 Sam. 5.2 would be superfluous since only the Micah text would be needed. But Matthew seeks to do more than simply validate Jesus' place of birth. By appending the Samuel text, he achieves some interrelated effects. He re-emphasizes the Davidic Christology with which he opened the Gospel and which will be featured prominently throughout it.[38] In addition, while Davidic kingship is the central thrust of the first portion of the infancy narrative, a corollary of this theme is the shepherd motif. Indeed, David is viewed in the HB as the ideal shepherd (e.g. Ps. 78.70-72; Ezek. 34.23), and when the HB and Second Temple Jewish authors use the metaphor for David, it refers to his ruling over Israel as its king.[39]

According to Matthew, Jesus represents the promised ruler who will shepherd God's people Israel. 'Shepherd' here specifically connotes 'rule' or 'kingship'. At the time of Jesus' birth, Israel had rulers/shepherds, viz. King Herod (v. 1a), as well as the chief priests and the scribes (v. 4).[40] But

---

34   אֶלֶף is used in this way, for example, in Num. 1.16; 10.4; 31.5; Josh. 22.14 and Judg. 6.15; cf. Davies and Allison, *Matthew*, 1.242–43, and Carson, *Matthew*, 87–88.

35   The LXX adopts a literal rendering of אֶלֶף with χιλιάσιν ('thousands').

36   Of the Synoptic Gospels, only Matthew employs ἡγεμών with any type of regularity: nine times, compared to once in Mark and twice in Luke. Matthew consistently applies the term to Pilate in the passion narrative (six times: 27.2, 11, 14, 15, 21, 27. Willitts asserts, 'The Matthean phrase τοῖς ἡγεμόσιν Ἰούδα in Matt 2:6 reflects the chapter's concern for the political power of Israel' (*Shepherd-King*, 108).

37   According to the wider context of Mic. 5.1, the coming Davidide shall rule over Israel in the majesty of YHWH, replacing Israel's former king who suffered humiliation at the hands of foreigners; see section 2.2.2 above.

38   While Davidic lineage is implied in the Micah text, it is more explicit in 2 Sam. 5.2, which represents words spoken by YHWH directly to David at his coronation over all Israel.

39   See sections 2.2.2 and 3.2.2 above.

40   It is possible that Matthew linguistically extends the shepherding contrast between Herod and Jesus in his description of the action Herod takes after he receives the Magi's news: he 'gathers together' (συνάγω) the chief priests and scribes of the people to learn where Jesus would be born (2.4). Frequently συνάγω bears shepherding imagery (e.g. Mt. 25.32; cf. use of the cognate verb ἄγω in the LXX: e.g. Gen. 46.32; Exod. 3.1;

according to this text, God is about to replace these shepherds with his own, the reason for which is only hinted at in this portion of the infancy narrative (i.e. they are disturbed by and disinterested in the arrival of God's new king), but more fully evidenced in the second section of it: they reject him and plan his destruction. This replacement of Israel's shepherds is implicit in the 2 Samuel 5 passage, where David not only replaces Saul as the king,[41] but the people acknowledge that even while Saul was king, David had been their true shepherd (2 Sam. 5.2a). This notion of the replacement of Israel's shepherds and the rejection of God's shepherd will be unfolded in the Gospel. And lastly, although 'shepherd' refers to Jesus as Israel's king in the context of the infancy narratives, it also reveals something of his mission, specifically its scope and to a lesser extent, its nature.

For Matthew, Jesus has been divinely appointed to shepherd God's people, Israel (v. 6b). Numerous scholars argue that 'Israel' refers to both Jews and Gentiles.[42] D. Hagner, for example, states that 'We may thus finally equate this λαός, 'people', with the ἐκκλησία, 'Church', of which Jesus speaks in 16.18'.[43] While Matthew can appeal in his Gospel to different levels of understanding,[44] Saldarini has demonstrated that the Evangelist never uses λαός with the sense of 'Church', but rather that he employs the word for the 'social and political entity of the land of Israel, that is, the Jewish people. He also uses it to specify subgroups within Israel.'[45]

It seems better to understand 'his people' in 2.6 as referring to Jews for several reasons. 'My people' (τὸν λαόν μου) is clearly an echo of 'his people' (τὸν λαὸν αὐτοῦ) in 1.21b. In 1.21 the angel tells Joseph that 'he [= Jesus] will save his [= Jesus'] people (τὸν λαὸν αὐτοῦ) from their sins'.[46] Since Jesus

---

Ps. 77.52; Isa. 63.12-14). Matthew had any number of linguistic options from which to choose (and which he employs elsewhere) other than συνάγω: e.g. καλέω (2.7), προσκαλέομαι (10.1), πέμπω (11.2), or ζητέω (12.46). That he opted for συνάγω here, particularly in view of its close syntactical (and conceptual) relation to ποιμαίνω in 2.6, may suggest a deliberate contrast on Matthew's part. Hence the contrast would be between the respective recipients of Herod's and Jesus' shepherding: Herod 'gathers' or shepherds his own, i.e. the religious elite 'of the people', whereas Jesus 'will shepherd [God's] people Israel'.

41   Herod's attempt on the life of Jesus – the one born and divinely appointed to be Israel's king – parallels Saul's attempts to destroy God's chosen replacement for him as king, David.

42   E.g. Davies and Allison, *Matthew*, 1.210; Nolan, *Royal Son*, 133; and Carson, *Matthew*, 88.

43   D. Hagner, *Matthew*, 2 vols, WBC 33a-b (Dallas: Word Books, 1998), 1.19.

44   Cf. R. France, 'The Formula-Quotations of Matthew 2 and the Problem of Communication', *NTS* 27 (1981): 233–51.

45   Saldarini, *Christian-Jewish*, 28 (cf. his analysis: *Christian-Jewish*, 28–34).

46   It could be argued that 'his' refers not to Jesus but to God, but this seems unlikely. On the one hand, in the phrase, 'for he (αὐτός) will save (σώσει) his people from their sins', the emphatic pronoun αὐτός would refer back to υἱός and Ἰησοῦς in the first half of the verse: 'You will bear a son (υἱόν) and you will call him, "Jesus" (Ἰησοῦν).' On the other hand, when σῴζω refers to acts of power it is unambiguously associated in the

is Jewish, 'his people' would more naturally refer to the Jews. The close proximity of 1.21 and its relation to the genealogy, which deals with Israel's history from Abraham to the Babylonian exile, suggests that the Jewish nation would be in view in 1.21. The double reference to the 'Land of Israel' – an expression used only by Matthew in the NT – in 2.20-21 would also echo 'my people Israel' in 2.6. Further, the literary context of Mic. 5.1 refers to a coming Davidic ruler who will gather together and shepherd the exiles of Israel, and in the literary context of 2 Sam. 5.2 David is commencing to rule as king over 'all the tribes of Israel'. In his appropriation of these texts, Matthew tweaks them to apply them specifically to Jesus; he does not, however, change their basic sense. Thus, while not denying the legitimacy of the inclusion of the Gentiles in the Jesus movement,[47] the focus of Matthew's Shepherd here is the nation of Israel.

This emphasis on the nation of Israel would explain why 2 Sam. 5.2b is inserted into the Mican quote, rather than, say, appending Mic. 5.3, in which the notion of a Davidic 'shepherd' explicitly appears.[48] On the one hand, Mic. 5.3 speaks only of the coming Davidide as shepherding 'his flock'. Matthew's interest in Israel, however, will not allow for so general an identification of the messiah's primary focus; hence, he appends the Samuel text which explicitly spells out the messiah's focus: '[God's] people Israel'.[49] On the other hand, Chae asserts that Mic. 5.1-4 'envisions the extension of [the Davidic Shepherd's] reign beyond Israel and over the nations, a point underscored by the phrase, עַד־אַפְסֵי־אָרֶץ ("to the end of the earth", v. 4b)'.[50] If he is correct, then this broader scope of the recipients of the coming Davidic ruler's shepherding may have contributed to Matthew's omission of what would be the more obvious choice of a

---

Gospel with Jesus (8.25; 9.21, 22; 14.30; 27.40, 42). Moreover, even if God was in view here, at this point in the story, God's people would plainly refer to the Jews and not the 'Church' of Jews and Gentiles.

47   E.g. Mt. 8.5-13; 15.21-28; 28.18-19.

48   Micah 5.3 reads: 'And he shall stand and feed (רעה) his flock in the strength of the LORD, in the majesty of the name of the LORD his God. And they shall live secure, for now he shall be great to the ends of the earth' (NRSV). R. Gundry is correct that 'shepherd' in Mic. 5.3 provides a good linguistic tie-in to the Samuel text (*The Use of the Old Testament in St. Matthew's Gospel with Special Reference to the Messianic Hope*, NTS 18 [Leiden: E. J. Brill, 1967], 92–93), but this link does not explain why Matthew appropriates 2 Sam. 5.2b rather than Mic. 5.3.

49   Soares Prabhu insists that the 2 Samuel insertion is 'not because it speaks about ὁ λαός but because it is a text about David, and so explicitly identifies Jesus as the "son of David" in whom the promises made to David are to be fulfilled' (*Formula*, 266). This understanding of the insertion, however, downplays the intra-textual reference between τὸν λαόν μου in 2.6 and τὸν λαὸν αὐτοῦ in 1.21. ὁ λαός and οἱ ὄχλοι play important roles for Matthew in delineating Jesus' mission and rejection in Israel (see Cousland, *Crowds*). Moreover, 2 Sam. 5.2 can easily function in both ways: it can specifically identify Jesus as locus of God's promise to David as well as establish the mission field for Matthew's messiah.

50   Chae, *Davidic Shepherd*, 177.

'shepherd' text, Mic. 5.3 – i.e. given his appropriation of Mic. 5.1. In other words, while the inclusion of the Gentiles in Jesus' messianic mission has already received some affirmation in the Gospel, Jesus' focus remains God's people, Israel and not the Gentiles. By inserting 2 Sam. 5.2 in place of Mic. 5.3, Matthew supports this pro-Israel point: 'Israel' (2 Sam. 5.2) becomes the explicit target of Jesus' anticipated mission; and furthermore, what would have been an implicit reference to the nations (i.e. 'to the end of the earth' [Mic. 5.3-4]) is omitted.

Thus, Matthew, in interpreting Mic. 5.1 and 2 Sam. 5.2 messianically, maintains the Jewish-national direction of these passages: Jesus is the Davidide from Bethlehem who will shepherd and rule over God's flock in the Land; and he is the Davidic heir who will rule over all Israel upon David's throne in place of Israel's corrupt leaders.[51]

Although the nature of Jesus' mission to Israel will be unpacked in the unfolding of the Gospel, it is nonetheless hinted at in and foreshadowed by the infancy narratives. The close linguistic connection between 2.6b and 1.21b suggests that Jesus' shepherding of God's people will focus on saving them from their sins. Here Davies and Allison represent standard opinion when they remark: 'The Messiah's first task is to save his people from their sins (1:21), not deliver them from political bondage.'[52] While it would clearly be wrong to minimize the moral or religious character of Jesus' mission – especially in light of the tone and plot of the entire story – the political dimension of his mission should not be overlooked for several important reasons.

First, σῴζω ('save') most often refers to the physical rather than moral realm; hence, it typically denotes 'deliverance' from some physical danger or impediment.[53] Although he adopts the moral direction for σῴζω, Hagner still notes: 'The natural expectation regarding the significance of σώσει "will save", would be that it refers to a national-political salvation, involving in particular deliverance from the Roman occupation.'[54] While the explicit mention of 'sins' in relation to 'save' leads commentators to override this

---

51   That only Matthew among New Testament writers uses the designation 'Land of Israel' (in 2.20 and 21), a title which indicates a unified concept of a land that was politically fractured at the time of the Gospel, may, on the one hand, represent another means of emphasizing that the appointed recipients of the messiah's shepherding/rule were the Jewish people, and may, on the other, foreshadow (for Matthew) the future political restoration of the nation.

52   Davies and Allison, *Matthew*, 1.174, 210; cf. R. Gundry, *Matthew: A Commentary on his Handbook for a Mixed Church Under Persecution*, 2nd edn (Grand Rapids: Eerdmans, 1994), 23–24; Charette, *Recompense*, 87, et al.

53   E.g. Matthew's use of σῴζω can be summarized as follows: deliverance from natural dangers (8.25; 14.30), deliverance from severe persecution (10.22; 16.25; 24.13, 22; 27.40, 42aβ, 49), and deliverance from physical ailments (9.21, 22; 27.42aα). Apart from the verse in question, only once does σῴζω denote something other than physical deliverance – in 19.25, where it clearly parallels 'having eternal life'.

54   Hagner, *Matthew*, 1.19.

'natural expectation' for 'save', this type of either/or position should be rejected because this distinction between the religious and political spheres represents a modern convention and did not hold in antiquity.[55] According to the biblical record, political figures like kings could exercise religious authority,[56] and biblical authors also make a direct connection between Israel's sins and their political oppression.[57] Additionally, during the Second Temple period, the priesthood begins to wield political power in increasing measure,[58] and Second Temple authors also link political oppression with Israel's sins.[59] Thus, according to biblical and Second Temple Jewish traditions, Israel's sins had political ramifications: foreign oppression.

A second reason for not overlooking the political dimension to Jesus' mission is because in the narrative 1.21 is followed by the account of Herod.[60] On the one hand, Herod is portrayed as a 'disturbed' monarch who seeks only to preserve power no matter what the cost – hence, the slaughter of the Jewish infants. It is from this cruel reign that God's people Israel need saving. On the other hand, the birth-prophecy of Jesus in Mt. 2.6 reinforces the Davidic ancestry of the messiah first introduced in Matthew's genealogy. Consequently, as the Davidic messiah, the salvation Jesus brings – consonant

---

55   W. Carter correctly observes, 'Matthean scholars, shaped by the contemporary separation of "religion" and "politics" and by their location in a long "spiritualising" (and confessional) tradition of reading Matthew, have avoided "political" interpretations of Jesus' mission to save from sins, preferring "spiritualized" interpretations' ('Matthean Christology in Roman Imperial Key: Matthew 1.1', in *The Gospel of Matthew in its Roman Imperial Context*, ed. J. Riches and D. Sim, JSNTSS 276 [New York: T&T Clark, 2005], 157). As far as Matthew is concerned, Verseput notes, 'There is certainly no attempt upon Matthew's part to distance Jesus from the Davidic hope. Nor does he in any way emphasize a discrepancy between Jesus and the Jews regarding the Davidic agenda' ('Davidic Messiah', 114).

56   David, for example, could wear the priestly ephod, sacrifice burnt offerings on behalf of the nation, and offer the divine blessing (2 Sam. 6.16-19); Solomon, too, could offer the blessing and prayer of dedication for the temple (1 Kgs 8.14-61). Sanders notes that Judaism did not stand as an exception in the ancient world in combining political and religious authority: 'Rulers whom we now think of as generals, conquerors, kings and emperors were also priests. Julius Caesar was a high priest [Pontifex Maximus; e.g. *Antiq.* 14.190]. Alexander the Great, in his triumphant conquest of much of the known world, sacrificed regularly. In Greece and Rome, it is difficult to understand just what a priest was because the 'distinction between civic magistracy and priesthood is elusive' (*Practice and Belief*, 49).

57   According to the Deuteronomic Historian, because the Israelites committed idolatry, God handed them over to their enemies to be plundered; but when his people cried out to him he 'raised up judges, who saved them out of the hands' of those who plundered them (Judg. 2.11-18; cf. 2 Kgs 17.3-20; 24.1-4).

58   The political power of the priesthood eventually culminates in the merging of the offices of high priest, military commander, and governor with Simon Maccabee (142–34 BCE) during the Hasmonaean Dynasty.

59   E.g. *Pss. Sol.* 17.5; 2 Macc. 6.1-16.

60   Verseput speaks of the contrast between Herod and Jesus as creating 'inevitable political implications' ('Davidic Messiah', 102).

with Second Temple Jewish expectation – would entail 'political and national' restoration.[61] A third reason is that in view of how the shepherd metaphor is deployed in the HB,[62] saviour qua ruler – particularly from a first-century Jewish standpoint – would be the expected direction of σῴζω in 1.21, rather than saviour qua 'spiritual' redeemer.

Therefore, in light of these reasons it would be highly unusual for a first-century Jewish reader not to understand salvation from sins as having political ramifications, viz. deliverance from political oppression. This is not to deny the centrality of Jesus' atoning sacrifice on the cross – indeed, the climax of all four Gospels. But to assume a mutual exclusivity or disconnect between the political and religious realms is to run completely foul of Matthew's first-century social context, for even YHWH, according to several HB texts, can simultaneously promise his people 'spiritual' renewal and political deliverance.[63]

Probably the major impediment to acknowledging the political aspect of Jesus' salvation in Matthew is that Jesus never acquires political power (or gives clear evidence of such aspirations), nor was Israel rescued from Roman rule. In what sense, then, could Jesus' salvation have included a political component? While political power is never realized during the days of Jesus' mission to Israel or thereafter, according to Matthew, the full realization of political power in Jesus and Israel's final political deliverance would come at Jesus' Parousia: upon his return with his angels, Jesus will sit as king on his glorious throne and judge 'all the nations' according to how they treated his followers.[64] Matthew sees Jesus as inaugurating God's rule, the kingdom of heaven (4.17), and extending it among Israel (9.35; 11.12; 12.26-29), but not consummating the rule of God's kingdom – of which the restoration of Israel is clearly a part (19.28) – until his return (23.39; 26.29).

Thus, according to the deployment of the shepherd motif in the birth and infancy narratives, a number of characteristics emerge concerning the coming Shepherd. Jesus the Messiah is the Davidic Shepherd. As prophesied by the scriptures, he was born in Bethlehem and he came to replace the Jewish leaders as Israel's Shepherd, a replacement echoed by the wider literary contexts of the 'shepherd' texts of Mic. 5.1 and 2 Sam. 5.2, which Matthew cites here. Since Jesus is the true heir to David's throne, those who occupy positions of leadership over the nation do so illegitimately (as evidenced by their reaction to the news of Jesus' birth).[65] The focus of the messiah's

61   Cf. J. Collins, *The Scepter and the Star: The Messiahs of the Dead Sea Scrolls and Other Ancient Literature*, ABRL (New York: Doubleday, 1995), 49–73.

62   See section 2.2 above.

63   E.g. Jeremiah 30–31 (especially 30.8-9 and 31.31-34); Joel 2.28-32.

64   25.31-46; cf. the more detailed discussion of this pericope in section 4.2.3 below.

65   Given the plot of the story, does Jesus actually replace the Jerusalem leadership? For Matthew he does in two ways. First, although Jesus never wielded any political power, according to Matthew only Jesus possessed the divine right to rule (upon David's throne); hence, of all kings, only Jesus had the authority to announce the coming of and to

shepherding is the Jews and the salvation he offers them is both religious and political, whereby he will rescue the people of God from their sins and the ramifications thereof, and in this way, the shepherd motif conveys definite overtones of Jewish nationalism for Matthew.[66] In saving his people from their sins, the presence and concomitant favour of God is shown to dwell uniquely with them, because Jesus, the one who shepherds Israel, represents Ἐμμανουήλ, 'God with us' (1.23).[67]

4.2.2 *The shepherd's mission: his works of healing*

The infancy traditions lead into the John the Baptist and the temptation narratives (3.1–4.11). Matthew 3.1–4.11 heighten the sense of expectation within Matthew's plot for Israel's salvation,[68] develops further Matthew's Christological portrait,[69] and sets the stage (geographically) for the beginning of Jesus' mission. The first major discourse of the Gospel, the Sermon on the Mount (chs 5–7), represents the consummation of the exodus typology developed in the first four chapters.[70] While the Sermon on the Mount showcases the authority of Jesus' teaching,[71] the so-called Miracle Chapters 8–9 demonstrate the authority of his

inaugurate God's kingdom rule (4.17), on the one hand, and to pronounce/predict divine judgement upon the Jewish leadership – as symbolized by the destruction of the temple (22.1-7; 23.37–24.2), on the other. In this way – i.e. insofar as he acted as God's emissary to inaugurate the kingdom of heaven (which begins with the restoration of Israel) – Jesus replaced Herod (also his successors and Caesar). Second, insofar as the Evangelist depicts Jesus as the authoritative interpreter of Torah, Jesus would be the supreme teacher for Israel, and thus replace the nation's teachers (priests, scribes, and other teachers of the Law; cf. 7.28-29).

66   Willitts argues that 'the political-territorial aspects of the Shepherd-King motif seem to have been intensified by Matthean redaction' (*Shepherd-King*, 114).

67   The placement of the Isa. 7.14 quotation after the significance of Jesus' name rather than after the initial mention of Mary's virginal conception or after Jesus' birth by a virgin, suggests that the emphasis of 'God with us' is the saving activity of YHWH in Jesus. This saving activity represents the establishing of God's rule – the kingdom of heaven – among his people, whereby even demons (as demonstrated by Jesus' exorcisms) no longer have a place to exercise power over the people.

68   The expectation of future salvation (1.21) wrought by the divinely appointed ruler (2.6) is amplified by the coming of John the Baptist: the Baptist comes preaching repentance 'in those days' (3.1a), a phrase closely tied to eschatology in the prophets (e.g. Isa. 4.2; Jer. 30.8; Ezek. 38.10; Hos. 2.16; Joel 3.1; Amos 9.11). Eschatological overtones would resonate in Matthew, especially in light of his citation of Isa. 40.3 in Mt. 3.3.

69   Jesus is featured in interwoven fashion as the Servant of the Lord (3.13-17), the Son of God, and Israel par excellence (3.17–4.11).

70   This typology centres primarily on the implicit parallels Matthew draws between Jesus and Moses in the circumstances of their birth and their respective missions. For a detailed discussion of these parallels, see D. Allison, *The New Moses: A Matthean Typology* (Minneapolis: Fortress Press, 1993).

71   At the conclusion of the Sermon on the Mount, 'the crowds were amazed by [Jesus'] teaching for he was teaching them as one having authority and not as their scribes' (7.28b-29).

deeds.[72] Together these chapters offer a window into Jesus' mission – the things he said and did. Matthew brackets these chapters with summary statements of Jesus' activity in 4.23 and 9.35,[73] the latter of which is explicitly connected to the shepherd motif.

The structure, theme, and function of these chapters have been seriously debated. Davies and Allison note the pattern of their arrangement as three triads: three sets of three miracle stories with each set followed by the words of Jesus.[74] While scholars have considered Christology, geography, discipleship, or the like to be the key to unlocking the structure of the Miracle Chapters,[75] the dominant (and multi-faceted) feature of these chapters would seem to be Jesus' mission to Israel. That is, the central theme of these chapters is missional – which would encompass Christology and discipleship.[76] The thrust of the 'prologue' (chs 1–4) is Christological; the Sermon on the Mount (chs 5–7) focuses on discipleship; the latter portion of the Gospel (chs 10–20), while continuing to possess Christological elements, showcases Jesus' teaching. But here in the Miracle Chapters, it is not so much who Jesus is (although this is not ignored), nor is it what Jesus teaches (although that, too, is included); rather, the focus of the Miracle Chapters is what Jesus does in Israel, i.e. his mission; hence, these chapters convey Matthew's concern for Jewish-national restoration.[77] While Jesus clearly evangelizes the villages of Galilee (8.5, 28; 9.1; cf. 4.23), the particular focus of the Miracle Chapters is the Land of Israel, as suggested by the inclusio, ἐν τῷ Ἰσραήλ ('in Israel'), in

---

72   After the healing of the paralytic, for example, the Evangelist states, 'the crowds were awestruck and glorified God who gave such authority to people' (9.8, cf. 9.33).

73   Matthew 4.23 (part of a more detailed summary extending to 4.25) reads: 'And he went around all of Galilee, teaching in their synagogues and preaching the gospel of the kingdom and healing every disease and every sickness among the people.' Matthew 9.35 states, 'And Jesus went around all the cities and villages, teaching in their synagogues and preaching the gospel of the kingdom and healing every disease and every sickness.' S. McKnight speaks of this inclusio as uniting the Sermon on the Mount and the Miracle Chapters ('New Shepherds for Israel: An Historical and Critical Study of Matthew 9.34–11.1' [PhD dissertation, Nottingham University, 1986], 14–15).

74   The triads of miracle stories and words of Jesus consist of 8.2-17 and 8.18-22; 8.23–9.8 and 9.9-17; 9.18-34 and 9.35-38. Davies and Allison note that while there are actually ten miracles, 'the two miracles in 9:18-26 are part of one indissoluble unit; hence there are only nine miracle *stories*' (*Matthew*, 1.67, their emphasis). For a similar view of a triadic composition of the Miracle Chapters, see B. Drewes, 'The Composition of Matthew 8–9', *SEAJT* 12 (1971): 92–101.

75   See the discussion of Kingsbury, 'Observations', 559–62.

76   In the Markan parallel to the material in the Miracle Chapters (viz. Mk 1.29–5.43), there is a much heavier dose of Christology and of Jesus' teaching than in Matthew.

77   The 'shepherd'-less shepherd imagery of 10.6 and 15.24 ('the lost sheep of the house of Israel') echoes this concern. These texts deal with the exclusivity of the disciples' and Jesus' missions, respectively. In 10.6, Jesus sends his disciples to the Jewish nation – 'the lost sheep of the house of Israel' – as opposed to sending them to the Gentiles or the Samaritans. In 15.24, in response to a Gentile woman's request for healing, Jesus states that he was sent only to the Jewish nation – 'the lost sheep of the house of Israel' – which is why he is reticent to grant her request.

8.10b and 9.33b.[78] The other thrust of these chapters would seem to be how the Jews should respond to Jesus' mission.[79] Since the former focus, i.e. Jesus' deeds, has the most relevance for the shepherd motif, the ensuing discussion shall concentrate on it rather than on the responses to Jesus' mission.

There are several distinguishing features of Jesus' mission to Israel according to the Miracle Chapters. First, Jesus reaches out to Israel with divine authority. Matthew previously noted at the conclusion to the Sermon on the Mount that the crowds recognized the authority of Jesus' teaching (7.28-29). Now he puts the authority of Jesus' deeds on display. In seeking the healing of his servant, the Roman centurion acknowledges Jesus' authority:

> But only speak a word and my servant will be healed; for I, too, am a man under authority, having soldiers under me. And I say to this one, 'Go' and he goes; and to another, 'Come' and he comes; and to my servant, 'Do this', and he does it.
>
> (8.8b-9)[80]

The centurion compares Jesus' position to his own: soldiers obey him because he is invested with the authority of Caesar: to defy him is to defy Rome; likewise, the centurion recognizes that Jesus possesses special authority such that he can heal with a single word. Matthew notes how Jesus can 'cast out spirits with a word' (8.16),[81] and calm a violent storm with words of rebuke (8.26-27). Consequently, after the healing of the paralytic, the crowds testify of the authority given to Jesus by God: 'When the crowds saw, they were afraid and they glorified the God who gives such authority to people' (9.8).

When the paralytic is brought to Jesus for healing, Jesus pronounces, 'your sins (ἁμαρτίαι) are forgiven' (9.2b, cf. 9.5a, 6a). Ἁμαρτία occurs seven times in Matthew, three times in this story of the paralytic's healing. The term first appears in the infancy narrative: '[Jesus] will save his people from their sins' (1.21), a verse which foreshadows the direction of the salvation Jesus will offer Israel. In the second use of the term, the inhabitants of Jerusalem and Judaea go out to John the Baptist to receive his baptism by 'confessing their sins' (3.6b). But as opposed to his Markan source, which records that

---

78   There is no such geographical delimitation in his Markan source (6.7-13).

79   This seems to be the common thrust of the words of Jesus appended to each set of miracle stories. Luz correctly recognizes that Matthew has a specific aim in mind for the Miracle Chapters, represented in 9.33-34: 'the final reaction of the people and the Pharisees ... to Jesus' miracles in Israel in general' (*Studies*, 228).

80   The story of the healing of the centurion's slave is absent in Mark and part of the Q tradition.

81   The authority required to cast out evil spirits is made explicit in 10.1: Jesus gathers his disciples together before sending them out and 'gives them authority over unclean spirits in order to cast them out'.

John, in preparing the way for Jesus, preached a 'baptism for the forgiveness of sins' (Mk 1.4b), Matthew (unlike Luke [3.3], who follows Mark) omits this phrase. For Matthew, only 'the Son of Man has authority on earth to forgive sins' (9.6a).

In light of Mt. 1.21, this joining together of physical healing and the forgiveness of sins in the healing of the paralytic demonstrates that Matthew considered Jesus' works of healing to be an intrinsic part of the salvation Jesus would bring to his people Israel,[82] since for the Evangelist, like the biblical authors before him, sin's far-reaching effects extend even into the physical realm. According to the Triple Tradition, Jesus viewed his acts of healing in terms of plundering Satan's house. Against the charge that he performed exorcisms through Satan's power, Jesus countered:

> [I]f Satan casts out Satan, he is divided against himself; how therefore will his kingdom stand? ... But if by the Spirit of God I cast out demons then the kingdom of God has come upon you. Or how can someone enter the strong person's house and take away his property unless he first binds the strong person? Then he will plunder (διαρπάσει)[83] his house.
>
>   (Mt. 12.26, 28-29; cf. Mk 3.26-27; Lk. 11.18, 20-22)[84]

---

82   Davies and Allison acknowledge, 'Matthew thought that Jesus saved his people from their sins in a variety of ways' (*Matthew*, 1.210).

83   Of its uses in the LXX, διαρπάζω can refer to what happened to Israel in exile: it was 'plundered' by its oppressors, e.g. Deut. 28.29; Ezek. 7.21 and 2 Kgs 17.20, the latter of which gives the reason for the Assyrian exile: because God was angry with Israel over their idolatry: 'The Lord rejected all the descendants of Israel; he punished them and gave them into the hand of plunderers (διαρπαζόντων), until he had banished them from his presence' (NRSV). Similarly, in a psalm recognized to have historical references to the desecration of Jerusalem by Pompey, the author of *Psalms of Solomon* 8 writes, 'They [= the Romans] stole (διηρπάζοσαν) from the sanctuary of God as if there were no redeeming heir' (8.11). Based on his genealogy, it is possible that Matthew perceived his nation to be in exile until the birth of Jesus: the Davidic line resided there 'until the coming of Christ' (1.17b). Thus, Jesus' mission could be conceived as delivering his people from the ravages of exile.

84   Matthew structures his triads of miracles stories and alters Mark in such a way as to elevate the significance of Jesus' exorcisms within the Miracle Chapters. On the one hand, each triad contains an exorcism: 8.16-17, 8.28-34, and 9.32-34, and the centre of the Miracle Chapters is the exorcism of the Gadarene demoniacs. On the other hand, Matthew emphasizes the demonic aspect of Jesus' healings in his summary statement (8.16-17) compared to Mark (1.32-34): only the demonized are brought to Jesus in Matthew vs the demonized and the sick in Mark; Jesus casts out spirits with a single word and heals in Matthew, compared to healing and casting out demons in Mark (i.e. exorcism then healing vs healing then exorcism); also, whereas the legion of demons merely 'drowns' in the sea in Mark (5.13), they actually 'perish' in the waters in Matthew (8.32). Although Drewes ('Composition') may slightly overstate his case (since exorcism is slightly more prevalent in Mark on the whole), this emphasis on exorcism in the Miracle Chapters material suggests that Matthew considered the sheep of Israel as demonically oppressed and in need of deliverance.

Of all the Evangelists, Matthew most unambiguously connects Israel's state of plunder by Satan[85] with Jesus' therapeutic activity. The connection between Israel's plundered state and Jesus' deeds of healing is made in three ways. First, the centre of this 'power source' controversy is Jesus' identity as the Son of David, which is Matthew's favourite title for Jesus' healing activity.[86] Second, in taking up Mk 6.34, Matthew considers the shepherd-less crowds as 'harassed and downcast (ἐρριμμένοι)', with the latter term being used one other time by Matthew to describe the 'lame, crippled, blind and dumb', who were placed at Jesus' feet to be healed by him (15.30). Third, because of Israel's 'harassed and downcast' state, Jesus commissions the Twelve to perform works of exorcism and healing, in an attempt to rectify their situation (9.36–10.8). Thus, when Jesus 'saves his people from their sins', an integral component of Israel's salvation is their deliverance from physical illness and satanic oppression.[87] The Miracle Chapters, then, demonstrate that the divine authority that Jesus exercised in healing Israel's sick represented expressions of him 'saving his people from [the ramifications of] their sins', viz. sickness and oppression.[88]

In addition to divine authority, Jesus' mission to Israel is characterized, second, by compassion.[89] A number of recipients of his healing would have

85   See Mt. 4.8-9: the kingdoms of the world belong to Satan and he can give them to whomever he desires.

86   See, for example, Gibbs, 'Purpose and Pattern', Burger, *Davidssohn*, 71–106, Kingsbury, 'Son of David', D. Duling, 'The Therapeutic Son of David: An Element in Matthew's Christological Apologetic', *NTS* 24 (1977): 392–410, and Novakovic, *Messiah*.

87   According to Carter (et al.), the deliverance from physical sickness and oppression would have been part of the political deliverance Jesus' initiated, viz. deliverance from the political ramifications of their sins. For Carter (*Empire*, 71), one of the consequences of Roman oppression was sickness, brought on and compounded by the squalor and harsh conditions the Jews experienced under Roman rule; cf. the hopeless picture R. Stark paints of life in a Graeco-Roman city in Stark, 'Antioch as the Social Situation for Matthew's Gospel', in *Social History of the Matthean Community: Cross-Disciplinary Approaches*, ed. D. Balch (Minneapolis: Fortress Press, 1991), 189–210. Not all scholars, however, agree with this portrait of severe oppression in Roman Galilee, e.g. M. Jensen, *Herod Antipas in Galilee: The Literary and Archaeological Sources on the Reign of Herod Antipas and its Socio-economic Impact on Galilee*, WUNT 2/215 (Tübingen: Mohr Seibeck, 2006).

88   While Jesus' healings deal with the consequences of Israel's sins, Matthew makes clear in the passion narrative (the seventh and final occurrence of ἁμαρτία) that Jesus' sacrificial death on the cross dealt with the problem of sin itself: 'for this is the my blood of the covenant which is about to be poured out for the forgiveness of sins' (26.28). Martin writes, 'The image of the shepherd which is evoked by the citation of Isa 53.4 in Matt 8:17 and which surfaces in the passion narrative with texts drawn from Dt-Zech. is one subtle way in which Matt connects the healings worked by Jesus and the saving action of the cross' ('Image', 277).

89   A related point is made by the parable of the lost sheep in Mt. 18.12–14: the well-being of Jesus' followers is of such grave importance that even if one should stray,

lived within the margins of first-century Jewish society: a leper, a Gentile slave, violent demoniacs, and a haemorrhaging woman.[90] Hence, in reaching out to the fringes of his society (something for which he incurred the disdain of the religious elite [9.10-11]), Jesus displays compassion. In approaching Jesus for healing, the leper assumes that Jesus is able to do it; he is merely uncertain if he is willing to do so. Jesus not only affirms his willingness, but rather than heal him with a spoken word (as he does with others elsewhere, e.g. 8.13; 9.6, 33), he cures him through the touch of the hand (8.3), thereby risking ostracism because of his physical contact with a ritually impure leper.[91] Jesus' compassion is also observed in the final healing story of the Miracle Chapters, where two blind men cry out to him, 'Have mercy on us, Son of David' (9.27b). Although Jesus' compassionate intervention is not limited to acts of healing,[92] it is only when healing is sought that 'mercy' is specifically requested. If, in the scriptures, YHWH shows his mercy by his saving acts,[93] then it is through the works of healing of 'Emmanuel' that YHWH, once again, demonstrates his mercy to his people.

Third, Jesus' mission to Israel represents the fulfilment of Israel's scriptures. At the conclusion of the first triad of healing stories, Matthew offers a brief summary of Jesus' healing activity, stating that he did these things 'in order to fulfil the word spoken through Isaiah the prophet saying, 'He took away our sickness and our diseases he carried away' (8.17). Just as the details of Jesus' birth and infancy fulfilled Israel's scriptures,[94] his acts of healing are viewed in the same way.

Jesus leaves the flock to recover it because it is not the Father's will that any of his followers turn away from following him. In view of their significance to God, disciples must therefore consider each other as valuable and offer one another the esteem that God has for each of them.

90   Kingsbury describes the recipients of Jesus' healings as 'no-accounts': 'the healing-activity of Jesus, Son of David ... is related to persons who in the eyes of contemporary society count for nothing' ('Son of David', 598).

91   There are likely two reasons for Matthew omitting Mark's use of σπλαγχνίζομαι ('to have compassion') for Jesus here. On the one hand, Matthew tends to shorten Mark's stories (Davies and Allison, *Matthew*, 1.103–106). On the other hand, Jesus' compassion for the leper would be self-evident and need not be explicitly stated: why else would Jesus touch a leper but for compassionate grounds? σπλαγχνίζομαι, however, does explicitly appear at the end of the Miracle Chapters: when Jesus sees the harassed and helpless multitude, he feels compassion for them (9.36).

92   Jesus miraculously intervenes in the lives of people by saving them from the violence of nature (8.23-27; 14.27-33), by feeding them (14.15-21; 15.32-39), and even by providing money for tax relief (17.24-27). In addition to these types of intervention, children are brought to him to receive his blessing (19.13-15).

93   See D. Williams, 'Mercy', *DJG*, 541-42.

94   E.g. his identity (1.22-23; cf. Isa. 7.14), his birthplace (2.5-6; cf. Mic. 5.1), his stay in Egypt (2.14-15; cf. Hos. 11.1), his dwelling in Nazareth (2.22-23 [according to 'the prophets']), and his activity in Capernaum (4.12-17; cf. Isa. 9.1-2).

The notion of a healing messiah does not seem to be a widely recognized feature of first-century messianic expectation.[95] Matthew obviously knew this and sought to emphasize this therapeutic element in the commission of the disciples.[96] Moreover, he grounds this rather unexpected element of Jesus' messianic mission in Israel's scriptures. Matthew implicitly restates this link between Jesus' acts of healing and the fulfilment of Israel's scriptures at the end of the Miracle Chapters.[97] After bracketing off the Miracle Chapters with a second summary statement of Jesus' mission (9.35), he writes that when Jesus saw the crowds, he 'felt compassion for them because they were harassed and downcast just like sheep not having a shepherd' (v. 36).[98]

Besides Ezek. 34.5 ('they were scattered because there was no shepherd'), the strongest contender for a possible allusion in Mt. 9.36 is Num. 27.17 ('so the Lord's people will not be like sheep without a shepherd').[99] While 9.36 is much closer to Num. 27.17 linguistically, an allusion to

95   J. Charlesworth correctly cautions that 'Early Jewish literature cannot be mined to produce a checklist of what the Messiah shall do' ('From Messianology to Christology: Problems and Prospects', in *The Messiah: Developments in Earliest Judaism and Christianity*, ed. J. Charlesworth [Minneapolis: Fortress Press, 1992], 6). Even putting Charlesworth's comment aside, of all of the numerous passages in the HB that are given a messianic interpretation by later Jewish and CB authors, only a few mention healing in connection with a messianic figure: Isa. 53.4-5; 61.1 and Ezekiel 34. In Second Temple Judaism, healing is not one of the roles assigned to the Son of David in *Psalms of Solomon* 17.

96   Healing has a much more prominent place in Mt. 10.1-15 than in the parallel of Mk 6.7–13: the Missionary Discourse is syntactically linked to the summary healing statement of 9.35, which itself is connected with the earlier healing narratives of the Miracle Chapters; and healing is referred to in 10.1 and 10.8 (where it is part of Jesus' charge to his disciples). By contrast, Mark's 'discourse' is linked to a summary statement in 6.6b, which condenses Jesus' mission to teaching with no mention of healing; while there is a description of the disciples healing, there is no charge to them to heal (unlike in Matthew); and when the disciples return from their expedition, they report to Jesus what they did 'and what they taught' (6.30) – teaching is underlined.

97   Cf. Mt. 11.5: in response to a doubting John the Baptist's query regarding Jesus' messianic identity, Jesus answers John by pointing him to his therapeutic acts, alluding to Isaianic passages that speak of healing.

98   D. Bauer notes the syntactical connection between 9.36 and 9.35: 'Matthew 9:36 is linked to 9:35 by means of the connective "and" (δέ) and by the circumstance that the subject (Jesus) is not expressly named in v. 36; the reader is forced to go back to the reference to Jesus in 9:35a. The reference to the crowds in 9:36 also points back to the mention of the crowds in 9:33' (*The Structure of Matthew's Gospel: A Study in Literary Design*, JSNTS 31 [Sheffield: Almond, 1988], 90).

99   Other possibilities include 1 Kgs 22.17/2 Chron. 18.16 and Zech. 10.2. First Kings 22.17/2 Chron. 18.16 can be ruled out, however, because in these passages, Israel is not without a shepherd. The phrase in Kings/Chronicles means that they are about to become shepherd-less. Zechariah 10.2 presents a closer contextual parallel than 1 Kgs 22.17/2 Chron. 18.16 and may possibly be in view; however, on the strength of other parallels to Ezekiel 34 (including the repetition of 'lost') and the lack of any such parallels in Zechariah 10, it would seem better to exclude Zechariah 10 from consideration as well; cf. Ham, *Coming King*, 86–87.

Ezek. 34.5 should not be ruled out for the following reasons. First, and perhaps most importantly, the literary context of the Numbers passage contradicts Matthew's meaning of the phrase, whereas the context of Ezekiel 34 fully aligns with it. In Numbers, Israel was far from shepherd-less: they had been led by Moses and were about to be led by Joshua – who was not succeeding an evil shepherd but one of the most central figures in Israel's history.[100] But Matthew's appropriation of 'sheep without a shepherd' is meant to convey Israel's terrible plight and what is needed to bring about its restoration – as evidenced by the mission of the Twelve (9.36–10.8). This appropriation closely lines up with the direction of Ezekiel 34.

Also there are three contextual parallels between Matthew and Ezekiel 34: Ezekiel's evil, self-absorbed, and neglectful shepherds find their match in the religious leaders, whom Matthew depicts as neglecting the outcasts (9.10-13) and being without compassion (12.7, 10); the exilic plight of Ezekiel's people (resulting from poor shepherding) that makes them the victims of slavery and oppression is paralleled by Israel's plunder by Satan (as evidenced by their sicknesses and demonization), whom Jesus plunders through his acts of healing (12.24-29, 43-45); and just as a unique relationship exists between YHWH and the Davidic shepherd whereby YHWH shepherds his people directly through the agency of his shepherd, so Matthew portrays Jesus as having a special relationship with God (1.18-23; 22.41-46).[101]

Additionally (and argued below), this verse should be taken with the Son of David title and the related controversy in 9.27-34: Matthew presents Jesus, the 'Davidic Shepherd' (2.6), as doing what Israel's shepherds had failed to do, idealized by the Evangelist in works of healing and exorcism.[102] Further, there is an important verbal parallel between Matthew's references to Israel being 'lost' ($\dot{\alpha}\pi o\lambda\omega\lambda\acute{o}\varsigma$) in the closely connected verse 10.6,[103] and $\dot{\alpha}\pi o\lambda\omega\lambda\acute{o}\varsigma$ in Ezek. 34.4 and 16 [LXX], referring to Israel.[104]

Last, there is an additional parallel between Matthew's presentation of Jesus in the Miracle Chapters in particular (and the entire Gospel, generally) and Ezekiel 34, viz. overt shepherding imagery.[105] According to Ezekiel, as

---

100   Cf. Deut. 34.10-11.

101   For a detailed discussion of parallels between Matthew and Ezekiel 34, see W. Baxter, 'Healing and the "Son of David": Matthew's Warrant', *NovT* 48/1 (2006): 36–50.

102   The only occurrence in the HB of a shepherding Davidide where 'David' is explicitly mentioned as 'shepherding' Israel is in Ezek. 34.23. Other prophecies speak either of a coming Davidic figure without invoking shepherding imagery, or of YHWH providing shepherds in the future but without explicitly linking them to 'David'.

103   Cf. 15.24, where $\dot{\alpha}\pi o\lambda\omega\lambda\acute{o}\varsigma$ occurs in relation to the Son of David title.

104   The only other occurrence of $\dot{\alpha}\pi o\lambda\omega\lambda\acute{o}\varsigma$ in the LXX is in Jer. 27.6 (MT 50.6) which, although it perhaps presents a close parallel to Mt. 10.6, should be excluded as an allusion here because the term appears twice in Ezekiel 34, which is clearly already in Matthew's sights; cf. Gundry, *Use of the OT*, 135.

105   Shepherding imagery is by no means confined to the Miracle Chapters. The promise is given in Ezekiel: 'In a good pasture [YHWH] will shepherd [his flock] ... they will lie down in good pasture and in fat pasture they will feed on the mountains of Israel.

Israel's true shepherd YHWH would do what Israel's shepherds had not done, viz. heal the sick, care for the marginalized, and deliver the flock from its bondage. These activities are witnessed in the Miracle Chapters: Jesus heals the sick, reaching out even to the outcasts and to those living on the social fringes of his society, and he delivers his people Israel from Satan's power. These are deeds that the Jewish leaders (i.e. Israel's shepherds) failed to do, causing Jesus to send out his disciples to extend his shepherding mission (9.36–10.8). In view of all this evidence, then, it would seem that the primary allusion in Mt. 9.36 is to Ezek. 34.5 (although not to the complete exclusion of a secondary/minor allusion to Num. 27.17).[106]

How does Matthew's appropriation of Ezek. 34.5 compare with the text as it appears in Ezekiel? In Ezekiel's prophecy the idea of sheep without a shepherd refers to the exilic state of the sheep: on account of their shepherds, the people of Israel found themselves weak, sick, injured, and lost, victims of foreign oppression. While the people had shepherds, because these shepherds had neglected them and had only sought their own good, the nation looked as if they lacked shepherds. Consequently, YHWH promised to gather his scattered sheep and tend them faithfully through the agency of his 'servant David'. This sense of the passage carries over into the Gospel. According to Matthew, Israel's masses live in a sick and harassed condition on account of the neglect of their shepherds.[107] Consequently, Jesus, who had been filling this void in leadership by his deeds of healing, commissions his disciples to continue his shepherding mission to Israel. Thus, there is a close correspondence between the appalling state of God's sheep (oppression), the cause of this state (poor leadership and sin), and its remedy: YHWH's deliverance.

The primary difference between Ezek. 34.5 and Matthew's deployment of it resides in the manner in which Israel's corrupt leadership is replaced. For Ezekiel, both YHWH and his chosen servant David shepherd Israel. For Matthew, YHWH appoints Jesus to shepherd Israel, thus fulfilling the role of the Davidic Shepherd of Ezekiel 34. But Jesus, in turn, commissions his disciples to continue shepherding Israel. Thus, within the parallel, Jesus would correspond both to the Davidic shepherd, insofar as he has been

---

I myself will shepherd my sheep and I myself will cause them to lie down' (34.14-15). For Matthew, the idealization of this scene takes place in the second feeding miracle (15.32-39): the setting for the second miraculous feed is a mountain in Israel (15.29) and there Jesus orders the crowds to lie down on the ground in preparation for the meal. While Heil attempts to link the first feeding miracle (14.14-21) to Ezekiel 34 ('Ezekiel 34', 703), this seems unlikely because of the different setting for the miracle: the first feed takes place in the desert (ἔρημος [14.13, 15]) rather than on a mountain. It is more probable that Mosaic imagery is at work in the first feeding rather than shepherding imagery.

106   Cf. Willitts, *Shepherd-King*, 122–23, who thinks along similar lines.

107   These shepherds have already been depicted in the infancy narrative as being more concerned about maintaining their own positions of power (which were threatened by the newborn king) than about witnessing and receiving the birth of the promised messiah, as the Magi did.

chosen by God to shepherd Israel, and to YHWH, insofar as he appoints the Twelve to shepherd Israel as an extension of his own mission.[108]

Fourth, not only does Jesus' therapeutic mission to Israel represent the fulfilment of Israel's scriptures, the allusion to Ezek. 34.5 (unlike the citation of Isa. 53.4 in Mt. 8.17) serves to accentuate the need for new leadership – which Jesus satisfies – and the replacement of Israel's failed leadership with the disciples.[109] The differences with the appropriation of the shepherd text in the Markan parallel demonstrate this. When Jesus notices the shepherd-less crowds in Mark, he is in the wilderness. In Matthew, however, the crowds are those Jesus encountered while travelling throughout the cities and villages of Galilee (9.35),[110] making it plain that the locus of the Davidic Shepherd's mission is the Land of Israel.[111] Mark records that Jesus saw the crowds and felt compassion for them 'because they were like sheep not having a shepherd' (6.34b). In Matthew, Jesus' compassion is aroused for the crowds because 'they were harassed and downcast like sheep not having a shepherd' (9.36b). For Matthew, it is not simply that Israel is (de facto) leaderless – i.e. because of the poor shepherding of their leaders; rather, he underlines the ensuing state that results from this failed leadership: the people are 'harassed and downcast (ἐρριμμένοι)'.[112] Consequently, although Jesus has been filling this void through his healing activity, he appoints his disciples to continue his mission to and leadership of Israel.[113]

Whereas in Mark Jesus' compassion compels him to teach the people (and eventually feed them miraculously in the wilderness), in Matthew he responds differently. Because of the crowds' afflicted state, Jesus feels compassion for them and commissions his twelve disciples to perform

108   Cf. Chae's 'two shepherds schema': YHWH (and Jesus) functions as the escha-tological shepherd, and the coming Davidide (and Jesus and his disciples) functions as the Davidic shepherd-appointee (*Davidic Shepherd*, 380–85, 92).

109   Cf. Mt. 19.28.

110   While 9.35 speaks of 'all the cities and villages' without specific geographi-cal details, these details would doubtless be filled in by the front end of the inclusio in 4.23-25, viz. Jesus travelled throughout Galilee, and crowds from Galilee, the Decapolis, Jerusalem, Judaea, and beyond the Jordan followed him as he went about.

111   Cf. Mt. 10.5b-6: 'In the way of the Gentiles do not go and any city of the Samaritans do not enter; but go, rather, to the lost sheep of the house of Israel.'

112   Cf. 15.30, the other use ῥίπτω to describe people: the crowds come with their lame, crippled, blind, and dumb and cast (ῥίπτω) them at Jesus' feet to be healed.

113   The manner in which Matthew's arranges Mark's miracle stories (in Mark 2–5) to compose the Miracle Chapters is noteworthy. In Mark 2–5, after Jesus appoints the Twelve, he still performs miracles: the stilling of the storm, the Garasene exorcism, the healing of the haemorrhaging woman and the raising of Jairus's daughter. In Matthew, however – insofar as Miracle Chapters are concerned – all of Jesus' miracles come prior to the appointment of the Twelve (including the four just listed from Mark), after which, the disciples are commanded to carry on Jesus' miracle-laden mission. Thus, there is more of a sense in Matthew than in Mark of the disciples taking up or completing Jesus' shepherding of Israel.

exorcisms and to heal illnesses (10.1),[114] sending them out exclusively to the 'lost sheep of the house of Israel' (10.6), and telling them to 'heal those who are sick, raise the dead, cleanse lepers, cast out demons' (10.8) – the very things Jesus has already done in the Miracle Chapters.[115] Although Jesus commissions his disciples to extend his work of shepherding Israel (10.1-6), Matthew clearly subordinates their mission to that of Jesus.[116] While they receive instruction to perform the (shepherding) works Jesus has been doing (as depicted in the Miracle Chapters),[117] nowhere does Matthew call the disciples 'shepherds' or even explicitly associate the verb ποιμαίνω with them. In fact, Jesus sends them out, not as shepherds per se, but as 'sheep in the midst of wolves' (10.16aβ). Hence for Matthew, unlike his contemporaries[118] – Christ-believing or otherwise – Jesus is uniquely the Shepherd of God's people Israel.[119]

---

114   Mark separates this commissioning of the Twelve in 6.7-13 and the shepherd-less sheep observation by the retrospective interlude concerning John the Baptist's execution in 6.14-32. Matthew brings them together thereby linking concern for leaders to his shepherd motif.

115   Here again, whereas in Mark Jesus' works of healing – particularly those corresponding to Matthew's final triad of healing stories in Mk 5.21-43 – are divorced from the shepherd metaphor in Mk 6.34, Matthew brings them together. While teaching is a part of Jesus' and his disciples' mission (Mt. 9.35a and 10.7, respectively), it is subordinate in the Miracle Chapters to healing, contra W. Tooley, 'The Shepherd and Sheep Image in the Teaching of Jesus', *NovT* 7 (1964), 15–16.

116   This Matthean emphasis on leadership distinguishes itself from the Markan parallel of Mk 6.7-13: the list of the names of the disciples is detached from the commissioning of the disciples, occurring earlier in the narrative in 3.13-19 (Luke follows Mark here). The list serves to emphasize their appointment as the Twelve (ἐποίησεν δώ δεκα ['he appointed twelve'] occurs twice [vv. 14a, 16a], contra Matthew, where it does not appear). For Matthew, however, the list of names underscores the disciples' mission to Israel: in contrast to Mark, the disciples are designated ἀπόστολοι ('apostles', literally 'sent-ones') and this list of people is 'sent out' (ἀποστέλλω; again unlike Mark) to the lost sheep of Israel.

117   Although Matthew clearly presupposes that the disciples can perform works of healing and exorcism, he never actually presents them as doing so, unlike Mark (6.13) and Luke (9.49; 10.17; cf. the book of Acts), and even describes on one occasion their inability to do so (17.14-20); cf. J. P. Heil, 'Significant Aspects of the Healing Miracles in Matthew', *CBQ* 41 (1979), 285.

118   As already observed in section 3.4.3 above, ποιμαίνω is explicitly associated with assembly leaders in Acts 20.28; Jude 12; Eph. 4.11; Jn 21.15–17; 1 Pet. 5.1-4; Herm. *Sim.* 108.5b-6.

119   This distinction that Matthew seems to make between Jesus as Israel's 'Shepherd' and the disciples who function as shepherds of Israel but are not called 'shepherds' finds a parallel in the Johannine corpus. That Christ-believers are υἱοί ('sons') of God cannot be disputed (e.g. Rom. 8.14, 19; Gal. 3.26); yet in the Johannine literature, only Jesus is explicitly called God's υἱός ('son' [Jn 1.34, 49; 5.25; 10.36; 11.4, 27; 19.7; 20.31; 1 Jn 3.8; 4.15; 5.5, 10, 12, 13, 20; Rev. 2.18]) – Christ-believers are never υἱοί but always τέκνα ('children') of God (Jn 1.12; 11.52; 1 Jn 3.1, 2, 10; 5.2). Thus, although Christ-believers would surely be υἱοί, the Johannine authors reserve this term for Jesus.

Additionally, Matthew has already foreshadowed an intended comparison between Jesus' deeds of shepherding and those of the Jewish leaders by the crowds' response to Jesus' teaching in the Sermon on the Mount, which represents an expansion of the first part of the summary description of Jesus' mission in 4.23, viz. his teaching. At the conclusion of the Sermon Matthew writes, 'And so it happened, when Jesus finished these words, the crowds were amazed at his teaching, for he was teaching them as one having authority and not as their scribes' (7.28-29). The point is not simply that Jesus taught with authority, but that in so doing, he differentiated himself from the scribes/teachers of the people. The comparison here between Jesus and the Jewish leaders is explicit. If, as has been widely recognized, the Miracle Chapters represent the second part of the summary in 4.23 (i.e. his works of healing), then although the comparison between Jesus' deeds and those of the nation's leaders is not as explicit as it is at the conclusion of the Sermon on the Mount, it would nonetheless be presupposed. And indeed, this shepherding comparison would be implicit in the background of Ezekiel 34, to which the Evangelist alludes at the end of the Miracle Chapters.

Finally, Matthew characterizes Jesus' mission to Israel in the Miracle Chapters as Davidic: Jesus' therapeutic deeds represent the acts of the Son of David. Matthew reintroduces the Son of David title towards the close of the Miracle Chapters in the account of the healing of the two blind men (9.27-31) and this serves to connect the 'Son of David' with Israel's 'Shepherd'.[120] Although this connection is only implied here, it becomes more explicit in the linguistically parallel pericope, 12.22-24, where, after Jesus heals a blind and dumb demoniac, the crowds ask, 'This is not the Son of David, is it?', to which the Pharisees respond by attributing Jesus' powers of healing and exorcism to Beelzebul, the ruler of the demons. Jesus' acts of healing, then, which comprise an important part of his shepherding of Israel, should be viewed in the Miracle Chapters in light of his identity as the Son of David. The reason this connection between the 'Son of David' and Israel's 'Shepherd' is merely implied in the Miracle Chapters, rather than explicit as it is in ch. 12, likely lies in their respective thrusts. The central theme of the Miracle Chapters is Jesus' mission to Israel. That is, the major thrust of the Miracle Chapters (as stated earlier) is missional: they offer a window into what Jesus does in Israel – i.e. his mission and how the Jews should respond it.[121] In chapter 12, however, the thrust of the passage is

120   Similarly, Verseput writes that 'the messianic character of the whole [section of chs 8–9] is placed into a distinctly Davidic garb by the final two pericopae (9:27-43)' ('Davidic Messiah', 111). Certainly if Martin is correct that 'an image may be the bearer of a theme and may become the vehicle by which two themes interpenetrate and mutually modify one another' ('Image', 264), then the audience would make this connection between the 'Son of David' and Israel's Shepherd more readily.

121   According to the example of the recipients of Jesus' healing in the Miracle Chapters, and the words of Jesus at the end of each triad of miracle stories, the Jews, in response to Jesus' mission in Israel, should respond with faith in Jesus (8.10; 9.2, 22, 29),

far more Christological: hence, the explicit mention of this fourth of four Christological titles (Son of Man [12.8], Lord of the Sabbath [12.8], Servant of the Lord [12.18], and Son of David [12.23]).

The implications of this Matthean connection between the shepherd motif and the Son of David title would be twofold. On the one hand, while the genealogy and infancy narratives make it clear that the Davidic Shepherd is a royal figure – the rightful heir to David's throne – the nature of his rule or shepherding includes works of healing. Thus, since Jesus' healing activity is most clearly associated with the Son of David title, for Matthew the Davidic shepherd is a healer who saves his people from their sins through his acts of healing.[122] On the other hand, this connection helps establish the important place Ezekiel 34 had for Matthew. Although explicit citations of the shepherd motif come from other parts of the HB (viz. 2 Sam. 5.2 in Mt. 2.6 and Zech. 13.7 in 26.31) and references to Ezekiel 34 are confined to allusions, the 'Son of David' motif would augment and extend the shepherd motif in the narrative. That is to say, insofar as Matthew presents Jesus as the therapeutic Son of David, he presents him as Israel's Davidic Shepherd.

By bringing into clearer focus the nature of Jesus' messianic mission to Israel, Matthew's deployment of the shepherd motif in the Miracle Chapters, similar to its use in the Gospel's prologue, conveys pronounced hopes for Jewish-national restoration, as Willitts comments, '[T]he Shepherd-King motif invoked by Matthew by means of the allusion contains real political substance.'[123] As the prophesied Davidic Shepherd, Jesus shepherded God's people by inclusively reaching out to the socially marginalized. When Jesus reaches out to the marginalized members of Israel, Chae constructively notes that this 'initiative towards sinners [was] fundamental to the eschatological restoration of Israel. ... Jesus' seeking sinners [represents] the inauguration of the process of restoration.' [124]

Matthew's Davidic Shepherd also performs deeds of healing and exorcism with divine authority. By these works, Jesus fulfils – in part – the angelic prophecy (1.21) and scripture (2.6), by saving his people from the physical ramifications of their sins.[125] Malina and Neyrey thus note, 'That

with obedience to him and to his interpretation of the Mosaic Law (8.4), and by serving (8.15) or following Jesus (8.19-22; 9.9).

122   Chae (*Davidic Shepherd*, 77) also points out that healing seems to be connected with shepherding. He notes that the LXX translators render Zech. 10.2cβ, רעה כי־אין רעה יענו כמו־צאן ('they are afflicted like sheep for whom there is no shepherd'), with ὡς πρό βατα καὶ ἐκακώθησαν διότι οὐκ ἦν ἴασις ('they have also been afflicted like sheep, thus there is no healing'). Since ἴασις is usually employed in the prophetic corpus of the LXX for physical healing (e.g. Isa. 19.22; Jer. 8.22; Ezek. 30.21; Nah. 3.19), it would seem that for the LXX translators, physical healing was associated with shepherding; cf. Ham, *Coming King*, 117, n. 54.

123   Willitts, *Shepherd-King*, 134.

124   Chae, *Davidic Shepherd*, 269.

125   The Evangelist perhaps underscores the therapeutic aspect of Jesus' mission to Israel by the frequency of healings that take place in these mission-oriented chapters: the

programmatic statement [1.21] is carefully worked out in the narrative of his ministry, in part by Jesus' exorcism of those possessed by Satan.'[126] Moreover, Matthew's concern for Jewish-national restoration is confirmed by the pericope of John the Baptist's deportation (11.1-6).[127] Here, Matthew invites his audience to reflect (along with John) on the nature of Jesus' messianic deeds. By implicitly appealing to Isa. 26.19; 35.5; 61.1 in Mt. 11.5 – which effectively recapitulate the healings recorded in the Miracle Chapters – Matthew identifies Jesus' messianic works of healing with signs of Israel's national restoration.

Additionally, by presenting Jesus' therapeutic activity as an integral component of his salvific mission to Israel, Matthew depicts him in rather pastoral terms, reminiscent of the portrayal of YHWH as Israel's Shepherd in the HB:[128] in saving the Jews from their sins, Jesus the Davidic Shepherd travels about the land of Israel healing the 'harassed and downcast', shepherd-less sheep of Israel.

4.2.3 The shepherd's eschatological role: universal judge

Jesus' final discourse in chs 24–25, the so-called Olivet Discourse, comes immediately before Matthew's passion narrative. Along with its strong eschatological orientation,[129] the Olivet Discourse could be seen as the climax of Jesus' teaching.[130] The logical flow within the Olivet Discourse would suggest that its own climax would be the pericope of the Final Judgement in 25.31-46 (which is without parallel in Mark and Luke).[131]

There are four features of this pericope that, for the purposes of this study, need delineation. The first is the identity of the judge: 'But when the Son of Man comes in his glory and all the angels with him, then he will sit

majority of specific accounts of healing in the Gospel occur within them (nine of fourteen stories).

126   Malina and Neyrey, *Names*, 123.
127   Verseput ('Davidic Messiah', 112–13) perceptively argues that the resumption of the narrative movement following the Missionary Discourse remains connected to the Davidic character of the Miracle Chapters by means of the Baptist's inquiry into Jesus' works.
128   Cf., especially, the portrayal of YHWH as a shepherd in Ezekiel 34: because Israel's shepherds have failed to heal the sick, YHWH promises to 'bind up the injured and strengthen the weak' (34.16).
129   Davies and Allison call Mt. 25.31-46 an 'eschatological testament' because of the many features it shares with Jewish and Christian apocalypses (*Matthew*, 3.326). Stanton classifies it as an apocalyptic discourse, discussing the common thrust between Mt. 25.31-46 and texts with similar social settings – according to Stanton – like *4 Ezra, 1 Enoch*, and *2 Baruch* (*Gospel*, 221–30).
130   Whereas the other major discourses deal primarily with ethics, Torah interpretation, mission, and the nature of God's kingdom, the Olivet Discourse deals with Jesus' Second Coming and the Final Judgement.
131   For supporting arguments of this point, see Baxter, 'Shepherd', 230.

upon the throne of his glory' (25.31). Matthew's depiction of Jesus as judge in the passage is noteworthy. He is called the 'Son of Man' – an echo of the son of man figure in Daniel 7[132] – who appears sitting on a glorious throne with attending angels. What is only implied by 'sitting on a throne' becomes explicit in v. 34a: the Son of Man is called 'the king'.[133] The uniqueness of the relationship between this royal judge and God can be inferred by his reference to God as 'my Father'.[134]

The second feature of this passage is the manner by which the Son of Man judges: 'And before him will be gathered all the nations, and he will separate them from each other, just as a shepherd separates the sheep from the goats, and he will put the sheep on his right and the goats on the left' (vv. 31-33). There are several observations to make here. The scope of the judgement is worldwide, i.e. 'all the nations' (πάντα τὰ ἔθνη) will appear before Jesus.[135] The passive form of 'gather' (συναχθήσονται) suggests that 'the nations' take their place before the judge at his initiative.[136] That judgement is pronounced swiftly without any form of trial demonstrates the expansive knowledge of the judge: he knows immediately who the sheep and goats are;[137] and the sheep are entitled to what has already – since the beginning of creation – been prepared for them. Matthew alludes in v. 32c ('just as the shepherd separates the sheep from the goats') to Ezek. 34.17, where YHWH promises (as Israel's true shepherd) to judge between the sheep, as well as between the rams and goats.[138]

---

132   While the precise nature of the allusion invoked by the Son of Man title is far from settled (cf. Davies and Allison, 2.43–52), the son of man's coming with angelic beings and a throne of glory, as well as the title's use in the passion narrative (26.64), would almost certainly suggest an allusion to Dan. 7.13-14. For a brief but helpful discussion of Matthew's appropriation of Dan. 7.13, see Gundry, *Use of the OT*, 231–33.

133   The appellation 'the king' in v. 34a harkens back, on the one hand, to its use in the infancy narrative for Herod (2.2), and it anticipates, on the other, the passion narrative (27.11, 37, 42), where Jesus is mockingly called 'the king of the Jews'. In the Synoptic Gospels, only here in this pericope does Jesus refer to himself (albeit indirectly) as a king.

134   A Davidic allusion may be implied by the appellation of 'Father' for God by the king, cf. YHWH's message to King David in 2 Sam. 7.12-14: 'I will raise up your offspring after you ... and I will establish the throne of his kingdom for ever. I will be a father to him, and he shall be a son to me' (NRSV).

135   While the precise identity of πάντα τὰ ἔθνη remains unsettled, the least that can be said is that, no matter which of the major positions is adopted on the issue (see the survey of U. Luz, 'The Final Judgment [Mt. 25.31-46]: An Exercise in "History of Influence" Exegesis', in *Treasure New and Old: Recent Contributions to Matthean Studies*, ed. D. Bauer and M. A. Powell, SBL Symposium Series 1, ed. G. O'Day [Atlanta: Scholars Press, 1996]: 271–310), the judgement is not limited to one locale – i.e. it involves people from many geographical locations.

136   Cf. Mt. 13.41; 24.31.

137   Cf. Mt. 11.27.

138   This act of judging, on the part of YHWH, is mentioned three times in Ezek. 34.17-22. Chae insists, 'No other comparable text exists beside Ezek. 34.17-22 that involves sheep and goats in the context of God's judgment to establish the eschatological community. The allusion is nearly irrefutable' (*Davidic Shepherd*, 221).

The third feature of the pericope is the criterion for judgement. The 'nations' are judged according to their deeds of mercy (or lack thereof; cf. Mt. 23.23): 'I was hungry and you gave me something to eat, I was thirsty and you gave me drink, I was a stranger and you gathered together with me; naked and you clothed me, I was sick and you visited me, I was in prison and you came to me' (vv. 35-36). [139] According to Matthew, Jesus' final judgement is based upon performing deeds of mercy to 'one of these brothers and sisters of mine, the least of them' (ἑνὶ τούτων τῶν ἀδελφῶν μου τῶν ἐλαχίστων). [140] While the identity of this group has received various interpretations, [141] in view of how Matthew uses ἀδελφός [142] and ἐλάχιστος, [143] it would seem best to identify this group with the Christ-believers generally, as opposed to restricting it to those serving as missionaries or prophets. [144] In other words, because Christ's presence resides with his disciples, [145] then how 'the nations' treat any disciple – whether great or small – will form the criterion of their final judgement at the Parousia. [146]

The final feature of the passage is the identity of the recipients of judgement. Who are 'all the nations' (πάντα τὰ ἔθνη) separated in judgement by the eschatological Shepherd? Davies and Allison list the most serious positions as all non-Christ-believers (Jews and Gentiles), all NCB Gentiles, and all of humanity. [147] A number of observations can be made here.

---

139   These acts of charity commonly appear in Jewish writings (see the survey in Davies and Allison, *Matthew*, 3.425–28 of early Jewish texts that include similar lists of deeds of mercy), e.g. Isa. 58.7. The criterion for judgement described in 25.31-46, then, is not necessarily restricted to Gentiles. Court speaks of Matthew converting the charitable ethic to an eschatological one ('Right and Left', 230).

140   The 'elative superlative' (so Turner, *Syntax*, 31), τῶν ἐλαχίστων, functions adjectivally, describing the extent or scope of ἑνὶ τούτων τῶν ἀδελφῶν μου, thus yielding the sense, 'one of these brothers and sisters of mine, *even* the least of them' (cf. Brown, 'Faith', 173).

141   See Davies and Allison, *Matthew*, 3.428–29.

142   Of its thirty-one occurrences in the Gospel, it usually denotes a biological relationship (1.2, 11; 4.18, 21; 10.2, 21; 12.46-48; 13.55; 14.3; 17.1; 19.29; 20.24; 22.24-25). In its other uses it refers to discipleship (12.49-50; 18.15, 21, 35; 23.8; 28.10; and probably 5.22-24, 47; 7.3-5).

143   Matthew employs this word two other times: once referring to Bethlehem (2.6) and once referring to the commandments of the Law (5.19). In both of these instances ἐλάχιστος is used to convey the smallness of the particular subject in order to show the overall significance of either the subject or the object to which it is related.

144   Here, then, ἐλάχιστος would convey the overall significance of Christ-believers whereby even the slightest member has immense worth in God's eyes (cf. Mt. 18.12-14). The saying would be similar to Mt. 11.11, where the least (μικρότερος) in the kingdom of heaven is greater than the greatest of prophets, John the Baptist.

145   Christ's presence with his disciples is evidenced by the phrase, 'inasmuch as you did it to these brothers and sisters of mine, the least of them, you did it to me' (v. 40, cf. v. 45; 18.20; also Acts 9.4-5).

146   Cf. Mt. 10.40-42.

147   Davies and Allison, *Matthew*, 3.422.

To begin with, Matthew uses the phrase 'all the nations' (πάντα τὰ ἔθνη) in 24.9, 14, and 28.19. In the eschatologically oriented ch. 24, 'all nations' refers to 'the whole world' (ὅλῃ τῇ οἰκουμένῃ).[148] 'All' probably should be given an inclusive meaning (i.e. 'every nation without exception' – including Israel),[149] rather than an exclusive one ('every other nation' – every nation except Israel), because of what follows in the discourse: according to 24.16-20, the disciples continue to live and evangelize in the land of Israel – since it is from there that they must flee – when all of these signs of the end transpire.[150] In the final chapter of the Gospel the disciples are commanded after the resurrection to make disciples of 'all the nations' (πάντα τὰ ἔθνη). While some scholars try to exclude Israel from 28.19,[151] 10.23 and 23.39 will not allow for this exclusion. In addition to this, the criterion of judgement (i.e. deeds of mercy) can apply equally to Jews and Gentiles. In addition, the language of patriarchal blessing ('you who are blessed of my Father') and of inheriting a foreordained kingdom (v. 34) refers to the Abrahamic covenant (cf. 1.1c), which can apply to both Jews and Gentiles.[152] And finally, as Cope observes:

> Perhaps it is impossible to say conclusively who 'all nations' are, but it is possible to say who they are *not*. From the pronouncements of vss. 40 and 45 it is clear that those who have been given or refused hospitality are not a part of the judgment proceeding and that they are 'the least of these my brethren'. ... 'All the nations' are those *other than the brothers of the Son of Man*.[153]

These four observations, then, suggest, on the one hand, that 'all the nations' excludes Christ-believers.[154] On the other hand, while it must include NCB Gentiles, it probably includes NCB Jews. The implication of this identification is that while Matthew sees Jesus' mission as directed to Jews, ultimately, his flock will consist, in the Eschaton, of both Jewish and Gentile Christ-believers.[155]

148   In 24.14, 'all the nations' (πᾶσιν τοῖς ἔθνεσιν) is clearly paralleled by 'the whole world' (ὅλῃ τῇ οἰκουμένῃ).
149   While Matthew can use ἔθνη as a point of contrast with Israel (10.5-6), he can equally use it in close association with Israel (4.12-15).
150   Cf. Mt. 10.23.
151   The basis for their exclusion would be, according to most of these scholars (Stanton, *Gospel*, 151–52), 21.43: 'Therefore I tell you that the kingdom of God will be taken from you [the nation of Israel] and given to a nation (ἔθνος [i.e. the Gentiles]) producing the fruit of it.'
152   Cf. Paul's appeal for Gentile inclusion in the Abrahamic covenant in Romans 4 and Galatians 3.
153   Cope, 'Matthew XXV', 37 (his emphasis).
154   Donahue ('Parable', 9–13) argues otherwise, but his argument turns largely on the Final Judgement pericope being a parable – which is not the case.
155   The inclusion of Gentiles in God's flock, prior to the final commission in 28.18-20, has already been anticipated at various points of the narrative: the title 'Son

Matthew's deployment of the shepherd motif in the Olivet Discourse, then, reveals that Jesus is the eschatological judge and king to whom all people must eventually answer, both Jews and Gentiles, according to their treatment of Jesus' followers. It is because the presence of Christ resides with his disciples, that those who accept and show hospitality towards them are rewarded as having accepted Jesus. Those who reject them – failing to show them hospitality – are punished as having rejected Jesus.

In appropriating Ezek. 34.17 for his shepherd motif, Matthew's deployment of the text differs noticeably from its use in Ezekiel's prophecy. In Ezekiel, YHWH's promise to 'shepherd the flock with justice' involves executing harsh judgement on the flock's leaders, who had failed to shepherd the sheep fairly. The leaders will be banished from the community of Israel and YHWH will save the flock from their tyranny by replacing them with his own shepherd. The recipients of judgement in Ezekiel 34, then, are both the flock in general (who receive the promise of salvation and a true [Davidic] shepherd), and their leaders (who are condemned).[156] While Matthew regularly targets Israel's leaders in his Gospel, in appropriating Ezek. 34.17, he broadens the scope of judgement to include Gentiles.[157] Hence in Matthew's Final Judgement, 'the nations' at large are separated into either membership in or exclusion from God's eschatological flock.

Despite the universal scope of Final Judgement, Matthew expresses clear aspirations of Jewish-national restoration in his deployment of the shepherd metaphor in this pericope. He explicitly binds the metaphor to Jesus' eschatological kingship: the shepherd-judge is twice referred to as 'the king' – an overtly political title. And those who prove themselves members of God's eschatological flock he describes in terms of patriarchal, covenant language: 'you who are blessed of my Father, inherit the [preordained] kingdom'. Matthew thus views the inclusion of Gentiles into God's flock not as forming a separate entity but as an expansion of CB Israel.

4.2.4 The shepherd's mission: his atoning sacrifice

The final explicit occurrence of ποιμήν comes in 26.31-35,[158] which foreshadows in outline the remainder of the Gospel.[159] On the Mount

---

of Abraham' (1.1c); the women of the genealogy (1.3a, 5, 6b); the homage of the Magi (2.10-11); the healing of Gentiles (8.5-13; 15.21-28); and the sowing of the Gospel in the world (13.37-38; 24.14).

156   In Ezekiel's judgement, sheep are separated from sheep, and rams are separated from goats, with the rams and goats representing Israel's leaders.

157   This broadening of the flock results in a different tone from the judgement scene: whereas the verses of judgement in Ezekiel 34 concentrate on the harsh punishment meted out to the corrupt shepherds, there is greater balance in Matthew's judgement scene between the giving out of rewards and punishment.

158   Luz suggests that 26.30 is a transitional verse and that vv. 31-35 represent a self-contained dialogue (*Matthäus*, 3.124).

159   The passage foretells the disciples' forsaking of Jesus, Peter's denial, the crucifixion and the resurrection; cf. Davies and Allison, *Matthew*, 3.482–83, 488.

of Olives, Jesus tells his disciples: 'All of you will fall away on account of me in this night, for it has been written, "I will strike the shepherd and the sheep of the flock will be scattered". But after I am raised I will go ahead of you to Galilee' (vv. 31aβ-32).

The Miracle Chapters offer one side of Jesus' shepherding activity: he performed works of healing and exorcism in the land of Israel to save his people from the physical ramifications of their sins. This text, however, presents the other, more central perspective of his shepherding: ultimate salvation from sin will come by Jesus' sacrificial, atoning death and resurrection from the dead. There are strong reasons for understanding the striking down of the shepherd in terms of atoning sacrifice, the most convincing of which would be the pericope's attachment to the Passover discourse, particularly, 26.26-30,[160] where Jesus speaks of his body being broken for his disciples; and he tells them to drink the cup of wine 'because this is my blood of the covenant, which is poured out for many for the forgiveness of sins' (26.28). Clearly, the blood of the covenant is poured out when Jesus is struck down in his crucifixion. For Matthew, then, forgiveness of sins, which Jesus pronounced during his mission to Israel (9.1-8), is ultimately secured by his death and resurrection.

Besides the immediate context of 26.31-35, another reason for understanding the striking down of the shepherd in terms of sacrificial atonement is its relationship to the passion predictions in 16.21, 17.22-23, and 20.18-19: it represents the climax of these predictions. They all, rather characteristically, bind Jesus' death and suffering to his resurrection, and they speak of Jesus' death as caused by the Jewish leaders – Israel's unfaithful shepherds. While the miracles of Jesus signify the inauguration and the ingressive coming of the kingdom of heaven, the striking down of the shepherd, beyond simply an act of martyrdom at the hands of the Roman authorities, represents the necessary prerequisite for the kingdom's future culmination.

The idea of a suffering messiah who dies ran against the grain of early Jewish messianic expectation, something observed in Matthew and other New Testament texts.[161] Hence, the Evangelist, consonant with his other use of scripture, where the identity and works of Jesus are said to fulfil or to be in accordance with the scriptures, states that the striking down of the shepherd and the scattering of the disciples happen 'because it has been written' (v. 31aγ).[162] According to the Gospel, although none of Jesus'

160   Matthew strengthens the connection between vv. 26-30 and vv. 31-35 by inserting τότε ('then') into his Markan source.

161   E.g. Mt. 16.21-23; cf. 1 Cor. 1.23. The frequent use of Isa. 6.9-10 (in Mt. 13.14-15; Mk 4.12; Lk. 8.10; Jn 12.40; Acts 28.26-27) and the 'stone of stumbling' passages (Isa. 8.14 in Rom. 9.33 and 1 Pet. 2.8; Ps. 118.22 in Lk. 20.17; Acts 4.11; 1 Pet. 2.7) represent a concerted effort on the part of early Christ-believers to explain the rejection and crucifixion of Jesus.

162   Matthew thus changes the first word of Zech. 13.7 from an imperative, 'strike [the shepherd]' to a future: 'I will strike [the shepherd]' – the striking down of the shepherd becomes prophetic.

followers or the religious authorities could understand this aspect of Jesus' mission, it was part of God's sovereign plan to bring about the redemption of Israel from their sins.

The death of Jesus is but one (albeit large) component of the kingdom's coming. The other according to the Synoptic Tradition is Jesus' resurrection from the dead: 'But after I have been raised I will go ahead (προά γω) of you into Galilee' (v. 32). Scholars like Luz assert that προά γω is best understood as referring to Jesus' arriving in Galilee prior to the arrival of his disciples and thus bears no shepherding imagery.[163] But the opposite seems more likely for several reasons. First, although προάγω is not explicitly tied to shepherding imagery in the LXX, when used with reference to God, it does speak of him as 'guiding' his followers – consonant with the shepherd metaphor.[164] Additionally, the cognates of προάγω are often associated with shepherding.[165] Finally, in view of its close proximity here with ποιμήν, πρόβατον, and ποίμνη, προάγω would almost surely carry shepherding connotations here. Moreover, the two thoughts of Jesus going ahead of the disciples like a shepherd, and of him going ahead of the disciples chronologically are not mutually exclusive: like a shepherd, Jesus leads his disciples to Galilee by first going there ahead of them. Hence, the Shepherd's redemptive mission does not end with his sacrificial death but with his resurrection from the dead.[166]

Another important feature of Jesus' mission according to this pericope is the reconstitution involved in this redemptive act. Zechariah 13.7 not only anchors the otherwise unexpected death of Israel's messiah, it explains the falling away of the disciples: 'All of you will fall away ... because it has been written, "I will strike the shepherd".'[167] Technically the falling away of the disciples occurs at Jesus' arrest (26.56). But something more can be said. The allusion to Zechariah 14 in 26.30 provides an eschatological backdrop to Jesus' solemn forecast concerning his disciples.[168] Additionally, when compared to Mark's citation of Zech. 13.7, Matthew seems to append an allusion to Ezek. 34.31:[169] while the Markan parallel has only 'and

163   Luz, *Matthäus*, 3.125–26. He insists: 'Ich kenne keinen Beleg, wo προάγω von einem Hirten ausgesagt wäre. Im übrigen gingen palästinische Hirten normalerweise hinter ihrer Herde und trieben sie, nur metaphorische Hirten gehen ihrer Herde voran' (*Matthäus*, 3.126).

164   E.g. in the LXX Prov. 4.27; cf. Ps. 22.1-3; 27.8-9; 2 Macc. 10.1.

165   There is a syntactical tie, for example, between ἄγω and ποιμαίνω in Gen. 46.32; Exod. 3.1; Ps. 77.52; Isa. 63.12-14, and Jdt. 11.19.

166   The author of Hebrews also makes this link between Jesus as a shepherd and his resurrection (Heb. 13.20), perhaps based on the Gospel traditions.

167   The γάρ ('for') introducing the quote from Zechariah is causative: it explains how it is that this turn of events could happen.

168   For a good discussion of the eschatology inherent in the neighbouring passage of 26.26-28, see Davies and Allison, *Matthew*, 3.475–77.

169   Cf. Willitts, *Shepherd-King*, 146–49, who also argues along these lines.

the sheep will be scattered' (14.27bβ), the second strophe of Matthew's citation of Zechariah reads, 'and the sheep of the flock (τὰ πρόβατα τῆς ποίμνης) will be scattered' (26.31bβ). Matthew also reverses Mark's order of the subject and predicate.[170] The phrase 'sheep of the/my flock' appears but once in the Jewish scriptures: Ezek. 34.31. In Ezekiel 34, the expression refers to Israel knowing that YHWH is their God and that they are his people – 'the sheep of my flock' (צֹאן מַרְעִיתִי [MT]/πρόβατα ποιμνίου μου [LXX]) – and that they will again enjoy the blessings of the covenant, after he gathers them from their dispersion and re-establishes them as his people in their own land. By inverting Mark's word order and inserting τῆς ποίμνης, Matthew would be emphasizing the dispersal of the flock, i.e. his disciples. Matthew also underscores their scattering by the additions of the emphatic pronoun ὑμεῖς ('you') and the phrase ἐν ἐμοί (lit. 'by me').[171]

In view of the importance of Ezekiel 34 to Matthew, coupled with the nearby words of the covenant's fulfilment through Jesus' blood (26.28), an allusion to Ezek. 34.31 here would contribute, first, to the Evangelist's sustained irony which runs throughout his passion narrative. Matthew has already identified Jesus as the Davidic Shepherd of Ezekiel 34, the one responsible for tending God's flock; yet, contrary to Ezekiel 34, the Shepherd's flock will actually scatter. Second, an allusion to Ezekiel 34 would emphasize the dispersion of the disciples more than Mark (and Luke); in other words, it is from this state of dispersal that the Shepherd will gather his people. This idea of a shepherd gathering his dispersed flock closely mirrors Ezekiel 34, which speaks of YHWH tending to his 'scattered' flock (Ezek. 34.5, 6, 12). Matthew not only adopts this direction of Ezekiel 34 here, but his appropriation of Zech. 13.7 also echoes the thrust of that passage: Deutero-Zechariah speaks of a Davidic ruler, who is struck down in judgement, causing the sheep of Israel to scatter; but the demise of the shepherd eventually results in the purification and restoration of the people of God. Matthew deploys this text in similar fashion: Jesus the Davidic Shepherd is struck down by God (by his crucifixion) and his disciples scatter as a result. But in the striking down of the Shepherd, Jesus atones for the sins of his flock, viz. his dispersed disciples, and by extension, those who receive their message (10.40-42; 25.35-40), securing their salvation and their reconstitution as the people of God through his death and resurrection from the dead.

Thus, according to his appropriation of the shepherd metaphor in this passage, the mission of Matthew's Shepherd to Israel climaxes in his sacrificial atonement on the cross. While not consonant with early Jewish messianic interpretation, it is nonetheless part of God's sovereign plan, as

---

170   Mark 14.27bβ reads, καὶ τὰ πρόβατα διασκορπισθήσονται, while Matthew has καὶ διασκορπισθήσονται τὰ πρόβατα [τῆς ποίμνης].

171   Carson captures the sense of these additions to Mark: '*you*, of all people, on account of *me*, your Messiah, by your own confession' (*Matthew*, 540, his emphasis); cf. Gundry, *Use of the OT*, 27–28.

forecast by the scriptures. Moreover, the Shepherd's mission does not end with his sacrificial death but with his resurrection from the dead and the reconstitution of his dispersed people in Galilee.

4.2.5 Other implicit features of the shepherd

While Mt. 27.9-10 does not employ 'shepherd', it nonetheless deserves special consideration for several important reasons. It explicitly cites a portion of Zech. 11.4-17 – one of the lengthiest and more significant biblical narratives involving the metaphorical use of 'shepherd'; based on Matthew's citations and allusions to Deutero-Zechariah elsewhere,[172] as well as his own elaborate shepherd motif, the shepherd of Zechariah 11 would have been squarely within his purview, and thus the entire context of 11.4-17 would be assumed for his audience; the Evangelist implicitly identifies Jesus as the rejected shepherd of 11.4-17 in 27.9-10;[173] and, as will be observed, this passage makes a special contribution to Matthew's shepherd motif.

Matthew 27.3-10 represents the Evangelist's version of what happened to Judas after he betrayed Jesus, an account in which the chief priests figure prominently.[174] This would suggest that the Evangelist intended his insertion[175] to explain not only Judas's fate and the aetiology of 'Field of Blood', but also to reinforce the responsibility of the Jewish leaders for Jesus' death – a culpability he underscores in three ways.[176] First, although the account of Judas makes better sense – from an emotional perspective – during the crucifixion scene (as Davies and Allison note),[177] because it comes

---

172   E.g. the citation of Zech. 9.9 in 21.5, 13.7 in 26.31, and the allusions to Zech. 9.11 in 26.28, 14.4 in 26.30, and 14.7 in 24.36.

173   In Zechariah 11 the thirty pieces of silver is the wage paid by the Jewish leaders to YHWH, care of the prophet (vv. 12-13a). In Mt. 27.9b the thirty pieces of silver is the price set (and paid for) by the Jewish leaders for Judas' betrayal of Jesus to secure his execution. Both YHWH and Jesus cost the respective Jewish leaders thirty pieces of silver.

174   Their actions and words occupy approximately the same amount of the story as Judas': two-and-a-half verses centre on Judas (vv. 3, 4a, 5) and two-and-a-half on the chief priests (vv. 4b, 6-7).

175   The story is absent in Mark. Without the insertion, Matthew's narrative reads quite smoothly: 'And when morning came, all of the chief priests and elders of the people took counsel against Jesus so as to put him to death. And after being bound they led him away and delivered him up to Pilate the governor. ... And Jesus stood before the governor and the governor questioned him' (vv. 1-2, 11a).

176   Gundry, for example, misses this last point: 'Matt felt no difficulty in the fact that in Zech. the prophet gives the money to the potter and in his own narrative the chief priests give the money, for the essential point is that the money is paid *to the potter*' (*Use of the OT*, 126, his emphasis). The appropriateness of this citation for Matthew, however, lay not simply in who received the money, but also in what the money – 'the established price which was set' – symbolizes: the rejection of YHWH in Zechariah, and the betrayal and rejection of Jesus in the Gospel.

177   That is, from the reader's point of view it would be emotionally more satisfying if, after Jesus died on the cross, Judas would have hung himself: Judas would have

immediately after the handing over of Jesus to Pilate, the account serves to connect the cause of Judas's fateful remorse to the action of the Jewish leaders and not to Jesus' suffering (vv. 1-2).

Second, when Judas returns the money to the leaders, telling them that he has sinned by betraying innocent blood, they callously respond, 'What is that to us? See to that yourself' (v. 4b). They do not deny Judas's assertion of Jesus' innocence – thereby implicitly confirming their own treachery. Third, they refer to the money with which they hired Judas to betray Jesus as the 'price of blood', and consequently recognize that it would be unlawful for them to donate it to the temple treasury (v. 6). Prior to the trial scene, then, which concludes with the ominous words, '[A]ll the people said, "His blood be upon us and upon our children"' (27.25), Matthew has in effect laid out in triplicate the responsibility for Jesus' death at the feet of the religious leaders.

The Judas narrative concludes with a citation from Scripture:[178] 'Then that which was spoken through Jeremiah the prophet was fulfilled, saying: "And they took the thirty silver pieces, the established price which the sons of Israel set, and they gave them to the field of the potter, just as the Lord directed me"' (vv. 9-10).[179] The citation functions in two ways. It affirms that Jesus' rejection and crucifixion took place according to the scriptures and was therefore an integral part of God's will in bringing about the salvation of his people Israel. Moreover, Matthew establishes a typological identification between the leaders who condemned Jesus and the leaders who rejected YHWH in Zech. 11.4-17. Support for this identification would be as follows.

As noted earlier, given the two citations and other allusions to Deutero-Zechariah, the full context of Zechariah 9-13 would be assumed and hence, the entire shepherd oracle of 11.4-17. A parallel exists not just between the rejected Shepherd of Deutero-Zechariah (YHWH) and Matthew's rejected Shepherd (Jesus), but also between the leaders who rejected the former shepherd[180] and those rejecting Jesus: the chief priests and elders.[181] This

---

thus received what he deserved, and poetic justice would have been more unambiguously served.

178   While the rest of the passion narrative is replete with scriptural allusions, 27.9-10 represents the final explicit citation ('formula quotation') in the Gospel.

179   On the text form of this quote, Stendahl states that its relationship to the LXX is 'very slight, and its form is definitely dependent on the Matthew's interpretation of the Hebrew text' (*School*, 124; cf. Gundry, *Use*, 122–27, and Luz, *Matthäus*, 3.230–31). While Matthew attributes his citation to Jeremiah, all scholars agree that the bulk of the words come from Zech. 11.13. For a survey of suggestions why Matthew attributes a quote from Deutero-Zechariah to Jeremiah, see Davies and Allison, *Matthew*, 3.568–69, and M. Knowles, *Jeremiah in Matthew's Gospel: The Rejected-Prophet Motif in Matthean Redaction*, JSNTSS 68 (Sheffield: Sheffield Academic Press, 1993), 60–67.

180   Deutero-Zechariah makes a careful distinction between the flock (11.4, 7a, 8b) and its leaders (11.5c, 7b, 11).

181   Just as the leaders in Deutero-Zechariah's oracle set the wages for the rejected

attention to the leaders is also evidenced by Matthew's insertion of 'the sons of Israel' (ἀπὸ υἱῶν Ἰσραήλ) into his citation.[182] Scholars recognize that ἀπό is a partitive particle that yields a sense of separation.[183] Thus, all Israel is not in view but a sub-group within Israel: the Jewish leaders.[184]

Support for a typological identification of Jewish leaders also comes from the allusion to Jeremiah embedded within the Zechariah citation, which actually prompts Matthew to attribute the entire quotation to this prophet.[185] Soares Prabhu suggests that 'in the διὰ Ἰερεμίου of Matt 27:9 there is a more or less conscious assimilation to the already closely parallel Matt 2:17: an assimilation perhaps prompted, and no doubt partly legitimized, by the allusion to Jeremiah in the text of the quotation introduced'.[186] If correct, then the implicit typological identification with the Jewish leaders in 27.9-10 would be strengthened: in 2.17, Herod the leader of the Jews fulfils Jeremianic prophesy by his evil act against Israel, viz. the slaughter of the innocent; in 27.9-10, the Jewish leaders fulfil 'Jeremianic' prophesy by their evil act of treachery against Jesus.[187]

If Matthew intends this identification of the Jewish leaders who condemned Jesus with the leaders of Zech. 11.4-17, then an important implication would follow: the Jewish leaders have been replaced but not the Jewish people. In Zechariah 11, the leadership of Israel is condemned for failing the people and, consequently, YHWH replaces those shepherds with his own. When his shepherd is rejected, divine wrath ensues: the desolation of the people and foreign oppression of the land.[188] Despite the outpouring of YHWH's wrath upon the nation, only the leaders were replaced according to the oracle of Zechariah 11. The same would follow for Matthew. Israel's leaders are judged for having failed the nation; consequently, Jesus (in his mission to Israel) replaces these shepherds. Jesus, however, is eventually rejected by the Jewish leaders,[189] bringing about God's wrath in the form

---

shepherd, so also in Matthew, the chief priests and elders set the price for Judas's betrayal and rejection of Jesus (26.14-15).

182   Neither the MT nor the LXX have this phrase.

183   See Turner (*Syntax*, 208), who acknowledges the use of a partitive construction here in which the ἀπό phrase stands as the subject of the verb: hence, 'which the sons of Israel set' for ὃν ἐτιμήσαντο ἀπὸ υἱῶν Ἰσραήλ.

184   Hence, Stendahl comments, 'Matthew distinguishes between the authorities and the people, putting the responsibility on the former' (*School*, 126, n. 1). Luz also recognizes that the construction refers to the Jewish leaders (*Matthäus*, 3.241). For more detailed arguments on this point, see Baxter, 'Shepherd', 246.

185   For a more detailed discussion of this citation, see Baxter, 'Shepherd', 246–47.

186   Soares Prabhu, *Formula*, 54; cf. Knowles, *Jeremiah*, 77–81.

187   Consonant with Zechariah 11, leaders are singled out from the rest of the flock in Jer. 19.1.

188   A similar scenario can be observed in Jeremiah: the entire nation is at fault for disobeying (e.g. Jer. 2.13-19; 5.1-13), but the leaders of the nation are particularly singled out for the nation's downfall (e.g. 8.8-12; 23.1-2, 15-40; 50.6), prompting YHWH to replace them with his own shepherds but not Israel as his sheep (e.g. 3.15; 23.4-6).

189   This rejection is crystallized in Matthew's report (absent in Mark) of the Jewish

of the destruction of Jerusalem in 70 CE by the Romans.[190] But despite the destruction of Jerusalem, it is the religious leaders who have been replaced by God – a replacement foreseen by the scriptures (i.e. in Zechariah 11, according to Matthew) – and not the nation.

Thus, Matthew's appropriation of Zech. 11.13 serves to emphasize the guilt of the Jewish leaders in the death of Jesus, as S. van Tilborg remarks, 'Mt wishes to minimize the guilt of Judas at the cost of the Jewish leaders.'[191] The Evangelist specifically implicates them in the destruction of Jerusalem and thereby scripturally justifies their replacement as Israel's shepherds.[192]

4.2.6 Summary

According to the birth and infancy narratives Jesus the messiah is the Davidic Shepherd. Like King David, Jesus is born in Bethlehem – as prophesied by the scriptures. Since he is the true heir to David's throne, those who occupy positions of leadership over the nation are illegitimate. The salvation and rule (of the kingdom of heaven) the Davidic Shepherd offers is ultimately for the whole world, but the primary scope of the messiah's shepherding remains the Jews – i.e. 'my people Israel' – whom Jesus came to save from their sins. Hence, the motif conveys strong aspirations of Jewish-national restoration for Matthew, thus echoing the sentiments present in the two texts he appropriates in 2.6, Mic. 5.1, and 2 Sam. 5.2. For Matthew, Jesus' salvation has clear political overtones in that he replaces Herod as the shepherd/king of Israel.[193]

Prior to his sacrifice on the cross, Jesus went about healing the people of Israel of their physical afflictions. Matthew connects Satan's plunder of Israel with Jesus' therapeutic activity, and his therapeutic activity to the Son of David title. Thus, when Jesus 'saves his people from their sins', an integral component of Israel's salvation is their deliverance from physical illness and satanic oppression. In this way, Matthew depicts Jesus as the Davidic Shepherd in the pastoral terms commonly associated with the activities of literal shepherds. In other words, according to the Miracle Chapters, Jesus, on the one hand, inclusively reaches out to the socially marginalized (8.2-4; 9.9-13): he thus has concern for the weak and the stray of the flock;[194] on

leaders' decision to put Jesus to death and the consequent handing him over to Pilate in 27.1-2 – a text which is closely connected to the Judas narrative and explains the placement of the Judas story here rather than later in the Gospel.

190   Matthew alludes to the destruction of Jerusalem in 22.7; 23.38; and 24.1-2.

191   Van Tilborg, *The Jewish Leaders in Matthew* (Leiden: Brill, 1972), 88.

192   This latter point extends Matthew's earlier assertion in the Miracle Chapters: what began as Jesus (and his disciples) filling the void left by Israel's failed shepherds has become an outright replacement.

193   Against the backdrop of Roman imperialism, Jesus would also replace the Emperor of Rome as the sovereign authority of the world; cf. the gathering of all the nations before Jesus to receive his final judgement in Mt. 25.31-46.

194   Cf., for example, the description of the ideal shepherd in Isa. 40.11; Ezek. 34.4-6, 11, 16, passim; Zech. 11.7a, 16; also CD XIII, 9–10; *Pss. Sol.* 17.40; *Apoc. Ezek.*

the other hand, he heals his people of their many sicknesses (8.16; 9.35): Jesus thus cares for and 'binds up' the wounds of his injured sheep[195] – correspondences which would be strengthened by Matthew's allusions to Ezekiel 34 in the Miracle Chapters.

The Miracle Chapters also bring clearer focus to the nature of Jesus' messianic mission to Israel. As the prophesied Davidic Shepherd, Jesus' works of healing and exorcism represent manifestations of YHWH's mercy to his people Israel, in fulfilment of scriptural prophecy (8.17; 9.36). But not only do his healings and exorcisms fill a significant void left by the Jewish leaders, Jesus also appoints his disciples to continue the therapeutic activity he began exclusively to the 'lost sheep of the house of Israel'. Thus, the missional theme of the Miracle Chapters, the special emphasis on the deliverance from physical illness and satanic oppression wrought by the Son of David, and the explicit restriction of Jesus' and the disciples' mission to Israel, all roundly reaffirm Matthew's Jewish-national outlook (expressed in Mt. 2.6) – similarly to the HB text to which the Evangelist alludes at the close of the Miracle Chapters, Ezekiel 34.

Matthew's deployment of the metaphor in the Olivet Discourse amplifies the royal character of the Shepherd (first introduced in the birth and infancy narratives): Jesus is the eschatological shepherd-king to whom all people – Jews and Gentiles – must submit. Additionally, the echo of 2.3a ('the king') in 25.34a would reinforce the national-political aspect, also seen in the text Matthew appropriates here, Ezek. 34.17. Moreover, the Shepherd is the eschatological judge, who will judge all the nations according to how they treat Jesus' followers.

According to the passion narrative, the deeds of Matthew's Shepherd climax in his sacrifice on the cross, forming an integral part of God's sovereign plan as forecast by the scriptures. Additionally, the Shepherd's mission does not end with his sacrificial death but with his resurrection from the dead and the reconstitution of his dispersed people in Galilee. Furthermore, Matthew appropriates Zech. 11.13 in the account of Judas's demise to affirm that Jesus' rejection and crucifixion took place according to the scriptures and were, therefore, a central part of God's will in bringing about the salvation of his people Israel. The use of Zech. 11.13 emphasizes the guilt of the Jewish leaders in the death of Jesus, specifically implicating them in the destruction of Jerusalem and thereby scripturally justifying their replacement as Israel's shepherds. In this way, Matthew mirrors the Jewish-national outlook of Deutero-Zechariah, echoing the prophet's concern for the leadership of the nation Israel.

---

195   Cf., for example, the 'healing shepherd' in Ezek. 34.4, 16; Zech. 10.2 [LXX]; Zech. 11.16; also *1 Enoch* 90.35.

4.3 Conclusions

Because Matthew's shepherd motif has not received much attention in the history of Matthean scholarship, the specific contributions it makes to the Gospel as a whole have been overlooked. Despite not being the central preoccupation of the Gospel writer, the motif represents a significant sub-theme that adds to the theological framework of the Gospel. Most obviously, the shepherd motif contributes to the discussion of Matthew's Christology. Matthew's presentation of Jesus has led scholars to paint diverse Christological portraits of Jesus.[196] According to Matthew's birth and infancy narratives, Jesus has been divinely appointed to shepherd the nation of Israel. The genealogy makes it clear that Israel's Shepherd is Davidic in his ancestry, thereby confirming his legitimacy as heir to David's throne. This connection between Jesus as Israel's Shepherd and Davidic messiahship (strengthened by the Evangelist's allusions to Ezekiel 34) underscores Matthew's concern to depict Jesus within a clear Jewish framework. That is, just as the Son of David motif 'adheres closely to the paradigm of salvation anticipated by at least a significant segment of [Matthew's] devout Jewish compatriots and hence to the hopes and dreams that were fertile soil of messianic yearnings',[197] so his shepherd motif – particularly in view of the metaphor's use in the HB – would underline Matthew's hopes for Jewish-national restoration.

In related fashion, his shepherd motif helps to bring out the national-political dimension of Matthean soteriology. While the explicit link between Jesus' kingship and his shepherding is not made until the Olivet Discourse (25.31-34a), when Matthew first introduces the motif in the Gospel, it is part of a sustained contrast between Jesus and Herod. Matthew portrays Herod as a 'disturbed' monarch who seeks only to preserve power at all costs. It is from this type of cruel reign that God's people Israel need to be 'saved' (1.21).[198] The Evangelist presents Jesus, in contrast to Herod, as the legitimate heir to the throne of Israel via divine sanction, as prophesied by the scriptures. In replacing Herod, Jesus' kingship would doubtless transcend the typical geo-political framework of kings and kingdoms, yet it would nevertheless bear essential continuity with it. Although the kingdom Jesus inaugurates would primarily be what would be considered

---

196   Cf. Stanton, 'Origin', 1922–25 and Saldarini, *Christian-Jewish*, 165–93.

197   Verseput, 'Davidic Messiah', 103.

198   Although Herod dies while Jesus is still an infant, the end of Matthew's infancy traditions suggests that the tyrannical threat Herod posed continued with his son Archelaus in 2.22. Consequently, just as God warned Joseph in a dream about Herod's threat (2.13), so he warns him about Archelaus (2.22b); and just as Herod's reign caused Joseph and his family to retreat to another region (2.14), so the reign of Archelaus causes them to retreat to Galilee (2.22); moreover, Archelaus reigning in place of his father Herod causes Joseph to become 'afraid' (2.22a).

today religious,[199] according to Matthew's birth and infancy narratives, it nonetheless involves replacing not simply Israel's religious leaders but its king. By employing the shepherd metaphor in this way, Matthew simply reflects its common usage in the HB: monarchs are shepherds and ruling is viewed as shepherding.

The shepherd motif provides additional insight into Matthew's Miracle Chapters. The Evangelist depicts Jesus' therapeutic mission to Israel in terms of shepherding the nation, primarily by drawing upon Ezekiel 34, whose imagery finds a natural resting place in the Miracle Chapters. According to Ezekiel, the Jews find themselves plundered and in exile because of their self-absorbed shepherds; YHWH, therefore, promises to do what these leaders failed to do, by searching for the lost, by healing and rescuing the people from their exilic plight, and by providing them with a Davidic shepherd.[200] According to the Miracle Chapters, Israel's leaders neglected the people and the social outcasts within Israel, ultimately resulting in the nation's 'harassed and downcast' condition. Jesus (YHWH's Davidic Shepherd), therefore, goes about doing what they failed to do – idealized by Matthew in works of healing and exorcism – and appoints his disciples to replace Israel's failed shepherds in order to heal and to save the nation from its woeful state. Matthew thus characterizes Jesus' mission to Israel in the Miracle Chapters as Davidic: his therapeutic deeds represent the acts of the Son of David, and this serves to connect the 'Son of David' title with Matthew's shepherd motif.[201] Jesus' acts of healing, then, which comprise (in part) his shepherding of Israel, should be viewed in the Miracle Chapters in light of his identity as the Son of David: insofar as Matthew presents Jesus as the therapeutic Son of David, he presents him as Israel's Davidic Shepherd. The implication of this connection would be that the royal Son of David's rule or saving of Israel includes works of healing and exorcism.

The Evangelist's use of the motif in the birth and infancy traditions as well as the Miracle Chapters thus serves to illustrate the connection between sin, political and physical suffering, and Satan. For Matthew, Satan's rule over Israel and the Roman Empire is most evident in the physical sicknesses which plague the people of God (8.16, 28-32; 9.32-36; 10.1, 8), and in the illegitimate rule of Herod (2.1-16), and the Jerusalem leadership (3.5-9; 21.43-46; 23.37-39). Consequently, when the Davidic Shepherd saves his people from their sins, he saves them in part, according to the Miracle Chapters, from the physical ramifications of their sins by healing his people from their illnesses and satanic oppression, thus demonstrating his power over Satan (12.28-29). Moreover, he saves his people by forgiving them their sins, and liberating them from their bondage to sin

---

199   Or 'not of this world' (Jn 18.36).

200   Martin comments, 'The whole tone of Ezekiel 34 already prepares the way for seeing the shepherd as a healer' ('Image', 275).

201   This link becomes explicit in Mt. 12.22-24.

(best symbolized in the healing of the paralytic in 9.1-8). The forgiveness of sins would be finalized in Jesus' sacrificial death on the cross (Mt. 26.26-35).

The shepherd motif sheds some light on the question of Israel's 'replacement' as the people of God. Numerous scholars insist that Matthew believed that Israel had been replaced by the church.[202] Although other important lines of argumentation need to be called upon in any attempt to resolve this thorny issue, the contribution of the shepherd motif here should not be overlooked. According to an analysis of this motif, it is not Israel who has been replaced as God's people, but Israel's leaders that have been replaced as shepherds of God's people. God appointed Jesus to replace King Herod (and his successors) and the Jerusalem leadership; Jesus subsequently commissions his disciples to extend his shepherding mission and continue doing the works (he began), which Israel's leaders had failed to do. In the passion narrative, Matthew casts the ultimate responsibility of Jesus' death on the Jewish leaders, whom he typologically identifies with the Jewish leaders who had rejected YHWH as their shepherd in Zechariah 11.

In view of Matthew's shepherd motif, how does his appropriation of the shepherd metaphor compare with its use by the NCB Jewish, Roman, and CB authors analysed in chapter 3 of this investigation? It is to this question of Matthew's socio-religious orientation that the study now turns.

---

202   So, for example, Gundry, 'A Responsive Evaluation of the Social History of the Matthean Community in Roman Syria', in *Social History of the Matthean Community: Cross-Disciplinary Approaches*, ed. D. Balch (Minneapolis: Fortress Press, 1991), 63–64, Hagner, '*Sitz*', 58–59, and Stanton, *Gospel*, 11–12.

Chapter 5

MATTHEW'S SOCIO-RELIGIOUS ORIENTATION

5.1 Introduction

The preceding analysis of Matthew demonstrates that the shepherd metaphor occupies a significant place within the Gospel narrative. Clearly, the
author exercised considerable care to present Jesus as Israel's Shepherd.
The question now becomes: what does the shepherd motif reveal about
Matthew's socio-religious orientation? Rather than adopting an either/or
configuration for Judaism and Christ-belief, and thinking of them as either
separate, intersecting, or concentric circles,[1] these groups are better thought
of as points on a spectrum. Belief in Jewish-national restoration would
represent one continuum whereby one end of the spectrum would represent
a Zealot-like nationalistic concern for the moral well-being and political-
national restoration of the people of Israel, while groups at the other end
would view Jews as absolutely cut off from and rejected by God.

To locate the Evangelist's place on this spectrum based on Matthew's
deployment of the shepherd metaphor, his appropriation of the metaphor
must be compared with the map of uses of the metaphor generated by NCB
Jewish, NCB Roman, and CB authors in the third chapter of the study. The
analysis of this chapter will begin by comparing the patterns of thought
exhibited by the use of 'shepherd' in Roman texts with those reflected
in its appropriation by NCB Jews, Christ-believers, and Matthew. In the
comparison with Roman texts, particular attention will be given to outlining
some of the social-historical realities concerning Roman emperors, and their
relationship to their subjects, as a way to underscore the different perspec-
tives on leadership that existed between NCB Romans, on the one hand, and
Jews and Christ-believers, on the other. The second set of comparisons will
be drawn between NCB Jews, Christ-believers, and Matthew. By discerning
points of continuity and discontinuity in the patterns of thought between
Matthew and these groups of writers, Matthew's socio-religious orientation
can be established and located on a socio-religious spectrum. The chapter
will then offer a sketch of some of the implications of Matthew's socio-
religious orientation for the institutional realities of the Mattheans within a
Roman imperial context.

---

1 See the discussion of section 1.2.1 above.

5.2 Comparing Patterns of Thought

5.2.1 NCB Roman authors vs NCB Jews, Christ-believers, and Matthew

As observed in section 3.3 above, Romans authors, unlike those of other ancient cultures, rarely liken their monarchs to a shepherd.[2] Common honorific titles ascribed to Roman emperors include 'God', 'Lord/Master', 'Saviour', 'Benefactor', and 'Founder'. These sorts of honorific titles, on the one hand, were consonant with what is known about Roman imperial theology.[3] According to Roman imperial theology, the gods willed for Rome to rule the world, and the Roman emperor represents the agent of their sovereignty, the manifestation of their presence among humans, and the conduit through which the societal gifts of peace, protection, provision, and the like flow.

While the Roman senate deified dead emperors, Goodman suggests that living emperors like Octavius sought to portray themselves merely as first among equals among senatorial aristocrats.[4] Later emperors, however, could on occasion demand worship during their lifetime.[5] In the case of Domitian – who probably would have reigned when Matthew composed his Gospel – the names ascribed to him include 'Favourite of God', 'Lord of the World', and 'Ruler of the Nations'. In addition to these titles, Suetonius asserts that Domitian sought to be called 'our Lord and God'.[6] These types of exalted ascription, as well as the directives for emperor worship, reflect in part the importance of social hierarchy in Roman society: wealth and elite social status were celebrated, while poverty and manual labour were despised.[7]

Thus, the ruler–subject relationship in Roman culture would have been characterized by absolute dominance, discrimination, and elitism on the part of the ruler, fear on the part of his subjects, and probably mutual hostility.[8] Rulers valued their economic, social, and even

2   When they do so, the metaphor's usage owes itself either to bi-cultural, Graeco-Roman authors borrowing from their ancient Greek literary and cultural tradition on the one hand, or to dramatic irony on the other. See section 3.3.5 above.

3   See Carter, *Empire*, 20–34, 57–74.

4   M. Goodman, *Roman World: 44BC–AD 180* (London: Routledge, 1997), 123–34.

5   E.g. Gaius, *Gaius*, 22.

6   P. Southern, however, remains less than convinced that this particular title was all that offensive, especially if it was limited to written correspondence not oral speech (*Domitian: Tragic Tyrant* [London: Routledge, 1997], 45). For more titles for Domitian, see section 3.3.4 above.

7   For a discussion of the Roman culture of social hierarchy, see Garnsey and Saller, *Roman Empire*, 107–25, and MacMullen, *Roman*, 88–120. Matthew 20.25 reflects an awareness of these Roman values.

8   This last point is debated, e.g. Kautsky, *Politics*. Mutual hostility, however, seems likely. In terms of basic conflict theory, resistance invariably follows assertions of

physical separation from the general populace. Carter perceptively comments that the various sorts of distinction 'maintain the distance between the aristocracy and peasants, and reminds the peasants of who they are and who they are not'.[9] The acute distinction between the emperor and his subjects would also be underscored ritually, inasmuch as Roman subjects offered vows, prayers, and sacrifices for the emperor's well-being, as well as, in the cases of Gaius and Domitian (at least), sacrifices *to* the emperor. In view of the stress on social hierarchy and class divisions, as well as the shape and tone of the ruler–subject relationship, it should come as no surprise that Roman rulers were not typically likened to lowly shepherds.

By contrast, NCB Jews took an entirely different view of shepherds largely because they had lived in an agrarian society for most of their history: hence, the overwhelmingly positive metaphorical use of the metaphor in the HB. Consequently, unlike in Roman culture, not only do NCB Jews call or liken God to a shepherd (e.g. *Agric.* 51; Sir. 18.13), they also use the metaphor for monarchs and rulers (e.g. *Virt.* 58; 4Q504). Based on his reading of biblical characters such as Moses and Joseph, Philo asserts that shepherding animals served as an effective training ground for and preliminary exercise in kingship (*Mos.* 60–62; cf. *Ios.* 2). Beyond political rulers, this group of authors also appropriates the metaphor for religious leaders and for teaching (e.g. CD XIII and *2 Bar.* 77.13-16, respectively). To shepherd their flock Jewish leaders were expected to provide care, protection, and guidance for their followers, and – at least according to the biblical tradition – were divinely reprimanded when they failed to do so (e.g. Ezekiel 34; Zech. 11.4-17).

Christ-believers employ the metaphor for Jesus as the messiah and for assembly leaders. Not only do Christ-believers apply 'shepherd' to Jesus, but they also ascribe to him some of the titles that Roman authors use for their emperors.[10] Similarly to their NCB Jewish counterparts, CB leaders were responsible for providing the proper religious care and nurture for their flock because of their role as 'under-shepherds' to Jesus, to whom they were accountable as leaders. In view of its usage in Eph. 4.11-13, where it is conjoined with 'teacher' (i.e. 'shepherd-teacher') and listed alongside other positions of leadership in CB assemblies (viz. apostles, prophets, and evangelists), it seems likely that 'shepherd' would have been used in some instances as an official title for CB leaders.[11]

---

power (cf. J. Barbalet, 'Power and Resistance', *BJS* 36 [1985]: 521–48).

9   Carter, *Empire*, 16.

10   E.g. 'Saviour' (Lk. 2.11; Jn 4.42; Phil. 3.20), 'God' (Jn 20.28; Rom. 9.5), 'Source of Creation' (Rev. 3.14; cf. Jn 1.3; Col. 1.16), and 'Lord' (or 'Master').

11   Its use as a title for leaders would be similar to the use of 'shepherd' in some modern, Christian circles as a synonym for 'pastor' – a transliteration of the Latin word for 'shepherd'.

Not unexpectedly, Matthew's use of 'shepherd' also differs markedly from its use by Roman authors. He applies the metaphor to Jesus as Israel's divinely appointed king; and he employs it to describe Jesus' salvific activity amongst his people: Jesus saved his people by performing deeds of healing and exorcisms, and by dying as an atoning sacrifice for their sins.

Thus, Roman culture represents very different thought patterns concerning 'shepherd' from those of NCB Jews and Christ-believers such as Matthew. The ruler–subject relationship in Roman culture would have been characterized by discrimination, elitism, fear, and hostility. The Emperor of Rome is depicted as a distant, ruling king, and not as a close shepherd. While emperors sought the support of their subjects, Roman writers do not portray them as associating with their subjects; class distinctions were even reinforced in the daily attire of togas and jewellery, which varied uniformly according to social rank, as Garnsey and Saller observe, 'Romans paraded their rank whenever they appeared in public.'[12] Jesus, however, is both king and shepherd: he exercises divine ruling authority, but he also remains his people's ever-caring shepherd, seeking out, gathering together, and spending time with the social outcasts. Assembly leaders were to follow the example of their 'Chief Shepherd': rather than separate themselves from the flock, they must abide with them, and shepherd the flock without any regard for social class distinctions. These points will receive further elaboration in section 5.4 below.

5.2.2 Matthew vs other Christ-believers and NCB Jews

A comparison of the basic referents for the shepherd metaphor in the texts of NCB Jews, Christ-believers, and Matthew are summarized in Table 5.1. Matthew's use of the metaphor parallels its use by NCB Jewish authors. This group typically employs 'shepherd' for rulers or for the activity of ruling. Matthew applies the term to rulers. He explicitly connects the metaphor to the activity of ruling in his infancy narrative: the messiah will 'shepherd' or 'rule' over God's people Israel – a rule clearly possessing a political-national dimension.

---

12   Garnsey and Saller, *Roman Empire*, 117.

Table 5.1 Shepherd metaphor referents[13]

Ruler	YHWH	Messiah	Assembly leader	Unique usages
Jeremiah	Gen. 48.15	*Pss. Sol.* 17	John	Philo
Num. 27.17	Gen. 49.24	John	Acts	*2 Baruch*
Ezekiel	Psalm 23	Mark	Ephesians	*Hermas*
Deutero-Zech.	Psalm 28	Hebrews	1 Peter	CD
Deuteronomistic History	Psalm 80	1 Peter	Jude	
Micah	Ecclesiastes	Revelation	*Hermas*	
Chronicles	Deutero-Isaiah	**Matthew**		
Psalm 78	Jeremiah			
Deutero-Isaiah	Ezekiel			
Trito-Isaiah	Hosea			
Nahum	Micah			
1 Enoch	Deutero-Zech.			
4Q504	*1 Enoch*			
1Q34	4Q509			
CD	Ben Sira			
Philo	Judith			
LAB	*Apoc. Ezek.*			
Josephus	Philo			
4 Ezra	*LAB*			
Revelation				
Matthew				

Christ-believing authors use the metaphor for Jesus as the messiah and for assembly leaders but not for political rulers. Not only are earthly monarchs never likened to shepherds, but seldom do Christ-believers even portray Jesus as a ruling shepherd. Conversely, Matthew never uses the metaphor for assembly leaders.[14] Moreover, he seems to distinguish between Jesus as Israel's Shepherd and the disciples whom Jesus commissions to extend his shepherding mission to Israel: on the one hand, the Evangelist uses ποιμαίνω (and ποίμην) for Jesus, but never for the disciples. Unlike John and 1 Peter, where the authors use ποιμαίνω for both Jesus and assembly leaders, and unlike Acts, Ephesians, and Jude, where the term is used only for assembly leaders, Matthew reserves the term for Jesus, whom he regards as the true Shepherd of God's people Israel;[15] on the other hand, while all of the

---

13   This table represents a slightly revised version of Table 3.16 in chapter 3 above.

14   In not using 'shepherd' for assembly leaders, Matthew resembles Second Temple Jews, who also refrain from using the term for synagogue leaders; cf. the massive primary source study of Runesson, Binder, and Olsson, *Ancient Synagogue*.

15   Matthew's reservation of 'shepherd' for Jesus would parallel the distinction

Synoptic Gospels have some version(s) of the account of the disciples' commissioning, and while Mark and Luke specifically make reference to the disciples' success – they did what Jesus did[16] – Matthew does not mention their success. Although their success would doubtless be implied, this omission may represent another way that Matthew distinguished between Jesus as Israel's true Shepherd and the disciples, who act on behalf of the Davidic Shepherd.

NCB Jewish authors tend to appropriate the metaphor in fairly pastoral terms – i.e. in terms commonly used to describe the duties of literal shepherds: the idyllic shepherd watches over the afflicted, binds up, heals, and feeds the troubled and the lame, protects the flock from danger, and the like. Matthew, in the Miracle Chapters, depicts Jesus the Davidic Shepherd in pastoral terms: in reaching out to the socially marginalized (8.2-4; 9.9-13), Jesus demonstrates his concern for the weak and the stray of the flock; in healing his people of their sicknesses (8.16; 9.35), he cares for and 'binds up' the wounds of his sheep. While Mark and Luke – and even Matthew elsewhere, for that matter – portray Jesus as engaged in these types of activities, only in Matthew are these activities related to the shepherding of Israel. Table 5.2 summarizes the pastoral imagery of the shepherd metaphor.

found in the Dream Visions section of *1 Enoch*: 'shepherd' is reserved for the evil angelic rulers who brutalize Israel. Israel's rulers such as Moses, David, and Solomon are not 'shepherds' – although they function as shepherd-rulers – they are depicted as herd leaders, while YHWH is the 'Lord' of the sheep. Manning is probably correct that the author avoids using 'shepherd' for YHWH and for Israel's heroes because he has decided to give the term a negative connotation (*Echoes*, 88–89). As mentioned in section 4.2.2 above, a parallel distinction is made in the Johannine corpus: only Jesus is explicitly called God's υἱός; Christ-believers are never υἱοί but τέκνα of God.

16   Mark 6.13 and Lk. 9.6; 10.17.

Israel's Only Shepherd

Table 5.2 Pastoral imagery used when idealizing a shepherd

Pronounced imagery	Modest imagery	Little or no imagery
Ps. 23.1	Gen. 48.15	Ecclesiastes
Ps. 28.9	Gen. 49.24	Ben Sira
Ps. 80.1	Judith	Philo
Isa. 40.11	*LAB*	Acts
Jer. 31.10	Mk 14.27	Ephesians
Ezekiel 34		Hebrews
Hos. 4.16		1 Peter
Mic. 7.14		Jude
Zech. 11.13		Revelation 2; 12; 19
1 Enoch		*Hermas*
CD XIII		
Pss Sol. 17		
Apoc. Ezek.		
Mk 6.34		
John		
Rev. 7.17		
Matthew		

Sentiments of Jewish-national restoration involving the shepherd metaphor by NCB Jews and Christ-believers are summarized in Table 5.3. Matthew's concern for the restoration of the people of Israel clearly corresponds with the tendency observed in the texts of NCB Jews – in clear contrast to the majority of Christ-believers.

Table 5.3 Overtones of Jewish-national restoration in the shepherd metaphor

Strong overtones	Modest overtones	Little or no overtones
1 Enoch	1Q34	Ecclesiastes
4Q504	4Q509	Ben Sira
CD	Judith	Philo
Judith	Mark	Acts
Pss Sol. 17	1Q34	Ephesians
1 Enoch	4Q509	Hebrews
4Q504	Judith	1 Peter
CD	Mark	Jude
Judith		John
Apoc. Ezek.		Revelation
LAB		Hermas
4 Ezra		
2 Baruch		
Josephus		
Matthew		

The most common referent for the metaphor among CB authors is the messiah. Its usage by these authors as well as by the author of *Psalms of Solomon* 17 are summarized in Table 5.4. Matthew's appropriation of the shepherd metaphor most closely resembles that of the other Gospels: Jesus the compassionate shepherd is sacrificed for his sheep but raised from the dead; he gathers together disciples, he is the object of scriptural prophecy, and his flock (ultimately) includes Gentiles.

Table 5.4 Profile of the appropriations of the shepherd metaphor for the messiah

Shepherd trait	Pss. Sol. 17	Mark	John	Heb.	1 Pet.	Rev.	Matthew
Is a sacrifice for the sheep		X	X	X	X		X
Offers abundant care		X	X		X	X	X
Raised from the dead		X	X	X			X
Gatherer of disciples	X	X	X				X
Moses-like		X	X	X			
Compassionate	X	X	X				X
Davidic ancestry	X		X			X	X
Object of scriptural prophecy		X	X				X
Relates uniquely to YHWH	X		X				X
Universal ruler	X					X	X
Universal judge	X					X	X
Relates intimately with flock			X				
Flock includes Gentiles	X		X		X		X
Teacher		X					
Healer and exorcist							X
Replaces failed shepherds							X

What is surprising, however, is the close correspondences between Matthew and *Psalms of Solomon*. In some ways, Matthew's appropriation of the metaphor actually resembles *Psalms* more than the writings of Christ-believers. Only Matthew and *Psalms* combine Davidic ancestry with pastoral imagery.[17] On the one hand, Matthew depicts Jesus in the Miracle Chapters as the messiah who inclusively reaches out to the socially marginalized, and goes about healing the flock of Israel of their physical afflictions. On the other hand, Matthew characterizes Jesus' mission to Israel in the Miracle Chapters as Davidic: Jesus' deeds of healing represent the acts of the Son of David. Since Jesus' acts of healing should be viewed in the Miracle Chapters in light of his identity as the Son of David, then insofar as Matthew presents Jesus as the therapeutic Son of David, he presents him as Israel's Davidic

17   While the messianic appropriations of Mark and Revelation 7 possess pastoral imagery, they lack the element of Davidic ancestry. John and Revelation 2 express the Davidic ancestry of the messiah but without much pastoral imagery. All the other texts of Christ-believers have neither of these elements.

Shepherd. Likewise, *Psalms of Solomon* 17 portrays the Davidic messiah using pastoral imagery: the '*son of David*' will '*gather* a holy people whom he will *lead* in righteousness' (v. 26a), he will '*distribute them upon the land*' (v. 28a), and 'faithfully and righteously [*shepherd*] the Lord's *flock* ... not [letting] any of them stumble in their *pasture*' (v. 40b).

Another way in which Matthew's use of the shepherd metaphor agrees with *Psalms* over and against other Christ-believers is in the overtones of Jewish nationalism. Matthew conveys definite Jewish-national sentiments in the birth and infancy traditions, by affirming that the primary scope of the messiah's shepherding is the Jews ('my people Israel') whom Jesus came to save from their sins (1.21; 2.6). These overtones also resonate throughout the Miracle Chapters:[18] in saving Israel from its sins and the satanic oppression that resulted from its unfaithful leadership, Jesus inaugurated Israel's restoration as the people of God, undoing the ravages of the nation's sins.[19] Similarly, the concern of the prayer in *Psalms of Solomon* 17 for the security and purity of Jerusalem, as well as for the righteous state of the Jewish nation, reflect the strong Jewish-national focus of the psalm's author.

5.2.3 Summary and assessment of the patterns of thought

In light of these comparisons, it is obvious that Matthew's employment of 'shepherd' stands in pointed contrast to the term's use by NCB Roman authors. Of the remaining two groups, it seems clear that the Evangelist's appropriation of the shepherd metaphor most closely resembles the patterns or general tendencies of thought reflected in the metaphor's use by NCB Jews. Matthew agrees with other Christ-believers against NCB Jews in applying the metaphor for Jesus;[20] and consequently, within the 'messiah as shepherd' category, he agrees with other Christ-believers against *Psalms of Solomon* in associating the metaphor with atoning sacrifice, resurrection from the dead, and abundant provision. These similarities in usage, however, must also be weighed against Matthew's agreement with *Psalms of Solomon*. Like *Psalms*, the Evangelist combines Davidic ancestry with pastoral imagery. Moreover, the metaphor reflects a strong concern for Jewish-national restoration. The Evangelist also stands with NCB Jews generally against Christ-believers in using the metaphor for the geo-political ruling of Israel, and in not using the metaphor, as other Christ-believers commonly do, for assembly leaders.

It might be argued that these similarities are somewhat ambiguous, and that Matthew's messianic appropriation of the shepherd metaphor resembles John, Mark, and Revelation more than *Psalms*; or that John, Mark, and

---

18   Cf. Mt. 10.5-6 and 15.24.

19   While Jesus inaugurated this national restoration during his mission to Israel, it would only be completed at his Parousia (19.28; 23.39).

20   This agreement would be expected since Matthew is, after all, a follower of Jesus.

Revelation show enough similarities with the patterns of usage of Second Temple Jews to warrant classifying them, with Matthew, alongside NCB Jewish texts. Such criticism, however, misunderstands the claim of the study, on the one hand, and under-estimates the diversity that existed within first-century Christ-belief and Judaism, on the other. This study contends that Matthew's patterns of thought concerning the shepherd metaphor more closely resemble those of NCB Jews *generally* than those of other Christ-believers *generally*. It does not follow that the Evangelist's thought patterns resemble those of *every* Jewish author. At points, for example, Philo's appropriation of the metaphor is strikingly different from Matthew's as well as from other Jews.

Nor does it follow that only the patterns of thought of the Mattheans – of all CB groups – resembled those of Second Temple Judaism. As argued in the General Introduction, interactions between Jews and Christ-believers are best configured spectrally: there were diverse strains of first-century Judaism and Christ-belief. Thus, on a Judaism–Christ-belief socio-religious spectrum, various CB groups would have fallen closer to the Jewish end of the continuum than others. It should not be surprising, then, to find that other Christ-believers – such as the authors of John, Mark, and Revelation – resemble some aspects of NCB Jewish thought patterns. This may especially be true if, as some scholars argue, these three texts reflect (at least in part) the traditions of Palestinian Jewish Christ-believers.[21]

Wilson's examination of second-century Jewish Christ-belief sheds further light on the diversity of Jewish Christ-belief. Although he admits that the information about kinds of second-century Jewish Christ-belief is limited to the scanty and somewhat problematic references in the early church fathers (who treat Jewish Christ-belief as a heretical sect), and the Pseudo-Clementines, Wilson recognizes that, while 'it may not be possible to delineate the sources [of Jewish Christ-believers] with great precision ... their general drift and the differences between them can be used to explore certain lines of development in the history of Jewish Christianity'.[22] Wilson, who (provisionally) identifies three clusters of second-century Jewish Christ-belief, concludes, 'The variety among, as well as within, these groups alerts us to the danger of speaking of Jewish Christianity as if it were a homogeneous entity, and this in turn suggests that *they may have related differently to non-Christian Judaism*.'[23] Direct lines of correspondence between the first-

---

21   In the case of Mark, for example, J. Marcus states, 'Mark himself is a Jewish Christian from Judea' ('The Jewish War and the *Sitz im Leben* of Mark', *JBL* 111/3 [1992], 461). Aune believes that there is strong evidence to suggest that the author of Revelation was a 'Palestinian [CB] Jew' (*Revelation*, 1.clxii).

22   Wilson, *Related Strangers*, 144. For a more sceptical view on isolating the sources in the Pseudo-Clementines, see J. Wehnert, 'Literarkritik und Sprachanalyse: Kritische Anmerkungen zum gegenwärtigen Stand der Pseudo-Klementinen-Forschung', *ZNW* 74 (1983): 268–301.

23   Wilson, *Related Strangers*, 157 (emphasis added).

century groups behind John, Mark, and Revelation need not be established with the second-century groups Wilson discusses. It seems clear enough, however, that based on a social-historical reading of the New Testament, the diversity that existed in the second century would also have existed in the first.[24]

Thus, three things become reasonably clear. First, John, Mark, and Revelation reflect to varying degrees thought patterns related to the shepherd metaphor of Second Temple Jews.[25] Therefore, on a socio-religious spectrum they would be located closer to various forms of Judaism than the other texts surveyed in section 3.4 above: Acts, Ephesians, Hebrews, 1 Peter, Jude, and *Hermas*. Second, this similarity merely attests to the diversity that existed among groups associated with the Jesus movement. Third, despite their similarities with NCB Jewish thought patterns, Matthew's patterns of thought align much more closely with those of NCB Jews than these three texts do. In other words, if John, Mark, and Revelation can be located closer to the Jewish-national restoration side of a socio-religious spectrum, then Matthew can be located still closer to the end pole.

Matthew's socio-religious orientation, then, reflects someone who operated within the conceptual framework of Second Temple Judaism, or as White puts it, 'the Matthean community must be viewed still as a *sect* within the larger fabric of Judaism in its day, rather than having obtained the status or self-definition of a separate religion'.[26] Thus, Matthew (and his followers) would have adhered to a Christ-centred form of Judaism, advocating among other things, in addition to faith in Jesus as the messiah, Jewish nationalism – as evidenced by his appropriation of the shepherd metaphor.

As previously mentioned, Matthew's socio-religious location can be described in terms of occupying a certain area on a socio-religious spectrum. Based on this study, Matthew would be located on a socio-religious spectrum mapping belief in Jewish-national restoration as shown in Fig. 5.1. That is to say, based on the Evangelist's shepherd motif – which gives evidence of a definite belief in Jewish-national restoration – Matthew's pattern of thought reflected by his appropriation of the shepherd metaphor puts him much closer to a form of Second Temple Judaism advocating Jewish-national restoration than the groups of Christ-believers who rejected Israel's restoration. To assert that Matthew resides on the left side of this spectrum is to say more than simply that Matthew is Jewish – a point that most scholars recognize.[27] The Gospel's shepherd motif suggests that its author advocated

---

24   See the discussion in section 1.2.1 above.

25   Revelation especially exhibits similarities in thought with NCB Jews. Besides associating the metaphor with the activity of ruling, followers of Jesus are described in very Jewish terms, e.g. they associate with the synagogues of the Jews (Rev. 2.9; 3.9) and they keep 'the commandments of God' (Rev. 12.17; 14.12).

26   White, 'Crisis Management', 222 (his emphasis).

27   Segal, for example, writes that to say 'Matthew represents Jewish Christianity ... is not very helpful because even Paul is a Jewish Christian' ('Jewish Voice', 15).

Jewish nationalism – like most strands of Second Temple Judaism – but quite unlike much of the Jesus movement. Additionally, in light of the political-national overtones that 'shepherd' possesses for Matthew, the Evangelist seemed to have a slightly different view of assembly leadership than many other segments of the Jesus movement. This point shall be revisited in section 5.3.2 below. To offer a more precise socio-religious location than the one offered here would demand a comprehensive treatment of other patterns of thought,[28] which clearly lies outside the purview of this study.

Belief in Jewish-   *Rejection of Jewish-*
national restoration   *national restoration*

Fig. 5.1 *Situating Matthew's socio-religious orientation*

Nevertheless, the results of this study of the Evangelist's socio-religious orientation can be integrated within broader Matthean scholarship. Scholars such as Clark, Strecker, and Meier[29] insist that Matthew was Gentile. In light of the unmistakeable divergences in 'shepherd' usage between Matthew and (near) contemporary Roman authors, this view seems highly unlikely. Numerous scholars argue that the Evangelist was Jewish (accounting for the strongly Jewish tone of the Gospel), but that he aligned himself with followers of Jesus who, in the mission to the Gentiles, rejected Jewish nationalism.[30] The Gospel's concern for the moral and geo-political restoration of the nation of Israel, conveyed in large measure by Matthew's shepherd motif, however, speaks against a non-Jewish-national, Gentile orientation.

The outcome of this study supports the position of Saldarini, Sim, et al.[31] Saldarini, in addition to employing sociological theory, investigates Matthew's understanding of terms such as 'Israel', 'people', and 'Jews', the Evangelist's polemic against the Jewish leaders, his understanding of the term 'nations', along with his view of the Mosaic Law, to arrive at the position that the Gospel reflects an 'author [who] considers himself to be a Jew who has the true interpretation of Torah and is faithful to God's will as revealed by Jesus ... [and who] seeks to promote his interpretation of Judaism over that of other Jewish leaders'.[32]

---

28   Matthew's view of the Mosaic Law, his attitude towards keeping the ritual laws, his view of Gentiles, etc.
29   Clark, 'Gentile Bias', Strecker, *Der Weg*, and Meier, *Law and History*.
30   E.g. Stanton, *Gospel*, Hagner, '*Sitz im Leben*', and Foster, *Community*.
31   Saldarini, *Christian-Jewish* and Sim, *Christian Judaism*.
32   Saldarini, *Christian-Jewish*, 7.

Matthew's shepherd motif reflects someone who thought within the conceptual framework of first-century Judaism. Right from the outset of the story, God appointed Jesus to shepherd his people, the nation of Israel (2.4b-6) – a messianic rule with definite geo-political dimensions. Consequently, the messiah's shepherding mission is exclusively Israel-centric (chs 8–9; cf. 10.5-6), on the one hand; thus only with reticence does Jesus heal those Gentiles who come to him (8.7; 15.24). The shepherd motif, on the other hand, makes it plain that Israel's Shepherd replaces the nation's leaders (2.1-6; 9.35-38), and that they are recipients of divine wrath – rather than the nation as a whole – according to God's sovereign design (27.1-10). While Jesus' death and resurrection represent 'die Wende der Zeit',[33] whereby Jesus' followers are directed to take the Gospel to the Gentiles, the inclusion of, among other things, the difficult logion of 10.5b-6 (cf. 15.24), suggests that the Jews remained at the centre of Matthew's mission.[34]

In offering support of Saldarini's position, this study complements his work in two ways. First, while Saldarini's analysis of various Matthean words (e.g. 'Israel', 'people', 'Jews') resembles the examination of 'shepherd' here, there remains one very important methodological difference. Saldarini's focus is inductive: he investigates what these terms mean within the narrative, claiming that their 'normal' usage by Matthew does not presuppose a non-Jewish or CB perspective. He does not, however, compare how these terms are used by Matthew's contemporaries (NCB Jews, NCB Romans, and other Christ-believers).[35] The present study employs both inductive and comparative approaches. Consequently, whereas Saldarini can conclude that Matthew uses these terms ('Israel', Jews', etc.) within the lexical parameters of NCB Jews – although they also fall within the lexical parameters of Christ-believers – the present study goes one step further. This study demonstrates that Matthew's patterns of thought concerning the shepherd metaphor, beyond simply falling within wide parameters of possible thought patterns, more closely aligns with those of NCB Jews than those of other Christ-believers, while largely contradicting those of NCB Romans.

Second, while Saldarini correctly acknowledges that '[Israel's] destiny and Jesus' mission to reform Israel and instruct it in God's will is central to the Matthean narrative and to Matthew's world view',[36] he does not discuss Matthew's belief in Jewish nationalism as a means of locating Matthew's socio-religious orientation. As observed, the Evangelist's shepherd motif provides powerful evidence for his Jewish-national sentiments, sentiments that were an integral part of Matthew's apocalyptic eschatology (25.31-46).

33   So Meier, *Law and History*, 65.
34   Cf. the comments of Brown, 'The Two-fold Representation of the Mission in Matthew's Gospel', *ST* 31 (1977): 28.
35   Cf. the similarly inductive approaches of other proponents of this position like Sim, *Christian Judaism*, Segal, 'Jewish Voice', and White, 'Crisis Management'.
36   Saldarini, *Christian-Jewish*, 83.

While Sim extensively analyses Matthew's apocalyptic eschatology,[37] he remains largely silent on the matter of the Evangelist's Jewish-national outlook. Furthermore, when discussing Matthew's socio-religious location, rather than attempting to use the Evangelist's apocalyptic eschatology as a possible line of argumentation for his position, he relies on the customary inductive approach.[38] Although he does not seek to analyse the similarities and differences in the apocalyptic eschatology of NCB Jews and Christ-believers, the way that they intersect in Matthew is noteworthy:

> The evangelist's distinctive portrayal of the Son of Man is *a combination of his Christian synoptic sources and certain Jewish traditions* which are also found in the Parables of Enoch. The climax of Matthew's eschatological scheme concerns ... the bestowal of rewards and punishments. ... The first of these themes is well represented *in both Jewish and Christian apocalyptic eschatology*, but the second finds *its closest parallels in Jewish tradition*. With the *notable exception of the book of Revelation*, the consignment of the wicked to the fires of Gehenna is *not particularly common in the early Christian literature*.[39]

Four observations from Sim's work are especially significant for the present study. First, some of the patterns of thought represented in the apocalyptic eschatology of NCB Jews and Christ-believers overlap with one another. Second, Matthew draws from both traditions. Third, at times his thought patterns more closely resemble those of the NCB Jewish tradition. Fourth, Revelation (at points) follows Matthew in reflecting this tradition. These observations of Matthew's apocalyptic eschatology resonate fully with this study. At times the thought patterns of NCB Jews and Christ-believers converge, but while Matthew's employment of the metaphor reflects both traditions, his use of it more closely resembles its appropriation by some forms of NCB Jews; and, Revelation seems to follow the same pattern as Matthew – although not to the same degree. Therefore, although Sim examines apocalyptic eschatology with a completely different purpose in mind,[40] his observations confirm the results of this study from an entirely different angle.

---

37   Sim, *Apocalyptic Eschatology in the Gospel of Matthew* (Cambridge: Cambridge University Press, 1996), 75–249 (especially).

38   Sim, *Apocalyptic Eschatology*, 183–95; cf. also the argumentation in his later work, *Christian Judaism*.

39   Sim, *Apocalyptic Eschatology*, 176 (emphasis added).

40   Sim's aims are to demonstrate that apocalyptic eschatology is of great importance to Matthew, and to show why this is the case.

5.3 Matthew's institutional setting

5.3.1 Introduction

Matthew's shepherd motif offers evidence that he operated within the conceptual framework of Second Temple Judaism: Matthew (and his followers) adhered to a Christ-centred form of Judaism, advocating Jewish nationalism; and on a socio-religious spectrum mapping belief in Jewish nationalism, the Evangelist's socio-religious orientation would be located much closer to the Jewish nationalistic end than the other. What kind of bearing would this have had on the institutional realities of the Matthean communities? Some of these social-historical realities will be outlined below.

5.3.2 Matthean leadership

Because 'shepherd' represents a core leadership symbol for Jews and Christ-believers, in light of Matthew's socio-religious orientation, his view of leadership would have differed in some respects from numerous other Christ-believers. For Matthew, the metaphor possesses strong political-national overtones. Consequently, unlike many other CB authors, who use the term for assembly leaders, the Evangelist does not employ 'shepherd' for Matthean leaders. For the Mattheans, leaders were likely called 'prophets' (10.41), 'righteous men' (10.41), 'disciples' (10.42), 'scribes' (13.52), 'servants' (20.26; 23.11), 'wise men' or 'sages' (23.34), and 'teachers' (διδάσκαλοι [5.19; 28.20]) – similar to Jesus for whom Matthew also uses these terms.[41] But leaders are never 'shepherds'.[42] For Matthew, only Jesus was Israel's Shepherd: the divinely appointed shepherd-monarch of the nation Israel, who inaugurated and who would consummate at his Parousia the rule of the kingdom of heaven on earth.

Elsewhere the Matthean Jesus forbids his followers from referring to their leaders as 'Rabbi', 'Father', or 'Leader' (καθηγατής [23.7-10]),[43] restricting the application of these titles to himself; however, this prohibition serves explicitly to distinguish the Mattheans from the Pharisees[44] – who enjoy

---

41   Matthew refers to Jesus explicitly or implicitly as: 'prophet' (13.57; 21.11, 46), 'righteous man' (27.19), 'scribe' and 'wise man' (23.34), 'servant' (20.26-28), and 'teacher' (8.19; 9.11; passim).

42   Cf. R. Ascough, 'Matthew and Community Formation', in *The Gospel of Matthew in Current Study: Studies in Memory of William G. Thompson, S. J.*, ed. D. Aune (Grand Rapids: Eerdmans, 2001), 121, and D. Duling, 'The Matthean Brotherhood and Marginal Scribal Leadership', in *Modelling Early Christianity*, ed. P. Esler (London: Routledge, 1995), 172–75.

43   This prohibition is without parallel in the other Gospels.

44   Williams ('Jews', 320) believes that the influence of Roman culture on the Jewish synagogue environment led to the adoption of the Latin term *pater synagogue* ('Father of the synagogue'). If she is correct then Mt. 23.9 may also represent an implicit polemic against Roman culture.

these titles (23.6-10) – a distinction that would have been of central importance if, as some scholars claim, Matthew was a CB Pharisee.[45] But the
restriction of 'shepherd' to Jesus would not have concerned the Mattheans
seeking to distinguish themselves from other groups; rather, the restriction
would have concerned the overtones of Jewish nationalism that the metaphor
often possesses for NCB Jews. Since for this group of writers a shepherd's
rule typically included a political-national element, this would have made it
more difficult conceptually for Matthew to apply the term to the assembly
leaders of his marginalized sect in the first-century Roman Empire.

Matthean terms for leadership are drawn from Jewish tradition.[46] Not
surprisingly, Matthew's leadership terms stand in sharp contrast to some of
the titles used by certain other CB authors, e.g. overseer (Acts 20.28; Phil. 1.1;
1 Tim. 3.2; Tit. 1.7; 1 Pet. 2.25), evangelist (Acts 21.8; Eph. 4.11), elder (Acts
14.23; 1 Tim. 5.17; Tit. 1.5; 1 Pet. 5.1; 2 John 1) and, of course, shepherd
(Eph. 4.11; Herm. *Sim.* 108.5b–6). Additionally, while three of Matthew's
leadership terms (prophet, servant, and teacher) are used elsewhere by other
Christ-believers, his other more Jewish terms for leadership (righteous man,
wise man/sage, disciple, and scribe) are not.

At this point two questions could be posed. First, do Matthew's leadership
terms represent a specific polemic against other CB groups? Sim, for one,
understands much of the Gospel as polemic against Pauline Christ-belief in
particular.[47] Certainly the evidence could be taken in this way. The Matthean
leadership terms that differentiate the Mattheans from other Christ-believers,
however, do not bear polemical overtones in the passages in which they
appear. The only passage bearing clear leadership-term polemic is 23.7-10;
and the injunction here against adopting 'Rabbi', 'Father', and 'Leader'
specifically targets Pharisees – not Pauline groups or other Christ-believers.

Second, of the Evangelist's leadership designations does 'shepherd'
represent a polemic against its use by other CB groups? Rather than being
rooted in specific interaction between the Mattheans and other Christ-
believers, it would seem better to understand their respective uses in light of
the metaphor's usage in the Jewish scriptures. The scriptures unambiguously
employ the shepherd metaphor to convey aspirations of Jewish nationalism,
and consequently routinely use it for political rulers. Because Matthew
operates within the religious framework of NCB Judaism, he embraces this
altogether Jewish dimension of the metaphor, freely giving expression to this
type of thought in his Gospel.

While some non-Matthean Christ-believers would have had similar
convictions as the Mattheans in this regard, many others would not have
and would have rejected any notion of Jewish-national restoration. Hence,

45   Cf. the discussions of Anders Runesson, 'Re-Thinking Early Jewish-Christian
Relations: Matthean Community History as Pharisaic Intragroup Conflict', *JBL* 127/1
(2008): 95–132, and White, 'Crisis Management', 224–25.

46   Cf. Saldarini, *Christian-Jewish*, 106.

47   See Sim, *Christian*, 165–213.

unlike Matthew, they would not liken political or civic rulers to shepherds,[48] especially in light of the increasing orientation towards Gentile, non-Jewish-national assemblies post 70 CE. While New Testament authors use the metaphor for their leaders, the concern for assembly leaders and their sphere of influence would not have been political but social and religious: Christ-believers sought to emulate Jesus' character; because they aspired to do and to become identified with the works of Jesus,[49] and because they considered Jesus the true and ideal shepherd, some believers would have sought to follow Christ as a 'shepherd', and consequently would have become identified as shepherds of the flock.

With respect to Matthean prophets and scribes, Williams asserts that the Mattheans were moving from a prophet-oriented leadership to a more scribal-oriented one;[50] but it is possible that prophets and scribes/teachers complemented each other. While their roles probably overlapped, scribes, on the one hand, may have been chiefly responsible for reinterpreting the biblical tradition in light of Jesus and his teaching; and they very likely remained with their local assembly, teaching, applying, and transmitting the tradition to the rest of the community.[51] Prophets, on the other hand, may have concentrated on mission and engaged in itinerant preaching. It is even possible that the command to heal and perform exorcisms in the disciples' commission to Israel in 10.5-8 and its absence in their commission to go to all the nations in 28.18-20 may reflect Matthew's Jewish-national outlook: part of Israel's restoration as God's people involved deliverance from physical illnesses and satanic oppression; while these activities were certainly not excluded generally in Christ-believers' mission to the Gentiles,[52] they would not have signified a 'restoration' for the Gentiles in the way that they would have for the Jews.

5.3.3 *The Mattheans and Israel's future*

While some groups of Christ-believers thought that the nation of Israel had been abandoned by God,[53] and consequently, no future national

48   See, for example, opportunities to do so in Acts 7.10; 13.22; Rom. 13.1-7; 1 Tim. 2.2; 1 Pet. 2.13-14.

49   E.g. to be a servant (Mt. 20.26-28; Phil. 1.1); to be a teacher (1 Cor. 12.28; Jas 3.1); to serve as a prophet (Acts 13.1; 1 Thess. 5.20); to be a 'sent-one' (ἀπόστολος [Rom. 16.7; Eph. 4.11]).

50   Williams, *Stewards*, 115–19; cf. Saldarini, *Christian-Jewish*, 107.

51   A. C. Wire summarizes the activity of a scribal community as reinterpreting a revered literary tradition to teach ritual and ethical behaviour in order to help establish and facilitate structure and order in a community ('Gender Roles in a Scribal Community', in *Social History of the Matthean Community: Cross-Disciplinary Approaches*, ed. D. Balch [Minneapolis: Fortress Press, 1991], 91).

52   See, for example, the book of Acts.

53   Some of Paul's statements in Romans suggest that some Christ-believers in Rome thought along such lines (e.g. Rom. 11.1, 11, 19) – a view which Paul seeks to combat. Even though Paul believed in the future restoration of Israel (cf. Romans 11), some

restoration awaited the Jews, according to Matthew's Jewish-national orientation, as conveyed (in part) by his shepherd motif, the people of Israel experienced a measure of Jesus-centred restoration. Jesus inaugurated Israel's moral renewal by offering divine forgiveness of sins and by healing the nation from the physical ramifications of its sins, including satanic oppression. To participate more fully in this national renewal required the acceptance of Jesus as Israel's messiah – expressed by faith in him and his claims, and by obedience and service.[54] Those who reject Jesus could only expect divine condemnation in the Eschaton (11.20-24; 25.41-46). Moral renewal secures the heavenly blessings of God's kingdom (5.3-9). It also guarantees individual well-being such as the material and physical sustenance needed to face living in the often impoverished conditions of the Roman Empire (6.25-34).

Although most Jews rejected Jesus, Matthew did not believe that God had abandoned the nation: God had merely condemned its leadership (21.43-45; 27.3-10) and had replaced them with the leaders of the Mattheans (9.36–10.6). A measure of restoration had already come to Israel – the evidence being the pronouncements of the kingdom's coming and divine forgiveness, the healings and exorcisms that Jesus performed in the Land of Israel, the followers that Jesus gained among the Jews, and the Gentiles that came to him to seek his favour. But Matthew held out hope for a future, more expansive restoration of the nation (23.37-39). In this regard Matthew sounds a note similar to Paul who, despite being rejected by other Jews and spending his life preaching to Gentiles, still believed that 'all Israel' would be saved.[55]

Final political-national restoration awaited Israel in the Eschaton. God appointed Jesus to rule over the nation upon his father David's throne (2.6). Jesus, through his works of healing and deliverance, and through his pronouncement of divine forgiveness, inaugurated the rule of God's kingdom on the earth – beginning in Israel. His death and resurrection secured the consummation of the kingdom, but its full realization would take place only at Jesus' Parousia (26.29). At that time, Jesus as the Shepherd-King will judge all the nations himself (25.31-34), but judge the nation of Israel through the agency of the disciples (19.28).

5.3.4 *The Matthean mission*

Matthew did not abandon the mission begun by Jesus to the Jewish people (10.23; 23.39). Only Matthew among the Synoptics fails to men-

---

of his other statements (e.g. Rom. 2.28-29; 10.4; Phil. 3.3) probably helped to plant the seeds of supersessionism; cf. Sim's discussion of Ignatius and Paul in *Christian Judaism*, 260–69.

54   See the Miracle Chapters, which depict how the Jews were to respond to Jesus' mission.

55   See Rom. 11.25-29.

tion the disciples' success on their pre-Easter mission.[56] Compared with the Gentile mission, the mission to the Jews was not as successful and therefore called for perseverance in the face of failure on the part of its missionaries.[57] Hence, despite its limited success – especially when compared to the relative triumph of the mission to the Gentiles – and despite the obvious attraction (because of its greater numbers) that the more flourishing Gentile mission held for Christ-believers, Matthew encourages his audience to maintain the Jewish focus of their mission, one that Jesus himself modelled. Although their messianic claims brought Jewish opposition, the Jewish nationalism of the Mattheans would have resonated with many first-century NCB Jews.[58]

The Matthean mission seems likely to have consisted of several different aspects. On the one hand, the mission would have been accomplished in fairly passive ways: by influencing their neighbours through their good deeds, which, according to the Evangelist, would result in praise to God by those who witnessed them (5.16); and by praying for more workers for the task of reaching others for the kingdom (9.37-38).[59]

On the other hand, their mission also employed more active strategies. It involved gaining followers through preaching and teaching the gospel of the kingdom (10.7; 24.14; 28.19-20). Matthew's followers were expected to preach the gospel beyond the confines of their own local cities (10.23; 24.14; 28.19). Among other places, the Mattheans (perhaps the scribes) would have debated with others in the public synagogues.[60] While the Mattheans (like other associations) had their own private synagogues, they would have disputed with the Pharisees and other Jewish groups in the public synagogues in order to gain greater sway with other Jews.

---

56   F. Beare makes this observation in 'The Mission of the Disciples and the Mission Charge: Matthew 10 and Parallels', *JBL* 89/1 (1970), 1–2. After Jesus sent out his disciples, Mark states that they performed exorcisms and healings (Mk 6.13); likewise, Luke mentions the success of the Twelve (Lk. 9.6) and the seventy/seventy-two (Lk. 10.17).

57   Sim offers the first part of the parable of the wedding feast as further evidence of the lack of success of the mission to the Jews: 'When the evangelist refers to the past missionary activity of his community, it is always in terms of the unsuccessful Jewish mission (cf. 22:1-6)' (*Christian Judaism*, 244–45).

58   According to Alexander, one of the reasons why Rabbinism bested Jewish Christ-belief in Palestinian Jewish communities is because 'Jewish Christianity would have found it hard to cope with Jewish nationalism, and nationalist sentiments were strong among the Jews of Palestine in the first two centuries of the current era' ('Parting', 22). While there were diverse types of Jewish Christ-belief, with some forms no doubt lacking this nationalist outlook, Matthew's version, with its strong Jewish-national perspective, would have been well suited in this regard to engaging first-century Jews.

59   Matthew 9.37-38 is without parallel in Mark and Luke. This type of petition would make particularly good sense if most Christ-believers sought involvement in the more successful Gentile mission.

60   See Runesson, 'Re-Thinking'.

Although the point is hotly debated in some circles, Matthew seems to have a positive attitude towards the Mosaic Law: faith in Jesus does not supplant obedience to the Law (5.17-19).[61] The sentiments of Jewish nationalism conveyed by the Evangelist's shepherd motif would offer some support for this view since biblical and early Jewish authors frequently interconnect Jewish nationalism and Torah-observance.[62] Consequently, Schwartz observes that 'the central national institutions of the Jews, the Jerusalem temple and the *Pentateuch* ... eventually became the chief symbols of Jewish corporate identity'.[63] What changed for Matthew was not the abolition of the Law, but how to interpret it in order to perform the Law rightly. Jesus, not the nation's scribes, Pharisees, or Sadducees, represented the final arbiter of the Mosaic Law (7.28-29): his interpretation was to be followed – even by Gentiles who became Christ-believers through the Matthean mission.

5.3.5 The Mattheans and Gentiles

Although it concentrated on the Jews, the Matthean mission acknowledged the legitimacy of the Gentile mission, if not without some dispute within the communities.[64] After the resurrection Jesus commanded his followers to preach the gospel of the kingdom to non-Jews; however, for Matthew this dominical injunction merely sanctioned the mission to the Gentiles *in addition to* the mission to the Jews – it did not authorize the latter's replacement.[65] Hence, Matthew had what could be called an inclusively Jewish approach to the mission, whereby the Mattheans concentrated on reaching Jews but not to the exclusion of Gentiles.[66]

---

61   Because Matthew believed Jesus to be Israel's messiah, the Evangelist sought to hold the authority of Jesus and the authority of the Law together coherently, rather than pit them against one another; cf. W. Loader, *Jesus' Attitude towards the Law*, WUNT 97 (Tübingen: Mohr Siebeck, 1997), 267–68.

62   When the people of Israel disobey the Law they are punished, and when they obey the Law they are blessed nationally; e.g. Jer. 31.31–34; Ezra 9.3-15; Dan 9.1-19; CD I–II; 1 QS I–II; 1QSb; *Pss. Sol.* 17.26-32; 2 *Bar.* 77.11-26.

63   Schwartz, *Imperialism*, 14 (emphasis added).

64   Brown remarks, 'The tension between Mt 10:5b-6 and 28:19 arises from a difference in viewpoint between the evangelist and some of his community' ('Two-Fold', 30).

65   Cf. A. von Dobbeler, 'Die Restitution Israels und die Bekehrung der Heiden: Das Verhältnis von Mt 10:5b-6 und Mt 28:18-20 unter dem Aspekt der Komplementarität: Erwägungen zum Standort des Matthäusevangeliums', ZNW 91 (2000): 18–44. Von Dobbeler argues that, rather than viewing the mission statements of 10.5-6 and 28.19-20 in a salvation-historical sequence whereby the latter cancels the former (either by substitution or by expansion), the two missions should be understood more as 'complementary'.

66   Cf. D. Senior, 'Between Two Worlds: Gentiles and Jewish Christians in Matthew's Gospel', CBQ 61 (1999): 1–23, and Saldarini, *Christian-Jewish*. An inclusively Jewish approach would stand in contrast with: an exclusively Jewish mission, where Gentiles were excluded (e.g. Sim, *Christian Judaism*), an exclusively Gentile mission, where Jews were excluded (e.g. Hare, *Jewish Persecution*), and an inclusively Gentile mission, where Gentiles were the focus but Jews were also included (e.g. Foster, *Community*).

Matthew's Jewish focus meant, on the one hand, that Gentiles comprised only a minority within Matthean communities,[67] even in a post-70-CE context. Few scholars doubt that Gentile Christ-believers came to outnumber significantly their Jewish counterparts during the final quarter of the first century, but despite being outnumbered generally, predominantly Jewish CB communities would have still existed in some locales.[68] It meant, on the other, that Gentiles were probably expected to keep the Jesus-interpreted Torah in the same way that the Jewish majority did.[69] Thus, Gentile members of the communities were probably expected to be circumcised.[70] This type of strict Torah observance by Gentile Christ-believers would have enabled table fellowship between Jew and Gentile in Matthean communities, something that had been a problem in other CB circles.[71] For Matthew, participation in God's kingdom required membership in God's covenant people, Israel (25.34) – hence, the close (but not synonymous) identification of ethnic identity with religious identity.[72] Membership among the people of God, however, could only come about by believing in Jesus as YHWH's appointed messiah and by following his messianic interpretation of Torah. While membership, then, would not be confined to the Jews, it would result in identification with the nation Israel, for according to the Matthean Jesus, in the Eschaton many will come from the east and west to dine in the kingdom of heaven – but they will do so alongside the Jewish Patriarchs, Abraham, Isaac, and Jacob (Mt. 8.11).

67   Saldarini agrees: 'In Matthew's version of a reformed Judaism, gentiles are peripheral, but firmly present' (*Christian-Jewish*, 83).

68   Cautioning against the consensus view, C. Barrett comments: 'It may well be true ... that if the numbers of Jewish Christians and of Gentile Christians were plotted against years on the same piece of paper the curves would probably intersect at a point somewhere between AD 70 and 100; they would probably intersect a number of times before the Gentile curve decisively took off and left the Jewish curve behind. This, however, would be an over-simplification. We should need a fresh sheet of paper for every centre of population; the rates of change would not everywhere be the same' (Barrett, 'What Minorities?', *ST* 1/49 [1995], 1–2).

69   This position would be echoed, for example, by the CB Pharisees (Acts 15), as well as by some of Paul's opponents (Galatians).

70   If the focus of the Matthean mission was the Jews, then circumcision would have been a non-issue since NCB Jews were probably already circumcised (contra Saldarini, *Christian-Jewish*, 158–60): hence its absence in the Gospel.

71   See Gal. 2.11-13; Rom. 14.13-17; and possibly 1 Tim. 4.1-4.

72   Cf. Runesson, 'Particularistic Judaism and Universalistic Christianity? Some Critical Remarks on Terminology and Theology', *JGRCJ*, online, vol. 1 (2000), 131 (Sheffield: Sheffield Phoenix Press, 2004 [print]).

5.4 *The Mattheans and the Roman Empire*

5.4.1 *Introduction*

For Matthew, God chose Jesus to 'save his people from their sins' (1.21b) by being Israel's Shepherd-ruler (2.6b). Against the backdrop of Roman imperial rule of Palestine, how did the Evangelist envision this messianic deliverance? And in what ways would Jesus, God's appointed ruler, relate to Rome's emperor? The remaining portion of this chapter shall discuss these two questions in light of Matthew's belief in Jewish nationalism.

5.4.2 *Matthew's Jewish-national salvation in the Roman Empire*

From what 'things Roman' did Israel need liberating? The Jews experienced Roman imperial oppression in several significant ways. The extreme hierarchical orientation of the Roman Empire meant that the lower social classes, which comprised the majority of first-century Christ-believers,[73] were severely exploited, especially in terms of excessive taxation. The majority of the lower strata residents of the empire consisted of the 'absolutely poor', whom E. Stegemann and W. Stegemann describe as 'not even [having] enough to live ... For the necessities of life they are dependent on the help of others.'[74] Because of high taxes, although the '[relatively poor] with effort somehow managed to achieve a minimum existence [they] were constantly in danger of falling into absolute poverty';[75] and doubtless many did. Consequently, their numbers included the chronically ill and disabled such as the blind, the lame, and lepers;[76] and as scholars have noted, extreme poverty would have exacerbated these health concerns, while creating others.[77] Hence, one of the consequences of Roman oppression was physical and emotional sickness, which would have ravaged the lower classes especially.

For Matthew, Jewish nationalism, as conveyed by his shepherd motif, entails liberation from the sicknesses and diseases resulting from living under Roman imperial rule. Matthew, of all the Gospel writers, takes a Jewish-nationalist perspective of Jesus' works of healing. The people of Israel were 'harassed and downcast' (9.36) because they lacked responsible shepherds to take care of them. Consequently, Jesus travelled throughout the towns of Israel (4.23-25; 9.35) healing all who were afflicted, thus inaugurating God's kingdom's rule among his people. Further, since

---

73   E. Stegemann and W. Stegemann, *The Jesus Movement: A Social History of Its First Century*, trans. O. C. Dean (Minneapolis: Fortress Press, 1999).

74   Stegemann and Stegemann, *Jesus*, 92.

75   Stegemann and Stegemann, *Jesus*, 92. Clearly, Matthew addressed people who had grave concerns about daily existence in the Roman Empire (e.g. Mt. 6.25-34).

76   Stegemann and Stegemann, *Jesus*, 92.

77   See Carter, *Empire*, 71, and Stark, 'Antioch', 189–210.

Matthew sees Satan as ultimately standing behind the Roman Empire,[78] by healing the demonized and those afflicted with disease, the Davidic Shepherd's therapeutic activity signifies not only the plundering of Satan's kingdom (12.22-29), but also the plunder of Rome. And to continue this national restoration of Israel, Jesus commissions his disciples to carry on his healing mission to the 'lost sheep of the house of Israel' (10.6) until his Parousia (10.23).

Jews and CB Jews, who like Matthew lived through the First Jewish Revolt, saw Roman imperial domination climax in the destruction of Jerusalem and the Temple. Jerusalem was the capital of Israel,[79] and its Temple the heart of the Jewish religion. While some Christ-believers viewed their destruction as an expression of God's judgement – either upon the nation or upon its leadership – their destruction would have symbolized the immensity of Rome's power over the Land of Israel and its inhabitants: the Jews were an utterly defeated people. The ruins of Jerusalem, the absence of the Jewish Temple, and its reconstruction as a temple for Jupiter would have served as an ever-present reminder of Israel's complete conquest and its dire need for national deliverance from the cause of their daily oppression: the Roman Empire.[80]

Matthew believes that this national deliverance can be found in the mission of Israel's Davidic Shepherd, Jesus. There are hints of national deliverance in some of the passages the Evangelist uses to develop his shepherd motif. In the prologue of the Gospel, Matthew states that Jesus is the promised Davidic 'ruler' of Mic. 5.1 (2.6). That Matthew combines this text with 2 Sam. 5.2, and that this combination receives further political-national associations from Matthew's story in 2.1-12, suggests that the Evangelist embraced the national deliverance overtones of the Micah passage. Micah prophesies that in shepherding God's people, this Davidic ruler will rescue Israel from the Assyrians, eventuating in God's destruction of the nations that fail to obey him. Micah's ruler, then, rescues his flock and judges its enemies.

A similar dynamic can be observed in the Davidic shepherd passage of Ezekiel 34, a text that underlies the Miracle Chapters. In bringing about national deliverance for Israel, God rescues his people from the harsh abuse of their evil shepherds, on the one hand, and pronounces and executes

78   In the temptation narrative, that Satan offers Jesus the 'kingdoms of the world' (4.8) presumes that Satan rules over these kingdoms – a point that Jesus does not dispute. Hence 'kingdoms of the world' would clearly include Rome.

79   Matthew seems to acknowledge Jerusalem's sacredness: he refers to it as the 'city of the great king' (5.35) and the 'holy city' – the destination of the resurrected saints (27.53).

80   Similarly, E. Smallwood (*The Jews Under Roman Rule from Pompey to Diocletian: A Study in Political Relations* [Leiden: Brill, 1981], 300–301) notes how prior to the first Jewish Revolt Jerusalem minted a half-shekel with inscriptions asserting Judaean freedom as the will of God; but post-70, Rome co-opted this coin to assert Rome's sovereignty as the will of Jupiter.

judgement on these evil abusers of the flock, on the other. Hence, YHWH the Shepherd both saves his people from their oppression and issues judgement for their captives.

Thus, besides saving his people from the harsh ramifications of Roman oppression, Matthew's Davidic Shepherd will ultimately exact judgement upon the empire. While the Roman Empire continued to rule during the days of Jesus (and Matthew), he announced its eventual demise with his proclamation, 'Repent, for the kingdom of heaven is at hand' (4.17). The coming of God's kingdom spelled the end of Rome: the two cannot coexist because they are diametrically opposed (4.8-10; 6.24). Therefore, the therapeutic mission of the Davidic Shepherd demonstrates two realities for Matthew.

First, in healing those victimized by Roman oppression, Jesus is announcing that God's kingdom has come to the Land of Israel, that it is forcefully advancing, and that people must make a choice to enter it (11.12; 22.1-14). When Gentiles travel from afar to pay homage to the infant 'King of the Jews' (2.1-2) or when they come to him to receive healing – despite Jesus' self-professed Israel-centred mission (8.5-13; 15.21-28), the inauguration of God's kingdom in the land receives confirmation, for the scriptures of Israel testify that the nations of the world will come to Jerusalem in order to honour the God of Israel.[81] Thus, besides inaugurating the kingdom of God, the works of the Davidic Shepherd signify the beginning of the end of the kingdom of Rome.

Second, for Matthew the ultimate end of the empire will come at Jesus' Parousia, when 'all the nations' – including Rome – will appear before the Shepherd-King in the final judgement (25.31-33). It will be at this time that source of Israel's domination will be definitively dealt with. Indeed, this is the direction of Ezekiel 34, where God promises to 'break the bars of their [enemy's enslaving] yoke'. As observed in chapter 4 of this book, Ezekiel 34 is an important text for Matthew, and he freely adopts the strong Jewish-national sentiments conveyed by the shepherd metaphor in that text.

Perhaps at the heart of Roman oppression was the values system of the empire. The ruling elite valued power, wealth, and status, which manifested in social hierarchies, dominance, and exclusion.[82] These values were highly intertwined: power was derived from wealth and status, and wealth increased a person's status. Consequently, people, who could, sought more power: by increasing wealth through, for example, taxation, property ownership, and production; or they sought power by increasing in position through, for example, political office, patronage, allegiances, and friendships. But people who had power also sought to display it frequently: through military aggression, forced labour, social and civic abuse, even through wardrobe distinctions.[83]

81   E.g. Mic. 4.1-2; Isa. 60.1-9; Zech. 14.16-18.
82   Cf. Carter, *Empire*, 9–12, and Stegemann and Stegemann, *Jesus*, 60–65, who use the categories of power, privilege, and prestige.
83   For a brief discussion of the latter as a means of displaying status, see Garnsey

Thus, for Matthew, Jewish-national restoration involves, on the one hand, rescue from the tyranny of Roman elitist values, i.e. of being on the receiving end of them. As previously stated, final deliverance from Rome would come at the Parousia, when all the nations of the world appear before the Davidic Shepherd-King in judgement. Of special note is the criterion for this judgement. The empire made judgements based on levels of power, wealth, or status.[84] Hence, those of little repute were mistreated. The upper class often expressed its elitist attitude towards the lower classes in terms of insults and ridicule. Based on the comments of Juvenal and Pliny, MacMullen remarks, 'The mockery and scorn [the lower class] endured was deliberate, unprovoked, and unresisted. In the very streets it pursued them. But it was better to be rudely ignored by "the Haughty" than to be stopped, bullied, and humiliated by some young drunken blueblood.'[85] But the final judgement of Matthew's Shepherd-King represents a reversal of Roman values. People are not judged based on their power or status but according to the level of mercy with which they treated Matthean Christ-believers (25.31-46).

On the other hand, the values of a morally restored nation would be the very opposite of Rome's. Hence, in God's kingdom power is not sought by its members but rather God's 'rule and his righteousness' (6.33). Residents of God's kingdom do not orient their lives around wealth because one 'cannot serve God and money' (6.24). Wealth is not meant to be hoarded but to help others. Consequently, resources should be used not to increase one's personal status but to extend God's kingdom; and community debts must be forgiven (18.21-35). Leaders must not dominate – 'lord it over' (20.25) – those in submission; rather, great leaders seek to serve their constituency in the manner of a slave (20.26-27). Furthermore, a morally restored nation is void of any social hierarchies, for Jesus the Davidic Shepherd set the example by reaching out inclusively not 'to those who are healthy ... but to those who are sick' (9.12), i.e. to the socially and physically marginalized.

5.4.3 Matthew's shepherd and Rome's emperor

If Matthew wrote his Gospel during the reign of Domitian, how does the Matthean Jesus, i.e. God's appointed ruler, challenge this emperor? Carter describes the essential tenets of Roman imperial theology as: the gods have willed for Rome to rule the world, they direct world history, the emperor is the agent of Jupiter, and the empire is the conduit for societal well-being.[86] Numerous features of Matthew's multi-faceted presentation of Jesus correlate differently to distinct aspects of Roman

and Saller, *Roman Empire*, 117.

84   E.g. Plutarch notes that people do not show respect for 'experience or virtue or age, but to wealth and repute' (*Mor.* 58D).

85   MacMullen, *Roman*, 111.

86   For a fuller discussion of these elements, see Carter, *Empire*, 20–34, 57–74.

imperial theology. The ensuing discussion of this interaction, however, will naturally be restricted to the Evangelist's shepherd motif.

Perhaps most obviously, Matthew's employment of 'shepherd' for Jesus may actually represent an explicit polemic against the emperor. As observed in section 3.3.4 above, numerous titles of honour were accorded Domitian, e.g. 'King', 'Peacemaker', 'Favourite of God [and Humans]', 'Lord/Master of the World', 'Lord and God', 'Lord of the Earth', and 'Ruler of the Nations'. Matthew uses a number of these honorific ascriptions or synonyms for Jesus: 'King' (2.2; 25.34; 27.42), 'Lord/Master' (7.21; 8.2; passim), 'God' (1.23), 'Ruler' (2.6), and 'Favourite of God' (cf. 3.17; 17.5). But Matthew also employs 'shepherd' for Jesus specifically within the context of kingship (2.6; 25.31-34). Domitian never receives this title. Further, Roman emperors are only rarely likened to shepherds because Romans tended to view shepherds very critically: to call the emperor a 'shepherd' would be insulting. But for Matthew, consonant with the traditions of the Jewish scripture and other ANE cultures, likening a king to a shepherd is not only acceptable, it is normative.

By connecting Jesus and his therapeutic activities to a shepherd caring for the flock, the Evangelist would, on the one hand, present one means of acknowledging Jesus' kingship and sovereignty over the Roman Empire. Jews, the primary mission focus of the Mattheans, would immediately perceive the significance of this reference. Romans, however, would have little reason in itself to understand this post-70, messianic title as treason. On the other hand, the Evangelist uses the shepherd metaphor to offer a portrait of the ideal ruler. The most obvious virtue associated with the metaphor is humility. Clearly the honorific titles ascribed to Domitian during his lifetime, his desire (according to Suetonius) to be called 'our Lord and God', as well as his aspirations to be worshiped,[87] belie humility. Royal arrogance was expressed in military domination and came through in lavish, self-laudatory ceremonies.[88] This type of self-exaltation is likely presupposed by the lengthy discourses by various Roman authors addressing the monarchy which stress the need for kings to define their greatness in terms of moral character rather than military conquests.[89]

In clear contrast to Roman imperial arrogance, Matthew presents Jesus as the humble Shepherd-King. Ham has argued that the Evangelist appropriates Deutero-Zechariah to mediate the kingship and shepherd motifs, with the shepherd motif serving to emphasize the rejection of Jesus' kingship.[90] In Jewish tradition, great rulers such as Moses and David were shepherds before being divinely 'promoted' to lead Israel; and in the case of the latter, David's royal appointment is contrasted with his humble beginnings as a

---

87   See Goodman, *Roman*, 123–34.
88   See W. Visser, 'T Hooft, "Triumphalism in the Gospels"', *SJT* 38 (1985), 491.
89   E.g. Dio Chrysostom, *3 Regn.*, 36–39.
90   Ham, *Coming King*.

shepherd.[91] Working within this tradition, Matthew's use of the metaphor for Jesus would accent Jesus' humble kingship – a point receiving further emphasis through other aspects of the Evangelist's Christology, especially his Servant of the Lord motif.

This association of humility with 'shepherd' would differentiate Matthew's use of the metaphor from its appropriation by Roman authors. As observed in section 3.3.2 above, Roman authors occasionally employ the metaphor to connote diligent care for their subjects. While Matthew's use of the metaphor involves this idea of benevolent, responsible care for the flock, it also connotes Jesus' humility – something entirely absent from the metaphor's use by Roman authors. Thus, while Dio Chrysostom uses the metaphor several times to depict a ruler's activity, the animal he believes best captures a ruler's character is a bull because it connotes strength and gentleness, affluence and generosity, and a striving for superiority.[92] Humility as a character trait for kings is never a consideration for Chrysostom.

Jesus' humble kingship also receives stress through other elements of the Evangelist's story. Consonant with being humble, Matthew's Davidic Shepherd of the Miracle Chapters rejects elitism. Elitism was the order of the day for the Roman Empire. Doubtless elites and commoners interacted professionally, as the patron–client relationship demanded, but on the one hand, the elite–commoner association was one-sided and exploitive.[93] On the other, it remained strictly professional and never extended beyond this business-like level to more intimate and informal interaction, lacking all of the attendant formalities and social protocols of an elitist society.[94] Elitism would never permit such an extension. Individuals of high rank refused and were even forbidden to socialize informally with commoners. Not surprisingly, Garnsey and Saller write:

> In the municipalities, the seating was arranged to give spatial definition to the distinction between the curial order and ordinary citizens. Caesar's law for the colony of Urso in Spain had already specified detailed regulations for seating in the amphitheatre and theatre, and laid down enormous fines for violations – an indication that something more was at stake than getting a good seat to watch the show. Putting everyone in his proper place was a visual affirmation of the dominance of the imperial social structure.[95]

91   E.g. Ps. 78.70-71; Amos 7.14-15.

92   *2 Regn.* 65–72. Interestingly, Dio mentions other animals that would suitably apply to kings: lions, boars, and eagles. By contrast, the animal associated with Jesus is the donkey – upon whose foal he rode into Jerusalem as king (Mt. 21.1-9).

93   Kautsky concludes that 'generally there is no reciprocity in the relationship between peasant and aristocrat in aristocratic empires' (*Politics*, 113).

94   Garnsey and Saller thus note that even the *salutatio* 'offered a visual demonstration of the social hierarchy in two ways. Clients were classed with reference to their place in the queue, and the patron in terms of the quality and number of his callers. The "crowded house" was a barometer of and a metaphor for power and prestige' (*Roman Empire*, 122).

95   Garnsey and Saller, *Roman Empire*, 117.

Thus, while the ideal king in Graeco-Roman tradition was to be 'a man for the people', he was by no means 'a man *of* the people'.

In sharp contrast to the elitist values of the Roman Empire, Jesus models inclusivity in his personal, social interactions. He physically reaches out to those separated and ritually cut off from mainstream society (8.2-4). He dines with notorious sinners, who were otherwise to be shunned (9.9-12). Jesus' socially inclusive lifestyle was even recognized by members of Herod's party, when they addressed him, 'Teacher, we know that ... you do not show partiality to anyone' (22.16b). Thus, while Matthew's Davidic Shepherd exercises divine ruling authority for Israel's betterment, quite unlike the ideal Graeco-Roman monarch, Jesus remains 'a man *of* the people'.

Finally, humility does not preclude authority for Matthew. Emperors were perceived by their subjects as wielding the authority of the gods. Thus, Seneca envisions Nero's authority, when he writes:

> Have I [Nero] of all mortals found favor with Heaven and been chosen to serve on earth as vicar of the gods? I am the arbiter of life and death for the nations; it rests in my power what each man's lot and state shall be ... without my favor and grace no part of the whole world can prosper ... what nations shall be utterly destroyed, which banished, which shall receive the gift of liberty ... what cities shall rise and which shall fall – this is mine to decree.
>
> (*Clem.* 1.2–3)

Yet despite exercising this kind of power, Matthew makes it clear that the authority of Jesus trumps even that of Rome. Caesar's own officer confesses as much (8.5-9). Despite being invested with the authority of Rome and being able to command with a single word the obedience of many soldiers (8.9), the Roman centurion is powerless to heal his paralysed servant – something Jesus is able to do – with a word: because he is endowed with the very authority of God (8.13; cf. 9.8). Similarly, although Rome was 'the arbiter of life and death' and consequently struck down – crucified – Jesus, his death was only in full accord with the ancient prophecies in Israel's scriptures (26.31); and moreover, the will of Rome was unambiguously overturned by the stricken Shepherd's resurrection (26.32).

Therefore, although the Matthean Jesus describes himself as 'gentle and humble in heart' (11.29), as the Davidic Shepherd-King he possesses sovereign authority, demonstrated by his therapeutic mission and resurrection from death; and he shall exercise this divinely endowed power over all the nations – including Rome – when he returns for the final judgement (25.31-46).

5.5 Concluding Remarks

According to his shepherd motif, Matthew clearly holds to a Jewish-national restoration of Israel, putting him much closer to the Jewish-nationalistic end of a spectrum mapping belief in Jewish-national restoration. This belief in Jewish nationalism is most characteristic of NCB Jews. His socio-religious orientation would explain (at least in part) the Evangelist's distinct – i.e. with respect to many other CB groups – views of assembly leadership, the Gentiles, and his Israel-centric mission.

Further, the Jewish-national salvation Matthew advocates would possess significant bearing in relation to the Roman Empire. Israel's Davidic Shepherd saves his people from the illnesses and demonization that result from living under Roman oppression. In this way Jesus' therapeutic shepherding of Israel represents the plunder of Rome, and indicates the beginning of the end for the Roman Empire. The culmination of Rome's demise will take place at the Parousia, when all the nations (including Rome) appear before Israel's Shepherd-King in final judgement, and are judged by him according to their deeds of mercy rather than their power or status – an overturning of the Roman imperial values system. Consonant with this reversal, Jesus embodies a radically different option to the emperor. Unlike Domitian's subjects, the followers of Jesus call him 'Shepherd'; and as a shepherd-ruler, Jesus models humility, on the one hand, and indiscriminately reaches out to the crowds, on the other, spending time with those living on the margins of society, who are eschewed by the ruling elite.

Chapter 6

CONCLUSIONS

Of all the texts examined in this investigation, Matthew deploys the shepherd metaphor most extensively and skilfully. The Evangelist introduces his shepherd motif in the prologue of his Gospel, linking it to the Davidic origin of Jesus and the royal nature of his messiahship. The author employs the motif to help describe and summarize Jesus' therapeutic mission to Israel in the Miracle Chapters. While the shepherd motif appears implicitly in the middle portion of the Gospel, it reappears explicitly near the end of the narrative: Matthew depicts Jesus as the eschatological shepherd-king who will one day judge all the nations at his Parousia. Prior to this event, however, Jesus is the rejected shepherd who is divinely struck down according to the scriptures, but his death provides an atoning sacrifice for his flock. Hence, Martin rightly notes, 'Mt, more than any of the other NT authors, has a consistent and well-developed message which he develops around the theme of shepherd.'[1] Since, as Martin recognizes, 'an image may be the bearer of a theme and may become the vehicle by which two themes interpenetrate and mutually modify one another',[2] the Evangelist's shepherd motif is comprised of the thematic clusters: Shepherd, Son of David, healing, and King of the Jews.

Thus, Matthew's shepherd motif contributes significantly in a number of different ways to the theological framework of his Gospel. It sheds light on the Gospel's Christology, specifically underscoring its Davidic Christology. The opening genealogy (1.1-17) makes it clear that Israel's Shepherd is Davidic in his ancestry, thereby confirming his legitimacy as true heir to David's throne. In addition to the Evangelist's citation of 2 Sam. 5.2 in Mt. 2.6 (which links the motif to the birth announcement in 1.21-23 and, less directly, to the genealogy), the connection between Jesus as Israel's Shepherd and Davidic messiahship is strengthened by the author's citation of Mic. 5.1, as well as by his allusions to Ezekiel 34, whereby he implicitly likens Jesus to Ezekiel's Davidic shepherd. All of these features reveal Matthew's concern to depict Jesus within a distinctly Jewish framework.

Verseput rightly notes that Matthew's Son of David motif bears the

---

1   Martin, 'Image', 271. Similarly Chae (*Davidic Shepherd*, 387) remarks: 'Matthew's story of Jesus can be read as the story of the Shepherd.'
2   Martin, 'Image', 264.

'earthly political agenda' associated with traditional, Jewish expectations concerning Davidic hope. Davidic messiahship helps to bring out the political-national dimension of Matthew's soteriology, but so does the Evangelist's shepherd motif. In being divinely appointed at birth to shepherd/rule God's people Israel (2.6), Jesus, as God's emissary, replaces the corrupt Jerusalem leadership, including King Herod.[3] The political-national overtones observed in the prologue echo the shepherd metaphor's use in the HB and in Second Temple Jewish texts, where the metaphor often symbolizes political and civic rulers: pre-monarchical rulers (e.g. Num. 27.17; 2 Sam. 7.7; *LAB* 19.3; *Virt.* 58), Israel's kings (e.g. Ezekiel 34; Mic. 5.3; *Psalms of Solomon* 17 [king-messiah]), and the nation's ruling class (e.g. Isa. 56.10-11; Zech. 11.5; *4 Ezra* 5.16-18). Doubtless Jesus' kingship would transcend the typical geo-political framework of kings and kingdoms, as the rest of Matthew's Gospel makes clear. Nevertheless, a measure of continuity is presupposed: although the kingdom Jesus inaugurates is primarily 'religious', according to Matthew's birth and infancy narratives, it nonetheless involves replacing not simply Israel's religious leaders but also its king.

The shepherd motif provides additional insight into Matthew's Miracle Chapters. The overarching concern of these chapters is missional: what Jesus does in Israel – i.e. his messianic mission to the nation. Matthew depicts Jesus' therapeutic mission to Israel in terms of shepherding the nation (9.35-36). If, as Heil writes, 'Matthew's shepherd metaphor is guided and unified by Ezekiel 34,'[4] then nowhere is this perhaps more evident than in the Miracle Chapters, where in addition to alluding verbally to Ezek. 34.5 (in 9.36),[5] the Evangelist draws close contextual parallels with Ezekiel 34, concerning the Jews' social and physical plight, the replacing of Israel's unfaithful leadership, and the shepherding activities of healing and delivering the nation from its afflictions. According to the Miracle Chapters, Israel's leaders have neglected the social outcasts, ultimately resulting in the Jews' 'harassed and downcast' condition (9.36). Therefore, Jesus goes about the land doing what the leaders failed to do: offering compassionate care for God's people (idealized in Jesus' works of healing and exorcism) and by appointing his disciples to replace Israel's failed shepherds by healing and saving the nation from its woeful state (9.37–10.8). For Matthew, Jesus' therapeutic deeds represent the acts of the 'Son of David.'

In delivering the people of Israel from their oppressed condition, then, Jesus' mission to Israel in the Miracle Chapters is characterized as Davidic (9.27-34; cf. 12.22-24) – similar to the connection the author makes in the

---

3   As mentioned in section 4.2.2 above, for Matthew, Jesus would replace Herod insofar as only Jesus possessed divine authority to announce the coming of God's kingdom rule (4.17) and to begin its inauguration. Further, because the Evangelist depicts him as the divinely authoritative interpreter of Torah, Jesus would be the supreme teacher for Israel, and thus replace the nation's teachers: the priests, the scribes, and the Pharisees.

4   Heil, 'Ezekiel 34', 708.

5   Cf. the probable verbal allusion to Ezek. 34.4 and 16 in Mt. 10.6.

birth and infancy traditions. Thus, the royal Son of David's rule/shepherding in the Land of Israel includes works of healing and exorcism, and consequently, the Miracle Chapters echo and develop the hopes for Jewish-national restoration, first introduced in the beginning of the Gospel. If Jesus is to 'save his people from their sins', then an integral dimension of Israel's salvation involves deliverance from physical illnesses and satanic oppression, consonant with the sin–sickness correlation in the biblical tradition. This concern for the physical and moral well-being of the Jewish nation appears frequently not only in the HB (e.g. Pss 28.9; 80.1-3; Jer. 31.7–11), but to varying degrees in the writings of NCB Jews (e.g. 4Q504; *Psalms of Solomon* 17; *4 Ezra*).

The shepherd motif sheds some light on the question of Israel's 'replacement' as the people of God. Numerous scholars insist that Matthew believed Israel had been replaced by the church. An analysis of the shepherd motif, however, shows that for Matthew, it is not the Jews who have been replaced as God's people, but Israel's leaders as the shepherds of his people. God appointed Jesus to replace King Herod and the Jerusalem leadership; Jesus subsequently commissions his disciples to extend his shepherding mission and continue doing the works that Israel's leaders had failed to do. Further, in the passion narrative Matthew squarely lays the final responsibility for Jesus' death at the feet of the Jewish leaders, whom he typologically identifies with the Jewish leaders who had rejected YHWH as their Shepherd in Zechariah 11 (Mt. 27.1-10). This replacement of the Jewish leaders is consonant with the shepherd/רעה metaphor in the HB, where judgement (usually of leaders) is often implicit in the literary contexts in which 'shepherd' appears (e.g. Jer. 22.22; 23.1-4; Ezekiel 34; Zech. 10.2-3; 13.7). It also echoes the literary context of the passages Matthew uses to develop his shepherd motif: 2 Sam. 5.2, Mic. 5.1, and Ezekiel 34 all contain the notion of failed leadership, whereby a Davidide replaces Israel's leaders who, in failing to execute their duties faithfully as shepherds of God's flock, have brought the Jews into disastrous circumstances – from which they need rescuing.

Besides contributing to the theology of the Gospel, the Evangelist's shepherd motif reveals distinctive patterns of thought. The Evangelist applies the metaphor for rulers or the activity of ruling (2.1-6). He explicitly connects the term to Jesus' ruling over Israel – a reign that, according to the narrative, possesses political-national overtones. Matthew thus associates the metaphor with monarchs and the activity of ruling, similar to HB texts and Second Temple Jewish authors – but quite dissimilar from other CB authors, who tend not to appropriate the metaphor in this particular way. Unlike other Christ-believers, the Evangelist never employs the shepherd metaphor for assembly leaders. Whereas Matthew can explicitly use a term such as 'prophet' for both Jesus and his disciples (13.57-58; 21.11; and 10.40-42, respectively),[6] he

---

6   Cf. other terms that either explicitly or implicitly do double duty for Jesus and his disciples: 'righteous man' (27.19 and 10.41, respectively), 'scribe' and 'wise man' (23.34), 'servant' (20.26-28), and 'teacher' (8.19 and 28.20, respectively).

reserves 'shepherd' for Jesus – similar to, for example, the specialized use of 'shepherd' in the Dream Visions, whose author reserves the term for the evil angelic rulers of God's people, never for YHWH nor for Israel's kings, even though they clearly function as shepherds in the text.

Matthew also depicts Jesus, especially in the Miracle Chapters, using pastoral imagery, i.e. in language that corresponds to the duties of vocational shepherds. Jesus the Davidic Shepherd inclusively reaches out to the lost and the marginalized throughout the Land of Israel (8.2-4; 9.9-13), tending to the physical needs of the crowds: he heals the sick, the lame, and the blind. This pastoral depiction of Israel's Shepherd echoes the deployment of 'shepherd' in the texts of NCB Jews, who similarly speak of shepherding in terms of gathering the flock together (e.g. *Virt.* 58), binding up and healing the wounded (e.g. *Apocalypse of Ezekiel*), and feeding them (e.g. *1 Enoch* 89.28). This employment of the metaphor contrasts with its not so pastoral use by Christ-believers, who tend to associate it with teaching.

Most significantly, Matthew's deployment of the metaphor resembles its appropriation by NCB Jews and diverges from other Christ-believers insofar as it conveys clear sentiments of Jewish nationalism. When he introduces the motif in the Gospel, it is to declare that Jesus the messiah has come to shepherd God's people Israel and to save them from their sins. The saving/ shepherding of Israel is partially unpacked in the Miracle Chapters. On the one hand, these chapters stress the exclusivity of Jesus' mission to Israel: he came to shepherd the Jews; on the other hand, his shepherding of Israel includes acts of healing and exorcism. Jesus' mission and his therapeutic deeds represent, for Matthew, the beginning of the restoration of the people of Israel which Jesus will complete at his Parousia. Matthew's Jewish-national sentiments are closely echoed by NCB Jews, who also show concern for the moral and/or geo-political restoration of the nation (e.g. *Psalms of Solomon* 17, *4 Ezra*, and Judith).

A comparison between Matthew and the texts of NCB Romans yields pronounced differences. Roman authors view shepherds critically; the Evangelist, however, presents Jesus as the Davidic Shepherd, who compassionately reaches out to the socially marginalized, through deeds of healing and exorcism. Roman writers infrequently employ the shepherd metaphor for Roman emperors, but Matthew deploys it in a fairly sustained way for Jesus as Israel's messianic king and for his messianic rule of and mission to the Jews.

Therefore, in view of the strong affinity shared between Matthew and NCB Jewish authors, the plain differences between Matthew and other Christ-believers, as well as the strong contrast between Matthew and Roman authors, Matthew's socio-religious location reflects someone who was more closely aligned with Jewish than with non-Jewish culture. The Gospel of Matthew could thus be described as a Jewish-oriented text authored by a person with messianic convictions focused around Jesus of Nazareth.

Consequently, on a socio-religious spectrum mapping belief in Jewish nationalism, Matthew's socio-religious orientation would be located as shown in Fig. 6.1.

Belief in Jewish-   *Rejection of Jewish-*
national restoration   *national restoration*
| ← Matthew → |

Fig. 6.1 *Situating Matthew's socio-religious orientation*

In light of Matthew's socio-religious orientation, a number of important implications would follow. In terms of leadership, because the metaphor possesses definite political-national overtones, Matthew, unlike many other CB authors, reserves 'shepherd' for Jesus. The Mattheans would probably have referred to their leaders as prophets, scribes, disciples, servants, sages, righteous men, and teachers – as opposed to some of the titles used by other CB authors, such as overseer, evangelist, elder, and shepherd. Matthew's specific names for leadership do not represent polemic against other Christ-believers as much as they demonstrate the Jewish orientation of the Mattheans, as is particularly evident from the Evangelist's avoidance of 'shepherd' for assembly leaders: the term possesses strong political overtones, making it inappropriate for assembly leaders.

Regarding Israel's status before God, in contrast to the groups of Christ-believers who insisted that the Jews had been forever rejected by God, according to Matthew's approaching-Jewish-national outlook (as expressed by his shepherd motif), Israel had experienced the beginning of a Jesus-centred restoration: moral renewal manifested in the remission of sins, the healing of their sicknesses, and the casting out of demonic spirits. Full participation in this national renewal required the acceptance of Jesus as Israel's messiah and obedience to the Mosaic Law as interpreted by Jesus (5.21-48). Moral renewal secures the heavenly blessings of God's kingdom (5.3-9), and guarantees the material and physical provisions to meet the difficulties of living in the Roman Empire (6.25-34).

Matthew did not believe that God had abandoned Israel; only that he had condemned the nation's leadership. Further, the Evangelist believed that God had replaced Israel's leaders with the leaders of his communities (9.36–10.6). While Jesus had begun Israel's restoration through his salvific and therapeutic activities in the land, Matthew believed in a more comprehensive moral and political renewal in the Eschaton, when Jesus, God's Davidic Shepherd, brings about the ultimate fulfilment of God's kingdom's rule at his Parousia, and judges all the nations of the world (25.31-46).

With respect to mission, because Matthew was strongly committed to his fellow Jews, he did not abandon the mission to Israel begun by Jesus (10.23;

23.39). Although their messianic claims brought Jewish opposition, the Mattheans' strong conviction for Jewish nationalism would have resonated with first-century NCB Jews. Also echoing many Jewish groups would have been Matthew's conservative attitude towards the Mosaic Law. Faith in Jesus did not supplant obedience to the Law (5.17-19); rather, Jesus was the final arbiter of the Mosaic Law (7.28-29).

Matthew had an inclusively Jewish and open-ethnic approach to mission, whereby Mattheans concentrated on Jews but not to the exclusion of the Gentiles. Matthew's Jewish focus meant that Gentiles comprised only a minority within Matthean communities. It also meant that Gentile members were expected to keep the Torah as interpreted by Jesus in the same way the Jewish majority did. Their obedience to Jesus would have enabled table fellowship between Jews and Gentiles in Matthean communities, which had become a problem in other CB assemblies.

Against the backdrop of Roman oppression, the mission of Israel's Shepherd offered a vastly different alternative to imperial rule and its ruler. For Matthew, when the Davidic Shepherd 'saves his people from their sins' (1.21), deliverance includes liberation from the ramifications of their sins, e.g. physical sicknesses and demonization, which resulted from living under Roman domination. The Shepherd's therapeutic activity signified the plunder of Satan's kingdom (12.22-29) – including the Roman Empire (4.8). Thus, in proclaiming the coming of God's kingdom in the Land of Israel, Jesus' works of healing and exorcism there also spelled the beginning of the end for Rome.

Although Jesus announces and initiates Rome's end, it will not finally take place until the Parousia, when Rome and the rest of the nations of the world appear before Jesus the Shepherd-King in final judgement (25.31-33). The final judgement of the Shepherd-King will represent a reversal of Roman values: the nations will be judged according to their deeds of mercy rather than their power or status (24.34-46). But even prior to the final judgement, a rejection of Rome's values is the norm for members of God's kingdom: God, his rule, and his righteousness are sought and served (6.24, 33) not power or status, nor do power and privilege permit discrimination (9.12); moreover, leaders serve their subjects rather than dominate them (20.25-26).

Jesus' mission represents a drastic alternative to the Roman Empire because he embodies a radically different option to the emperor. While the subjects of Domitian and Jesus refer to their respective masters as 'King', 'Lord', 'Ruler', etc., only Jesus' followers call him 'Shepherd' – a title which would have been sternly rejected by a Roman emperor. Israel's Shepherd distinguishes himself from his Roman counterpart by, among other things, his humility – something not associated with nor even desired by ideal Graeco-Roman kings, but an attribute routinely connected with shepherds in the Jewish tradition. Subsequently, whereas Domitian ruled the masses without actually living with them, Jesus the Davidic Shepherd-King spent time reaching out to crowds, even to those socially marginalized and shunned by the ruling elite.

Despite the range and the depth of research involved in this investigation of Matthew's shepherd motif, numerous related matters offer potentially fruitful areas for further exploration. The second chapter of this study noted a shift in thought concerning the shepherd metaphor in the HB, whereby the metaphor becomes extended in Ecclesiastes 12 to include the teaching of wisdom. Whether this extension was brought about by some type of claims of authority for the sages of the time, whether it was the result of the emphasis on the public reading of Torah, or something else, the social-historical factors that would have contributed to this shift in the metaphor commend themselves for additional study.

Other social-historical implications of the use of the shepherd metaphor commend themselves for additional study. For Second Temple Jewish texts, is there a relationship between the breadth of the stream represented by a text and its particular use of the metaphor? For example, do narrower streams of Judaism employ the metaphor more innovatively than wider, more 'mainstream' forms, or vice versa?[7] This study used the patterns of thought related to the shepherd metaphor to locate Matthew on a socio-religious spectrum mapping belief in Jewish nationalism. Besides socio-religious orientation, can the metaphor be used to determine other aspects of social location, e.g. provenance? More broadly, what other patterns of thought or religion can be used, and for what type of socio-religious spectrum?

This study opened with the question, 'When did Christianity and Judaism part company and go their separate ways?' While scholars will continue to debate this question, and no single research project can ever settle the matter in a once-and-for-all fashion, the present investigation makes an important contribution to this very central issue for biblical studies. Matthew's appropriation of the shepherd metaphor reveals that although the author of the Gospel was a Christ-believer and firmly believed that Jesus was Israel's promised messiah, he nevertheless remained conceptually within the orbit of Second Temple Judaism and not separated from it. That is to say, more than simply being what many scholars consider the most Jewish Gospel, the patterns of thought reflected by Matthew's shepherd motif give evidence that faith in Christ, at least for some in the first century, did not demand or necessarily result in a socio-religious divorce from 'Judaism'.

---

7   De Robert was the first to suggest something like this: 'Il n'est pas sans intérêt de remarquer que ces textes appartiennent tous à une littérature qui se rattache à la branche ésotérique du Judaïsme' (*Berger*, 94–95).

The results of this study demonstrate that the multiplicity of 'Judaisms' and 'Christianities' permitted a great deal of socio-religious overlap between groups, such that one stream of Christ-belief could diverge from other streams so as to resemble a form of Judaism. Therefore, it is not legitimate to speak of Judaism and Christ-belief in terms of false opposites, as many scholars do. A bipolar configuration ignores the immense religious diversity of these groups, on the one hand, and the complex socio-religious interactions that characterized much of their early histories, on the other. While Dunn claims that hindsight makes the 'Parting' an inevitable development, he rightly questions if this would have been so at the time: 'would these outcomes have appeared inevitable to those *in via*?'.[8] Clearly for Matthew, this was not the case. In the words of Stanton, 'a long lingering embrace' could exist not simply for 'many ordinary believers',[9] but even for leaders of the early Jesus movement – like Matthew.

8   Dunn, 'Concluding Summary', 386.
9   Stanton, *Partings*, xxiv.

Select Bibliography

Aaron, D. *Biblical Ambiguities: Metaphor, Semantics, and Divine Imagery*. Leiden: Brill, 2002.

Balch, D., ed. *Social History of the Matthean Community: Cross-Disciplinary Approaches*. Minneapolis: Fortress Press, 1991.

Barbalet, J. 'Power and Resistance'. *British Journal of Sociology* 36 (1985): 521–48.

Barclay, J. *Jews in the Mediterranean Diaspora: From Alexander to Trajan 323 BCE–117 CE*. Edinburgh: T&T Clark, 1996.

Baxter, W. 'Healing and the "Son of David": Matthew's Warrant'. *NovT* 48/1 (2006): 36–50.

———, 'Matthew's Shepherd Motif and Its Socio-Religious Implications'. PhD dissertation, McMaster University, 2007.

Becker, A. and A. Y. Reed, eds. *The Ways that Never Parted: Jews and Christians in Late Antiquity and the Early Middle Ages*. Tübingen: Mohr Siebeck, 2003.

Bracewell, R. 'Shepherd Imagery in the Synoptic Gospels'. PhD dissertation, Southern Baptist Theological Seminary, 1983.

Brown, R. 'Not Jewish Christianity and Gentile Christianity but Types of Jewish/Gentile Christianity'. *CBQ* 45 (1983): 74–79.

Brown, S. 'The Two-Fold Representation of the Mission in Matthew's Gospel'. *ST* 31 (1977): 21–32.

Burger, C. *Jesus als Davidssohn: Eine traditionsgeschichtliche Untersuchung*. Göttingen: Vandenhoeck & Ruprecht 1970.

Carter, W. *Matthew and Empire: Initial Exporations*. Harrisburg: Trinity Press, 2001.

Chae, Y. *Jesus as the Eschatological Davidic Shepherd: Studies in the Old Testament, Second Temple Judaism, and in the Gospel of Matthew*. Tübingen: Mohr Siebeck, 2006.

Davies, W. D. and D. Allison, Jr. *The Gospel According to Saint Matthew*, 3 vols. ICC. Edinburgh: T&T Clark, 1988–97.

De Robert, P. *Le Berger D'Israël: Essai sur le Thème Pastoral dans l'Ancien Testament*. Neuchâtel: Delachaux et Niestlé, 1968.

Duguid, I. *Ezekiel and the Leaders of Israel*. Leiden: Brill, 1994.

Duling, D. 'The Therapeutic Son of David: An Element in Matthew's Christological Apologetic'. *NTS* 24 (1977): 392–410.

Dunn, J. *The Partings of the Ways: Between Christianity and Judaism and their Significance for the Character of Christianity*. 2nd edn. London: SCM Press, 2006.

Fernandez, J. *Persuasions and Performances: The Play of Tropes in Culture*. Bloomington: Indiana University Press, 1986.

Fikes, B. 'A Theological Analysis of the Shepherd-King Motif in Ezekiel 34'. PhD dissertation, Southwestern Baptist Theological Seminary, 1995.

Fitzgerald, T. *Metaphors of Identity: A Culture-Communication Dialogue*. New York: State University of New York Press, 1993.

Garbe, G. *Der Hirte Israels: Eine Untersuchung zur Israeltheologie des Matthäusevangeliums*. Neukirchen-Vluyn: Neukirchener Verlag, 2005.

Garnsey, P. and R. Saller, *The Roman Empire: Economy, Society and Culture*. London: Duckworth, 1987.

Gibbs, J. 'Purpose and Pattern in Matthew's Use of the Title "Son of David"'. *NTS* 10 (1964): 446–64.

Goodblatt, D. *Elements of Ancient Jewish Nationalism*. Cambridge: Cambridge University Press, 2006.

Goodman, M. *The Roman World: 44 BC–AD 180*. London: Routledge, 1997.

Hagner, D. *Matthew*, 2 vols. WBC, vols 33a–b. Dallas: Word Books, 1998.

Ham, C. A. *The Coming King and the Rejected Shepherd: Matthew's Reading of Zechariah's Messianic Hope*. Sheffield: Sheffield Phoenix Press, 2005.

Heil, J. P. 'Ezekiel 34 and the Narrative Strategy of the Shepherd and Sheep Metaphor in Matthew'. *CBQ* 55 (1993): 698–708.

Huntzinger, J. 'End of Exile: A Short Commentary on the Shepherd/ Sheep Metaphor in Exilic and Post-Exilic Prophetic and Synoptic Gospel Literature'. PhD dissertation, Fuller Theological Seminary, 1999.

Hunziker-Rodewald, R. *Hirt und Herde: Ein Beitrag zum alttestament-lichen Gottesverständnis*. Stuttgart: Kohlhammer, 2001.

Kautsky, J. *The Politics of Aristocratic Empires*. Chapel Hill: University of North Carolina Press, 1982.

Lakoff, G. and M. Johnson, *Metaphors We Live By*. Chicago: University of Chicago Press, 1980.

Luz, U. *Das Evangelium nach Matthäus*, 4 vols. Zürich: Benziger/ Neukirchener Verlag, 1985–2002.

McKnight, S. 'New Shepherds for Israel: An Historical and Critical Study of Matthew 9:34–11:1'. PhD dissertation, Nottingham University, 1986.

MacMullen, R. *Roman Social Relations: 50 BC to AD 284*. New Haven: Yale University Press, 1974.

Malina, B. and J. Neyrey. *Calling Jesus Names: The Social Value of Labels in Matthew*. Sonoma: Polebridge, 1988.

Martin, F. 'The Image of the Shepherd in the Gospel of Sant [*sic*] Matthew'. *Science et Esprit* 27 (1975): 261–301.

Novakovic, L. *Messiah, the Healer of the Sick: A Study of Jesus as the Son of David in the Gospel of Matthew*. Tübingen: Mohr Siebeck, 2003.

Price, S. *Rituals and Power: The Roman Imperial Cult in Asia Minor*. Cambridge: Cambridge University Press, 1984.

Riches, J. and D. Sim, eds. *The Gospel of Matthew in Its Roman Imperial Context*. New York: T&T Clark International, 2005.

Saldarini, A. *Matthew's Christian-Jewish Community*. Chicago: The University of Chicago Press, 1994.

Sauter, F. *Der Römische Kaiserkult bei Martial und Statius*. Stuttgart-Berlin: Verlag Von W. Kohlhammer, 1934.

Seibel, J. 'Shepherd and Sheep Symbolism in Hellenistic Judaism and the New Testament'. PhD dissertation, Yale University, 1963.

Senior, D. 'Between Two Worlds: Gentiles and Jewish Christians in Matthew's Gospel'. *CBQ* 61 (1991): 1–23.

Sim, D. *The Gospel of Matthew and Christian Judaism: The History and Social Setting of the Matthean Community*. Edinburgh: T&T Clark, 1998.

Smith, J. Z. *Drudgery Divine: On the Comparison of Early Christianities and the Religions of Late Antiquity*. Chicago: University of Chicago Press, 1990.

Stanton, G. *A Gospel for a New People: Studies in Matthew*. Edinburgh: T&T Clark, 1992.

Taylor, L. *The Divinity of the Roman Emperor*. Philadelphia: Porcupine Press, 1975.

Tilley, C. *Metaphor and Material Culture*. Oxford: Blackwell Publishers, 1999.

Tooley, W. 'The Shepherd and Sheep Image in the Teaching of Jesus'. *NovT* 7 (1964): 15–25.

Vancil, J. 'The Symbolism of the Shepherd in Biblical, Intertestamental, and New Testament Material'. PhD dissertation, Dropsie University, 1975.

Verseput, D. 'The Davidic Messiah and Matthew's Jewish Christianity'. *SBLSP* (1995): 102–16.

Willitts, J. *Matthew's Messianic Shepherd-King: In Search of 'the Lost Sheep of the House of Israel'*. Berlin: Walter de Gruyter, 2007.

Index of Biblical and Other Ancient Sources

INDEX OF AUTHORS